BLACK
AND
MORE
THAN
BLACK

BLACK AND MORE THAN BLACK

AFRICAN AMERICAN FICTION IN THE POST ERA

CAMERON LEADER-PICONE

University Press of Mississippi / Jackson

Margaret Walker Alexander Series
in African American Studies

The University Press of Mississippi is the scholarly publishing agency of
the Mississippi Institutions of Higher Learning: Alcorn State University,
Delta State University, Jackson State University, Mississippi State University,
Mississippi University for Women, Mississippi Valley State University,
University of Mississippi, and University of Southern Mississippi.

www.upress.state.ms.us

The University Press of Mississippi is a member
of the Association of University Presses.

Chapter 1 was published in an earlier form as "Post-Black Stories: Colson
Whitehead's *Sag Harbor* and Racial Individualism," *Contemporary
Literature* 56.3 (Fall 2015): 421–49. Chapter 4 is an expanded version of
"An Unhyphenated Man: Alice Randall's *Rebel Yell* and the Literary Age of
Obama," *MELUS* 42.1 (Spring 2017): 53–73. I want to thank the University
of Wisconsin Press (*Contemporary Literature*) and Oxford University Press
(*MELUS*) for publishing my work and for providing permission to republish
revised versions of those articles.

First printing 2019
∞

Library of Congress Cataloging-in-Publication Data

Names: Leader-Picone, Cameron, author.
Title: Black and more than black : African American fiction in the post era / Cameron
Leader-Picone.
Description: Jackson : University Press of Mississippi, [2019] | Series: Margaret Walker Alex-
ander series in African American studies | Includes bibliographical references and index. |
Identifiers: LCCN 2019003531 (print) | LCCN 2019011228 (ebook) | ISBN 9781496824530
(epub single) | ISBN 9781496824523 (epub institutional) | ISBN 9781496824554 (pdf single)
| ISBN 9781496824547 (pdf institutional) | ISBN 9781496824516 (cloth : alk. paper) | ISBN
9781496824561 (pbk. : alk. paper)
Subjects: LCSH: American literature—African American authors—Criticism and interpreta-
tion. | American literature—21st century. | Racism in literature. | LCGFT: Literary criticism.
Classification: LCC PS153.N5 (ebook) | LCC PS153.N5 L385 2019 (print) | DDC
813/.609896073—dc23
LC record available at https://lccn.loc.gov/2019003531

British Library Cataloging-in-Publication Data available

For Ann

CONTENTS

ACKNOWLEDGMENTS

Though it is a cliché to say that it would be impossible to write a book without the work and support of a whole range of people, it is certainly true. As a junior faculty member, I made a decision that I would start an entirely new book project rather than revise the manuscript that I had already drafted. Making that decision was difficult, and would not have been possible without the support of my colleagues and students at Kansas State University. A Faculty Enhancement Grant from the university helped underwrite the early research and drafting process and additional funding allowed me to hire research assistants. I was able to present early work on the book at the department's faculty colloquium, where I received great questions and useful ideas. The Cultural Studies Interdisciplinary Research Group on campus also gave me an opportunity to present research from chapter 5. In particular, I want to thank Lisa Tatonetti for her advice at every step of the process, and her willingness to read (and re-read) sections of this manuscript as they were drafted and at every stage of review. I also want to thank Dan Hoyt, Phil Nel, and Joe Sutliff Sanders for reading portions of the book. Karin Westman, Tanya González, Abby Knoblauch, Mark Crosby, and Anna Goins all provided needed support. I remember being stressed out during one reappointment meeting, wondering whether I had made a mistake by starting an entirely new book project. After that meeting, Elizabeth Dodd knocked on my door and told me how exciting she thought the project was. That meant a lot in the moment, so I want to say thank you to her for that. Also, I want to thank my research assistants, including Melissa Prescott and Ashley Denney, as well as Jalen Thompson and Alejandra Valadez.

The intellectual groundwork for this book came in the Department of African and African American Studies at Harvard University. I could not have made it through that period without the support, friendship, and intellectual fellowship of Peter Geller, Laura Murphy, Hua Hsu, Namwali Serpell, Julia Lee, Linda Chavers, Ashley Farmer, Lyndon Gill, Michael Jeffries, Amber Moulton,

Amber Musser, Jennifer Nash, Kaya Williams, Josef Sorett, and Wendy Grant. I want to thank Henry Louis Gates Jr. for always challenging my ideas and for his ability to recall an entire library of useful sources at any moment to help with research. Even before I got to campus, Glenda Carpio took me under her wing and helped me to become a better scholar and a better teacher. She made me feel, even as someone right out of college, that my ideas were valuable and that I could become a better writer. I want to thank her for always pushing me, and for sharing her love of humor, music, and contemporary African American literature with me. Tommie Shelby helped push my engagement with literature in new philosophical and political directions. Jennifer Hochschild, Werner Sollors, Evelyn Higginbotham, Lawrence Bobo, Michael Dawson, and Susan O'Donovan were all indispensable to my time at Harvard. My year as a fellow at the W. E. B. Du Bois Center for African and African American Research helped lead to the development of this book project. I want to thank Vera Grant, Abby Wolf, and everyone in my cohort of fellows for making that such a special and intellectually stimulating year.

A Summer Stipend grant from the National Endowment for the Humanities helped me complete an initial revision of this manuscript. I also want to thank everyone involved with the National Endowment for the Humanities summer institute "Don't Deny My Voice: Black Poetry after the Black Arts Movement," especially Maryemma Graham, Evie Shockley, and Howard Rambsy, and the Project on the History of Black Writing at the University of Kansas who organized such a fantastic group. The institute helped me to clarify how the ideas I was analyzing in relation to fiction related to contemporary Black poetry.

A significant portion of this book was written or revised at Radina's Coffee Shop in Manhattan, Kansas; PT's Coffee in Topeka, Kansas; and Decade Coffee Shop in Lawrence, Kansas, so I want to thank each of them for providing space and comfort during the process.

I want to thank my editor Vijay Shah, Lisa McMurtray, and everyone at the University Press of Mississippi for helping make this book a reality. In addition, I want to say a special thank you to the anonymous reviewers who read this manuscript as it went through the publication process. Your comments were invaluable and helped make this book better than it would have been otherwise. In addition, I want to thank Kristy Johnson for her copy-editing work on the manuscript.

Many years ago, I read through Paul Gilroy's acknowledgements for *The Black Atlantic*, where he thanked various musicians for getting him through the writing process. While the list of artists and albums that soundtracked my own writing process is far too long to thank individually here, I want to give a collective acknowledgement to their indispensable help along the way. I do, however, want to highlight Kendrick Lamar, whose work has found its way into my writing and teaching, and whose albums provided the soundtrack to several years of writing this book.

I wouldn't be where I am today without the support of my best friend Matthew Schneider-Mayerson. Ever since our first semester at Yale, he has helped me see the world in new ways and consider new ideas. During the writing of this book, he was always willing to read something when I couldn't tell if I was making any sense, or to talk about books, music, movies, or the NBA if I needed that instead. My parents, Linda and Malcolm, have always been there for me no matter what, as have my siblings Drew and Whitney. My dad was one of my first readers and I want to thank him for always taking my writing and ideas seriously, no matter how young I was. My mom taught me to examine the world critically and imagine how I could help make it a better place. I can never thank them enough for everything they've done for me.

Most of all, I want to thank my partner and the love of my life Ann Sagan, who supported me throughout the entire process. Thank you for sharing your prodigious intellect and empathetic spirit with me these last ten years. This book (and so much more) would not be possible without you.

BLACK
AND
MORE
THAN
BLACK

INTRODUCTION

The Post Era

I take this book's title from Barack Obama's description of his initial encounter with Reverend Jeremiah Wright at Chicago's Trinity Church in his memoir Dreams from My Father ([1995] 2004). In his account of his experience in that moment, the cynicism and alienation laced throughout the book slide away, and Obama feels a transcendent connection to both a larger Black community and humanity as a whole. Articulating these simultaneous connections, he describes the communal history of which he feels a part as "black and more than black." I am struck by the broader resonance of this description. Each of this book's chapters trace the tension between the sense of rootedness—histori-cally, culturally, socially—signified by Blackness and the simultaneous tran-scendence embedded in the sense of being "more than" that same Blackness. Whether conceptualized as the tension between the individual Black artist and limitations of what it means to be classified as a "Black artist" or the experience of racialization by immigrants who become Black on American soil despite the diversity of their backgrounds, the sense of being "more than" maps the larger effort to imagine a twenty-first century Blackness that is simultaneously an extension of past meanings and a transcendence of those same definitions. In this context, the sense of being "more than" evokes optimism and aspiration and yet also pessimism and mourning. Charting the tenuous path being laid by African American authors, this book traces these attempts to name, define, and otherwise rearticulate racial identity in the twenty-first century through "post" categorizations that illuminate the push and pull between the power of historical meanings and attempts to explore new meanings. In doing so, it illuminates a critical period of transition that continues to influence the course of African American culture and ongoing movements for Black liberation in the twenty-first century.

The proliferation of "posts"—post–civil rights, post-soul, post-Black, pos-trace, and post-racial, as well as analytically related concepts such as New Blackness and NewBlack—mark the attempt to map the meaning of Black identity and the direction of Black politics for a community increasingly distant in time from the still-dominant iconography and history of the civil rights and Black Power movements. I am not the first to note the relationship between the increased prominence of African American authors and artists and an emphasis on the diversity of their aesthetic: as just one example, Bertram Ashe edited a special issue of *African American Review* devoted to the "post-soul aesthetic," as part of what he called "this 'post' era" (Ashe 2007, 609), in 2007. However, this is the first book-length effort to analyze the implications of the post era holistically in the historical and political context of the early twenty-first century—especially through a focus on the presidency of Barack Obama. My argument that the proliferation of these various post terms constitutes a post era accentuates that their range maps a transitional period in which the privileging of individualistic conceptions of racial identity exists in dialogue with entrenched structural racism.

The temporality of the post era explicitly aligns questions of continuity and rupture with teleological narratives of progress. Joseph R. Winters, for example, argues that the "postracial fantasy" occasioned by Barack Obama's election as president reveals broad investment in such narratives. This is true not just of white people who seek to use Obama's election to avoid engaging with systemic racism. As Winters explains, "Even individuals and figures who might reject the postracial fervor tend to cling to the proverbial idea of progress, invoking this trope to make sense of present and past struggles, achievements, and losses" (Winters 2016, 4). My explication of the post era accords with Winters's argument that to neglect this ideological commitment in progress would be to ignore ideas that "heavily influence Americans in particular, and modern denizens more generally" (Winters 2016, 4). This is not to say that the sequential logic of "post" necessarily designates progressive claims (better, freer, etc.). Instead, post can more effectively be read as a "space-clearing gesture," in Kwame Anthony Appiah's terms (Appiah 1991, 348; see also Taylor 2007, 629).[1] The turn to post carves an opening for new performances of Black identity and new forms of Black art. "Post," then, designates a period during which the relationship to the past is one of both rejection and indebtedness. In centralizing post in my analysis of twenty-first century African American fiction, this book argues that the post era makes visible several tensions that play out through generational shifts in the definition and meaning of Blackness itself: resistance to claims of authenticity; assertions of individual agency over the meaning of Black identity and Black art; rejection of the idea that Black art is primarily concerned with responding to the ongoing history of American white supremacy; and an often parodic relationship to key figures and historical moments in Black history.[2] For African American literature in particular, these tensions play out through the negotiation of prescriptions about what Black art can or should look like and through the post era's primary "space-clearing gesture": the acknowledgement and rejection of a narrative in which the Black Arts Movement and Black Aesthetic (BAM) stand in for essentialist and restrictive modes of Blackness and Black writing. Recent scholarship by Margo Natalie Crawford (2017) and Gershun Avilez (2016) has sought to counter such reductive narratives of BAM aesthetics by showing the continuity between the ideas and cultural production of that era and the present one, but the post era explicitly defines itself against that past, whether it is a caricature or not.

Many scholars have disputed the idea of progress embedded in post categories along a range of metrics, from economics to politics to culture.[3] Without disputing the existence of the ongoing structures of racial hierarchy, others have aligned post categories with other liberating forms of identity performance. Most prominently, Derek Conrad Murray and Francesca Royster explicitly link the post era to queer critiques of BAM to celebrate the possibilities embedded in the post temporality. Royster's *Sounding Like a No-No: Queer Sounds and Eccentric Acts in the Post-Soul Era* (2012) connects post-soul to queer theory to embrace liberatory identity performances within Black popular music. Murray goes even further than Royster in connecting post era theories with queer studies in visual art to argue that "if post-black represents a threat, it is to the hegemony of hetero-patriarchal expressions of blackness that, in their essentialist logics and racial nostalgia, relegate African-American identity to a series of limiting scripts" (Murray 2016, 3). Both Murray and Royster celebrate post theories for embracing the performative aspects of racial identity, thus placing Blackness more and more within the space of individual agency. Royster's and Murray's analyses build on E. Patrick Johnson's theories on the performative nature of Blackness. Johnson rightly argues that Blackness itself is the terrain through which power structures compete over definitions, resulting in a post era typified by moments in which "the authenticity of older versions of blackness is called into question" (Johnson 2003, 2). However, while Johnson argues that such moments are periods of "crisis," I would argue that the post era serves as a period of transition during which negotiations over the boundaries of Blackness are engaged in an attempt to map the next steps of this contested narrative of ongoing American progress.

To analyze this period of transition, *Black and More than Black* covers the years from the turn of the millennium to the end of 2016 to explicitly link the post era with the person who has become one of its central exemplars,

President Barack Obama. While the intellectual underpinnings of post-era theorizing precede the year 2000—important examples include Trey Ellis's 1989 essay "The New Black Aesthetic," the writings of Reginald McKnight and Greg Tate, Henry Louis Gates Jr.'s declaration of a "fourth renaissance" in Black arts and letters in 1997, and Nelson George's work on post-soul—the turn of the new century accelerated the formulation of these ideas as an epochal discourse that found its culmination in the rapid rise of the nation's first Black president.[4] Obama's biography (especially his self-narrativizing across two major books) and the history of his political career offer an example that writers like Touré have connected specifically to post-Blackness (see Touré 2011, chapter 7).

The Obama presidency concretizes the sense of post as progress, marking the symbolic ascension of a Black person to the highest position of power in a nation founded on the enslavement of Black people followed by their exclusion from full citizenship. The immediate context of Obama's election was a financial crisis that further deepened the racialized dimensions of economic inequality. According to a range of metrics, the supposed progress trumpeted by the post prefix is more elusive than concrete. Michelle Alexander's now-canonical designation of this same era as "the New Jim Crow" speaks to a range of crises in policing, public health, and incarceration. The expansion of the Black middle and upper class that found unprecedented access to positions of power within both the Obama administration itself and the larger culture accompanied a retrenchment of opportunity for the large numbers of Black people below or near the poverty line (see Jeffries 2013, 157–62). Despite these metrics, the national press, including conservative commentators, trafficked in a grotesque version of this idea of progress in the immediate wake of Obama's election, claiming that it designated the inauguration of a post-racial era, by which most meant the end of the era of legitimate grievance over past and ongoing systemic racism. As attacks rooted in Obama's racial otherness or putative foreignness mounted over the course of his presidency, the ridiculousness of claims about a post-racial America was equaled only by the obscene argument that references to the racism of the president's opponents were a violation of the progress Obama's election supposedly signified.

Indeed, if November 4, 2008, serves as the ubiquitous reference point for a narrative of progress, then the racialized backlash to the Obama presidency, especially the so-called "birther" movement spearheaded by now-President Donald Trump, the mobilization of Black Lives Matter and related movements in response to the sequence of high profile murders of Black people by police officers and others show the limits of post era claims of progress, especially following the 2016 election of Trump. The existence of reductive versions of post-era discourse does not, however, undermine my argument that the early twenty-first century generated a range of attempts by African American writers to claim a more nuanced and qualified version of progress than that contained within the popular idea of post-racialism. In constructing this parallel between the post era and the Obama years, I argue that the new century emphasized a racial discourse in which resistance to claims of authenticity elevated racial individualism.

The fiction analyzed in this book resists imperatives towards both a post-racial erasure of Blackness and claims of obligation rooted in racial unity. Approaching the iconography of past struggles and Black history as repertoires through which to construct a performative Blackness, characters in early twenty-first century African American fiction negotiate a spectrum of expectations tied to citizenship, belonging, and community. As Sandra Adell (1994) and Adolph Reed Jr. (1997) have noted, W. E. B. Du Bois's "double consciousness" serves as both master trope of African American literature and as an assumed universal psychological state of Black identity. Unsurprisingly, then, the tension between racialization and self-expression within these texts occasions an explicit revision of double consciousness. While Du Bois emphasizes the power of the white gaze to define and fragment Black subjectivity, authors of the post era emphasize individual agency in the choice to both identify oneself as Black, as Hamza Walker highlights, and to define its meaning (Walker 2001, 16–17). This individual focus does not dismiss the power of structural racism; rather, it rejects the prescription that responding to racism is the defining structural feature of Black identity.

Critics often mistake the meaning of the post era. Some see the current discourses as simply new iterations of longstanding debates about African American literature. Many authors across the African American literary tradition have resisted the essentialist argument of a monolithic Blackness, and scholars argue that even the Black Arts Movement, against which so many post era critics position themselves, acknowledged and made room for diverse Blacknesses. Other critics argue that various post categories are merely facile embraces of a neoliberal approach to identity tied to the relative class privilege of so many writers. Neither of these arguments is entirely wrong, per se. "Post" is neither simply a restatement of ideas from BAM nor a triumphalist post-racialism. Instead, it is an anxious assertion of individual liberation from racial prescriptiveness. Critically, this is about distinguishing the individual from a broader collective, and questioning the validity of the collective as a coherent whole. It is an argument for embracing Blackness as something elective: the move from being Black to choosing Blackness.[5]

To outline the dominant concerns of the post era, it is necessary to first historicize the cultural discourses of the early twenty-first century. I do this by looking back to precedents across African American literary history (especially periods such as the postwar era and the 1980s), situating post era theorizing's origins in the New Black Aesthetic and post-structuralism, and then detailing the various permutations that post era discourses take. Following this, I discuss the salience of a continued focus on racial identity and literature in the present, despite potent arguments against such a focus (see, especially, Fields 2012). In doing so, I explain the centrality of double consciousness to literature of the period. I then connect the post era with the Obama era by examining the post-Black political context of his election and presidency. The parallel between the post era and the ascension of Barack Obama mirrors this book's structure to highlight a cultural discourse that maintains its influence even as some of its optimism has dampened in a period of renewed explicit racism and anti-racist movement activism. Engaging with the post era's representations of Black identity traces ongoing attempts to construct a liberatory framework through which to imagine further progress as the legal triumphs and cultural and political movements of the civil rights era retreat further into the past.

THE POST ERA

On March 18, 2008, Barack Obama, soon to be the first African American candidate nominated by one of the two major parties, traveled to Philadelphia, Pennsylvania, to give a speech about race. Up until this point, Obama's campaign had largely avoided the explicit discussion of race, believing that highlighting Obama's Blackness only served to exacerbate any racialized backlash and opened him up to charges that he was more interested in serving the supposedly narrow issues of African Americans than the general American populace. At this moment in the campaign, however, Obama was forced to speak on the subject because of the discovery of past controversial comments by Reverend Jeremiah Wright, who had been his pastor at Trinity Church on the south side of Chicago. Wright's comments, captured on a video recording sold through the church, reflected the dissatisfaction of a consistent strain within the African American church and Black culture overall. Speaking soon after the events of September 11, 2001, Wright argued that the attacks had been the product of American imperialism abroad, citing Malcolm X's words following the assassination of President John F. Kennedy, "America's chickens! Are coming home! To roost." The constant barrage of cable news stories repeatedly playing this and other supposedly inflammatory clips finally prompted Obama to make a public statement about Wright, and about race in the United States more generally (see Remnick 2010, 515–22).[6]

Prior to embarking on the campaign trail, race had not been a subject that Obama shied away from. His memoir *Dreams from My Father* has the subtitle "A Story of Race and Inheritance," and even his more policy-oriented second book *The Audacity of Hope* includes a full chapter on race-related public policy, albeit one that argues for more universal programs than race-specific ones. Further, the title of that second book comes directly from Wright. In *Dreams from My Father*, Obama describes hearing Wright's "Audacity of Hope" sermon in words he would quote during his March 18, 2008, speech:

> Those stories of survival and freedom and hope became our stories, my story. The blood that spilled was our blood; the tears our tears; until this black church, on this bright day, seemed once more a vessel carrying the story of a people into future generations and into a larger world. Our trials and triumphs became at once unique and universal, black and more than black. In chronicling our journey, the stories and songs gave us a meaning to reclaim memories that we didn't need to feel shame about—memories that all people might study and cherish and with which we could start to rebuild. (Obama [1995] 2004, 294)

The context of their expression radically transforms the meaning of these words. Glenda Carpio (2011) argues that this is the decisive moment in Obama's memoir, one that provides synthesis for a young Obama searching for the meaning of his racial identity.[7] That Obama defines the history of the "people" within which he situates himself as "black and more than black" signals the tension in the first decade plus of the twenty-first century between optimism regarding the increasing opportunities for African Americans in American society on the one hand, and pessimism over the persistence of racial hierarchies and racial violence on the other.[8] With an emphasis on progress and transcendence that mainstream commentators would subsequently interpret as post-racialism, Obama's 2008 speech centralizes cross-racial identification and unity in service of universal needs and values.[9] Though the speech makes it clear that the nation has not yet become "perfect" with regard to race, he clearly articulates the ways in which it has become, and is becoming, "more perfect."

Across the first sixteen years of the twenty-first century, the post era adopted a similar qualified linear progress narrative that associates the transcendence of limitations rooted in collective racial identities with greater freedom. The context for this understanding of freedom, however, is not simply the abstract consideration of sociological metrics or the philosophical meaning of identity. Instead, the various discourses that make up the post era situate themselves as an explicit counternarrative to an essentialism frequently associated with the aesthetic movements of the late 1960s and early 1970s, particularly the

Black Arts Movement, and what Rolland Murray defines as the "incorpora-tion" of African American literature into the dominant institutions of both publishing and academia (Murray 2017, 731).[10] In both cases, authors resist aesthetic prescription, due to essentialism in the case of BAM and through market stereotypes articulated by publishers, readers, and curricula. Because of its temporal alignment with the early institutionalization of Black Studies and African American literature on college campuses, the Black Arts era has played a foundational role in academic criticism of African American literature, lending it a potent institutional force for post–civil rights authors to rebut. Furthermore, because the dominant narrative of BAM tends to emphasize its essentialism, sexism, and homophobia, it provides a convenient stand in for multiple discourses of authenticity.

The post era's relationship to BAM is ultimately not one involving a complex analysis and negotiation of actual aesthetic arguments. Instead, it takes the nationalism of the era as a frame through which to reject claims that certain themes or literary forms are more authentically Black. Crawford makes the most comprehensive version of the argument that twenty-first century Black aesthetics are actually a continuation of those present within BAM, especially during its later years in the early 1970s. In her book *Black Post-Blackness: The Black Arts Movement and Twenty-First Century Aesthetics*, she argues that "As the BAM became the first cultural movement determined to make art that is specifically and unapologetically black, the artists' search for the specificity of black art led to a wide horizon of shaping and unshaping blackness that I call 'black post-blackness'" (Crawford 2017, 1–2). Notably, though, Crawford does not address the implications of the specificity that she notes for the post era's repudiation of BAM aesthetics. While she is right that BAM encompassed a diverse range of definitions of Blackness and Black art, the dominant objec-tion of post era theorists is not to any exact definition but rather to the polic-ing of the category that necessarily attends to the "specificity" she mentions. Crawford's book persuasively expands our understanding of BAM (particularly during the 1970s), but it is equally important to engage with post era authors as they situate themselves against a caricature of BAM even if it is indeed a caricature. In *Radical Aesthetics and Modern Black Nationalism*, Gershun Avilez intentionally connects artists of the Black Arts era and the post–civil rights era who superficially appear distinct in their ideas and aesthetics. By doing so, Avilez seeks to "[uncover] the afterlives of Black Arts critical frameworks and the impact nationalist thought continues to have on artistic production" (Avilez 2017, 25). Building on Crawford's and Avilez's research, my intention here is not to argue that the Black Arts Movement itself encompassed one single, essentialist framework through which art was produced or critiqued. Instead, my analysis highlights that the authors of the post era tend to rely on such a caricature of the Black Arts Movement in opposing their work to its dictates.

Many of the dominant concerns of post era authors echo longstanding tensions within the African American literary tradition, particularly around publishing-industry and critical expectations about what constitutes Black art. These previous moments in the African American literary tradition have seen writers shift their focus to the personal politics of identity. J. Martin Favor, in his book about the Harlem Renaissance and racial authenticity, argues that "artists and intellectuals of the era were especially self-conscious about their (re) construction of African American identity" (Favor 1999, 3), particularly as they sought to move beyond the conflation of vernacular culture and authenticity. Writing about the postwar period, which he labels the "existential school" of African American literature, Robert J. Washington explains that "in the wake of the postwar political changes, the dominant ideological preoccupation of black American literature shifted from public issues of racial oppression to private issues of personal identity" (Washington 2001, 190–91). The key shift that Washington identifies parallels the post era, emphasizing individual choices about identity performance and self-identification, and viewing public claims of responsibility as limitations on agency.

More proximately, the 1980s produced important critical precedents for turn-of-the-millennium post theorizing. During that decade, authors such as Ishmael Reed and Trey Ellis celebrated experimental and non-traditional African American literary expression and critiqued more mainstream Black writers for feeding into white stereotypes (see Reed's *Reckless Eyeballing* [1986] and Ellis's *Platitudes* [1988] in particular). Problematically, however, such authors mocked the growing market share of Black women writers, echoing the historical misogynistic association of the mainstream with the feminine and the esoteric with the masculine. In other words, the initial post–civil rights framework for aesthetic liberation was intensely gendered and classed, critiques that lie at the core of historian Tera Hunter's response to Trey Ellis's generation-defining essay "The New Black Aesthetic" (Hunter 1989; Ellis 1989).

Ellis's essay attempts to define a specific post–civil rights aesthetic as a direct repudiation of Addison Gayle's key BAM-era volume *The Black Aesthetic* (1972). Ellis argues that the New Black Aesthetic is defined by what he calls "cultural mulattoes," who, he emphasizes, "no longer need to deny or suppress any part of our complicated and sometimes contradictory cultural baggage to please either white people or black" (Ellis 1989, 235). Ellis's essay makes it clear that the liberation sought by the artists encompassed by his label is from the dictates of the essentialist Blackness that defined such anthologies as *The Black Aesthetic*. Describing his own childhood growing up in wealthy areas of Ann Arbor,

Michigan and New Haven, Connecticut, Ellis admits that his aesthetic ideals are likely the specific product of his class privilege, a charge that Tera Hunter (1989, 247–49) elaborates on in her critique. Furthermore, Hunter and Eric Lott, whose critiques were published in *Callaloo* alongside the original essay, are wary not just of the exclusively middle- and upper-class origins of Ellis's aesthetic but also of what Lott describes as its "evasion of politics" (Lott 1989, 246).

However, while Hunter and Lott assail the ambiguous politics of Ellis's essay as a defect, its lack of a unified definable ideology is actually one of the New Black Aesthetic's distinctive features. In the body of the essay, it is clear that filmmakers such as Spike Lee and musicians such as Fishbone and Public Enemy often make sharply political art. However, it is Ellis's approach to understanding the relationship between politics and art that presages post era concepts such as "post-black art," post-soul, and the postrace aesthetic. Ellis is less dismissive of structures of institutional racism than he is of the responsibility of the artist to engage with them with the primary motive of overturning them. "Neither are the new black artists shocked by the persistence of racism as were those of the Harlem Renaissance, nor are we preoccupied with it as were those of the Black Arts Movement. For us, racism is a hard and little-changing constant that neither surprises nor enrages" (Ellis 1989, 239–40). Similar to the New Black Aesthetic, the post-soul aesthetic pushes against the institutionalization of "previous—and necessary—preoccupations with struggling for political freedom, or with an attempt to establish and sustain a coherent black identity" (Ashe 2007, 614).

As Hunter's critique of Ellis highlights, the post–civil rights era has seen class distinctions grow within the Black community, even as various economic metrics comparing median wealth between Black and white communities have stagnated or seen little long-term change. Recent statistics show that the number of Black households earning more than $75,000 a year "more than doubled" between 1975 and 2016, while those earning more than $100,000 a year "quadrupled." There has not been an equivalent decrease in the number of Black households with "incomes below $15,000," leading to an increase in economic inequality within the Black community (Wilson 2018). Consequently, intraracial distinctions in class experiences drive several aspects of the post era. An emphasis on diversity in Black representations frequently manifests as the inclusion of depictions of the Black middle and upper class and a resistance to popular cultural focus on urban crime. The shift towards racial individualism also reflects a certain class privilege not available to a Black underclass disproportionately subject to over-policing and mass incarceration. This is not to say that the Black middle and upper class are not also disproportionately policed and economically precarious relative to their white peers. Indeed, as

Thomas Shapiro explains, "racial inequality" is actually "increasing" during the twenty-first century (Shapiro 2004, 3). However, those ongoing structural racial inequalities have joined with shifting class inequalities within the Black community during the post era to transform critical discourses on representation. In marking themselves as temporally post the civil rights and Black Power eras, Black authors of the post era position themselves as liberated specifically from the political work of the previous era, even as they repeatedly acknowledge the necessity of that same work. In other words, the freedom imagined in the transcendence of the post era is defined by the absence of prescriptions seen as residing within specific ideologies or aesthetic movements. Bertram Ashe argues that this position constitutes a kind of privilege born out of the struggles that post-soul artists now resist. "Many post-soul writers critique the events or mindset of the Civil Rights movement in their fictions, and I believe it is important to this sense of African Americans' being 'post' that these artists have no lived, adult experience with that movement" (Ashe 2007, 611). The temporal distance that Ashe describes enables what the curator Christine Y. Kim labels "nonstalgia" in connection with Thelma Golden's concept of "post-black art" (Golden and Kim 2005). Golden, who coined the term when curating the *Freestyle* exhibition at the Studio Museum in Harlem in 2001, argues that post-black art is "characterized by artists who were adamant about not being labeled 'black' artists, though their work was steeped, in fact deeply interested, in redefining complex notions of Blackness" (Golden 2001, 14). Importantly, the term "black artist" here is not abstract, but instead a direct reference to the construction of a specific form of politicized Black art in the context of the Black Arts Movement.

Because of this, post-Blackness underscores the simultaneous turn towards the privileging of individual agency over racial identity and expression and concurrent recognition of the continued centrality of race in contemporary American society. Opening at the turn of the new century, the Thelma Golden-curated *Freestyle* exhibition focused on young African American artists as a means of interrogating whether the specific Black Power-era ideologies that motivated the Studio Museum of Harlem's opening remain relevant in the present. In her introduction to the volume accompanying the exhibit, Golden labeled the work displayed in *Freestyle* as "post-black art" to argue that while race remains relevant to these artists' work, it does so in a way distinct from previous eras. "How would black artists make work after the vital political activism of the 1960s, the focused, often essentialist Black Arts Movement of the 1970s, the theory driven multiculturalism of the 1990s, and the late globalist expansion of the late 90s? 'Freestyle' was the answer to those questions" (Golden 2001, 14). During the more than fifteen years since Golden first floated the term, "post-black art" has turned into a broader concept of post-Blackness, emphasizing the possibility of freedom from the potential confinements of a normative racial identity, though not necessarily from race itself. Moving beyond Golden's initial conceptualization, Touré, in his 2011 book *Who's Afraid of Post-Blackness?: What it Means to be Black Now*, and Ytasha Womack, in her 2010 book *Post-Black: How A New Generation is Redefining African American Identity*, expand the scope of Golden's term (see Womack 2010, 23).[11] While the definitions of what constitutes "post-black art" or characterizes post-Blackness are distinct in each of these texts, they draw a parallel between the transition from the civil rights era into a post–civil rights generation and the transition from an emphasis on group-based organizing to a contemporary definition of Blackness that centralizes individual agency.

Despite Ashe's insistence that the post-soul aesthetic distinguishes itself from post-Blackness because of its more definable boundaries, both frameworks stress the obsessive focus on Blackness by Black artists and uneasiness with the restrictiveness of labels such as "Black artist." Ashe's more concrete definition for "the post-soul aesthetic" highlights its open nature, focusing on "blaxploration" (Ashe 2007, 614). The combination of self-referentiality and the propensity to push against or "trouble" the implications of those references—what Ashe describes as the *"allusion-disruption* strategy" (Ashe 2007, 615, italics in original)—generates a diverse body of writers who are obsessed with the various meanings and expressions of Blackness while simultaneously resisting its limitations. Far from avoiding the subject of racism, contemporary African American literature celebrates the dynamic, the shifting, and the exceptional in order to trouble the boundaries of what constitutes Black identity and imagine a liberating Blackness. However, such playfulness is not without its problems. As Mark Anthony Neal argues, post-soul art has a distinct "willingness to undermine or deconstruct the most negative symbols and stereotypes of black life via the use and distribution of those very same symbols and stereotypes" (Neal 2002, 120). As the comedian Dave Chappelle discovered, a performer who everyone from Touré (who dubbed him a "Post-Black King") to Glenda Carpio cites as one of the definitive artists of the post era (see Touré 2011, 57–74; Carpio 2008, 103–16; Haggins 2007), such play with stereotypes, particularly within the interracial forums and audiences carved out as the product of the struggles of previous generations, can easily reinforce the very structures one seeks to undermine.

Expanding beyond just African American literature, Ramon Saldívar (2013) argues that this reactionary stance towards restrictive definitions of identity exists throughout contemporary ethnic American literature. Risking conflation of his term with post-racialism, Saldívar identifies a "postrace aesthetic" which seeks a cultural politics able to account for the increasingly global, mobile, and itinerate present, as social realist fiction did for a previous generation. Each of the theorists mentioned goes to great pains to underscore their unwillingness to institute their own restrictions on the scope and character of Black art, positioning their aesthetics as descriptive rather than prescriptive. Similarly, this book does not intend to litigate the merits of the various terms in service of endorsing one of the diverse aesthetics as more accurate in its presentation of contemporary African American literature.

Leaving aside Touré, who is a novelist and short story writer in addition to a journalist, critics dominate the published use of "post" categories such as post-Black, postrace, and post-soul. Indeed, in the rare instances when they are asked about such ideas, authors themselves express reluctance to apply such labels to their work, if not outright distaste for the terms.[12] Examining their public statements, however, reveals that while authors may not like the terminology, their understandings of their work typify the same tensions and shifts I argue epitomize the post era. Across interviews, for example, Paul Beatty declares his investment in iconoclasm: "I'm trying to look beyond expectations of what a black book is supposed to be. I am trying to be new—it is a 'novel,' right? The hardest thing doing interviews is that you run into a wall of expectations" (Beatty 2017). Responding to an interviewer's question about the degree to which he defines himself as an author about race, Colson Whitehead demurs, "Very little. In some books, race is a topic I'm exploring; it's more or less present in each work. . . . I like to explore different ideas of race, how the concept of race has evolved in the country. It's one thing I enjoy talking about, but I don't feel compelled to talk about it" (Whitehead 2012). Whitehead makes a subtle distinction here. The interviewer attempts to impose the label of "a writer of race" on Whitehead, which the author resists. In doing so, however, Whitehead does not deny the ubiquity of "ideas of race" across his oeuvre. Instead, he emphasizes that such a subject matter is a product of individual choice and interest rather than any obligation rooted in his own racial identity. In doing so, he, like Beatty, seeks to carve out space for his writing outside of expectations about what Black writing can or should look like specifically by focusing on his individual agency over the meaning of Blackness. Alice Randall extends the power of this elective relationship to Black identity to argue against the inherence of racial divisions in American life. Claiming that "profound things have changed" even since the early Civil Rights Movement, Randall laments that too many Black people still buy into a "one drop rule" racial essentialism in defining themselves and others (Randall 2004). Though references to post categories are largely absent from these and other interviews with twenty-first century African American authors, their emphasis on aesthetic freedom and individual agency over the meaning of Blackness directly mirrors post era critics.

This is true even among authors who are more explicitly hostile to claims of racial progress. As I argue in chapter 2, there is an explicit counternarrative among some writers to the idea that the African American literary tradition imposes a burden on contemporary Black writers. Kiese Laymon, for example, embraces his inheritance of a specifically southern Black literary tradition: "Being a black writer means that I have the wonderfully huge responsibility of building on the black literary traditions before me while writing to the next generation of courageous black readers and writers. We must claim it. I want everything I write to be honest and in the real and imaginative service of black folks, particularly Mississippi black folks" (Laymon 2015). Laymon's injunction that the African American literary tradition must be claimed counters charges that such a tradition is at all limiting, yet he does so by highlighting its instrumental value rather than by resorting to statements of a definable Black identity. Even Jesmyn Ward, whose work, like Laymon's, I argue directly counters post-Blackness's insistence on moving beyond the idea of the "Black artist," frames her description of the struggle against anti-Blackness as the expression of conscious choice: "I remembered that in choosing to identify as black, to write about black characters in my fiction and to assert the humanity of black people in my nonfiction, I've remained true to my personal history, to my family history, to my political and moral choices, and to my essential self: a self that understands the world through the prism of being a black American, and stands in solidarity with the people of the African diaspora" (Ward 2016, 94). In this single sentence, Ward moves from arguing that her racial identity and the substance of her artistic work are the product of elective choice to claiming a form of pan-African essentialism rooted in history. Most importantly, however, the progression of Ward's argument makes clear that her exercise of choice is an expression of freedom, and the essentialism that follows gains its weight precisely because she claims it rather than having it imposed on her.

Because I argue that literature constitutes a central site for the negotiation of racial identities in the twenty-first century, I contend with a central strand of contemporary argument about the meaning of race in the new century that maintains "African American literature" is itself an obsolete category. In his controversial 2010 book *What Was African American Literature?*, Kenneth Warren argues that "African American literature took shape in the context of this challenge to the enforcement and justification of racial subordination and exploitation represented by Jim Crow," and that "with the demise of Jim Crow, the coherence of African American literature has been correspondingly, if sometimes imperceptibly, eroded as well" (Warren 2011b, 2). Warren's contention is more nuanced than his provocative title suggests. He argues that what we call African American literature is the product of theorizing and writing explicitly oriented toward overturning structures of legal discrimination, and such structures have largely disappeared, along with the capability of defining a coherent literature. As with the post theorists analyzed earlier, Warren is not arguing that racial discrimination itself has disappeared. On the contrary, he is arguing that a continued analytical insistence on reading African American literature produced in the present in the same terms as that produced under Jim Crow risks undermining the capacity of recognizing and understanding current structures (Warren 2011b, 5). Unfortunately, as Warren's analysis makes clear, one cannot so easily separate the current regime from its past. Indeed, even if some of the defining characteristics of contemporary African American literature are its growing distance from firsthand experience with, and the struggle to end Jim Crow, along with an increasing willingness to critically engage with those periods from that position of distance, African American literature still remains focused on the changing meanings of Blackness in the United States.

Warren's argument, which has already prompted substantial and useful critique, is ultimately too stark in its declaration of African American literature as something of the past. As Erica Edwards notes, not only does Warren miss that much of the process of constructing the tradition of African American literature is a product of post–civil rights era institution building, he also mischaracterizes twenty-first century African American literature's investment in the literary linked fate he attempts to rebut (Edwards 2011). For example, Warren's analysis of Michael Thomas's 2007 novel *Man Gone Down* strongly echoes Henry Louis Gates Jr.'s elevation of class as the central issue facing African Americans in the new century (Gates, Jr. 2012, ix–x). Thomas's novel is suffused with the burden of the post–civil rights legacy. As a writer, Thomas's protagonist experiences the slow deterioration of his interracial marriage as he attempts to come up with sufficient money to pay for his children's Brooklyn private school. Throughout, the narrator recalls his Boston childhood in the midst of the racial strife that defined that city during the struggle for school integration in the 1970s and 1980s, going through life as "a social experiment" (Thomas 2007, 201). Warren assails how the narrator "needs to believe" that his actions have implications for the broader racial community, otherwise he might be forced to reckon with the meaningless complacency of his own life (Warren 2011b, 139). However, in conflating the narrator's anxious interrogation of racial linked fate with the author's, Warren positions the novel as typical of the post–civil rights perpetuation of the argument that African American literature still plays a role in the "broader political work . . . [that] remains to be done by black Americans through the writing and critiquing of literary fiction" (Warren 2011b, 120). What he fails to recognize is that what Thomas's novel actually typifies is the anxious consideration of that very question rather than an unqualified insistence on any particular answer to it. Thomas's novel, like theories of post-soul, postrace, and post-Blackness, produces a dynamic rewriting of the African American literary tradition that resists ossification and whose declension Warren too optimistically trumpets.

Warren's argument echoes the materialist claims of scholars like Barbara and Karen Fields (2012), who lament a growing focus on the individual's relationship to their racial identity within both the political and literary discourse of Blackness. Other authors, with Charles Johnson (2008) serving as the most important example, celebrate the freeing of the individual Black person from the burden of collective politics as enabling the possibility of a more diverse and better literature, less oriented around narratives steeped in "victimization" (37). In a sense, the arguments by Warren and Johnson about the obsolescence of African American literature as a meaningful tradition construct their own "post" argument; one that seeks to assess the continued meaning and relevance of Blackness in the present in relation to literary criticism and academic institutionalization. Despite his use of the novel as evidence of his point, Warren's work echoes Michael Thomas's *Man Gone Down* (2007) in its assertion of a definable—if still quite abstract, for Thomas—distinction between the twenty-first century and the past. Warren's own teleological claim that the present is "post" Jim Crow may not argue for progress in the way that Johnson most certainly does, but it must still be located in the broader post era transition.

By situating Warren's arguments in this way, I align with Gene Andrew Jarrett's *Representing the Race: A New Political History of African American Literature* (2011)—the whole of which serves as something of a rebuttal to Warren's book—in arguing that it is the politics of the post era that have changed, not the political importance of African American writing. The "indirect cultural politics" of twenty-first century African American literature uses issues of representation and identity as a platform through which to interrogate the increasingly ambiguous position of Black people in American society with regard to concrete political, legal, and economic structures (Jarrett 2011, 7). It is no accident then that Jarrett ends his book with a discussion of Barack Obama as both author and subject. After all, Obama, as I discuss at length in chapters 3, 4, and 5, serves as an avatar not just of neoliberal aspirations of exceptional success but also for larger questions of citizenship and legal equality framed within the temporal context of American history. More broadly, in each of the literary texts analyzed in this book, African American literature as an institutionalized category and commodity becomes an object of contention within the larger framework of debating the question of racial progress. While none of these texts voice a valedictory optimism about the present and the future, each seeks to balance the proper attention that the past should be paid in the present and future as it attempts to open new ways of thinking about and through African American literature.

So, if Warren's argument goes too far in declaring African American literature the mere product of the old Jim Crow, what form of African American literature is appropriate to an age that encompasses both what Michelle Alexander (2010) calls "the New Jim Crow" and the first Black president? Contemporary African American literature is distrustful of claims to collective meaning, recognizing the untenable essentialism that many such claims rest on. At the same time, such individualism is always in dialogue with the recognition that group-based racial identification remains the font of many of the vibrant traditions out of which African American art and literature continues to arise. Furthermore, the institutionalization of African American literature in publishing and the academy risks inscribing accepted performances of Black writing that are more likely to sell or be taught, potentially limiting the scope of aesthetic and thematic possibility (see Chow 2002, 107). In other words, the assertion of subjectivity by marginal groups may generate terms of inclusion—into society or the literary canon—contingent on maintaining a distinctive performance of ethnic identity. For example, Aida Levy-Hussen (2016) traces how engagement with African American literature has fallen into limited methodologies—which she names "therapeutic reading" and "prohibitive reading"—that fail to address its complexities.[13] As a consequence of the circumscription of reading practices and engagement in relation to ethnic literature, Jodi Melamed (2011, 39–45) argues that the incorporation of texts from diverse traditions and the politics of multiculturalism on college campuses is part of a broader neoliberalization which substitutes the superficial performance of reading works by diverse authors with the engagement of substantive issues relevant to such communities.

Although a major struggle of the civil rights era, the demand for recognition in popular culture and the academy has been only superficially successful. While programs such as Ethnic Studies remain a contentious element of America's culture wars, the expanding presence of texts by diverse authors on K-12 and post-secondary syllabi formalizes many of the demands that students protested so strongly for in the late 1960s and early 1970s. However, if the diversification of syllabi provides a way to know difference, it has the concomitant effect of essentializing Black writers, arguing that to read their work is to, on some abstract level, experience Blackness (Melamed 2011).[14] Furthermore, this concept of diversity has the potential to premise inclusion on the superficial performance of certain forms of writing designated as "Black" or certain representations of Black characters, further circumscribing the recognition that African American authors receive. Indeed, this very topic generates the oft-cited satire of Percival Everett's *Erasure*, as "the historical condition of creating black literature during a period in which African American literature has become more centralized both as a commodity and within the university" (Murray 2017, 728). However, institutionalizing African American literature, and other ethnic literatures, risks concretizing essentialist assumptions about the meaning of Black writing that potentially elide the shifting meanings of race in America.

Overall, the literature of this period both resists and reifies Blackness. In negotiating a shifting social landscape in which Black people's premature death at the hands of the police remains distressingly common, even while people of color are increasingly visible culturally, politically, and economically, twenty-first century African American authors face charting a transition that acknowledges the persistence of structural racism while imagining its transcendence. These authors ruminate on how racial identity can serve as a mere marketing label or brand to limit the aesthetic possibilities of Black artists. They offer optimistic visions of worlds in which Blackness no longer constrains either artistic expression or basic life chances. They also document continuing injustices to mourn both those lost in struggle and the distance between the present and a transcendent future. Such literature privileges individual agency over racial identity performance and emphasizes the heterogeneity contained within what are often framed as stifling or oppressive collective identities. Often, authors represent this neoliberal shift towards situating individual self-definition within the realm of private choice as liberating, in contrast to structures of external racialization that they associate with an oppressive state. Indeed, the post era emphasis on self-definition highlights authorial resistance to labels or categories even when those same authors are cynical about progress or claims that things have changed.

The emphasis on the "self," in this context, fits with a post-racial emphasis on individual success in opposition to the broad structural critiques aligned with racial collectivism. In other words, the desire to transcend the limitations posed by structural racism takes the form of an emphasis on self-affirmation, choice, and the insistence that the individual is not bound by racialist assumptions. Often, the desire for racial transcendence resembles the utopianism of Paul Gilroy's *Against Race* and its celebration of cultural hybridity and new science (Gilroy 2000). Responding to this shift, authors such as Barbara and Karen Fields (2012) emphasize the reality of racism but argue that the elision between racial identity and racism prevents the confrontation of the actual causes of racial disparity. Arguing that such "racecraft" erroneously implies a causal link between being racialized as Black or Latino and the material outcomes of structural racism, Fields and Fields (2012, 40–41) highlight the focus on racial identity as a smokescreen for racism and capitalism's continuing oppressions. In the same vein, Adolph Reed (1997, chapter 9) and Kenneth Warren (2011b, 122) argue that the emphasis on identity indulges petit bourgeois narcissism and masks class inequality both within the Black community and American society as a whole.

Notably, the class backgrounds of most of the authors analyzed in this book all reflect the expanding educational and economic opportunities available to the Black middle and upper class. Whitehead, Beatty, and Randall all attended Harvard University. Laymon and Adichie are the children of professors, though Laymon, at least, certainly did not grow up wealthy. Ward is the only exception, as a first-generation college graduate (from Stanford University). While on one level this educational background is unsurprising, and likely mirrors the similar class background among widely-published white authors, it does provide a foundation for a potentially limited repertoire of class experiences depicted across African American literary fiction. In contrast to the relative mainstream invisibility of so-called "street lit" (cf. Chiles 2006; Early 2014; Norris 2014), which circulates mainly within the Black community, the popularity of twenty-first century African American literary fiction constructs an interracial marketplace within which questions of individual identity hold wide currency. In interviews, Beatty (2015a) and Randall (2004) both comment on the distinct reading habits of white and Black readers, and note how their works may not all participate in the same conversation. The dominant white readership of these authors may create some of the unique pressures to resist expectations of Black writing imposed by the white gaze.

So why then do I insist on centralizing racial identity as the locus of my analysis of twenty-first century African American literature? I am mindful of the caution that Fields and Fields and others urge. Moving beyond essentialism, the assumption of static lines of delineation embedded in the term and concept of identity lacks foundation. Rogers Brubaker and Frederick Cooper argue that in a post-essentialist world, identity "tends to mean too much . . . too little . . . or nothing at all" (Brubaker and Cooper 2000, 1). My investment in identity, however, is rooted more in its currency than its analytical robustness. Indeed, the tension that I outline and locate at the center of twenty-first century Black cultural production arises from the ambiguity of the various texts' answer to Brubaker's and Cooper's question, "What constitutes the 'groupness' of these 'groups?'" (Brubaker and Cooper 2000, 32). I am not arguing that the texts of twenty-first century African American fiction articulate a stable or coherent definition of Blackness as a racial identity category. Instead, I am invested in the terrain of identity because it serves as the topography across which competing visions of Black political, economic, and cultural understandings are negotiated. Precisely because race provides the metalanguage through which individuals, as social beings, are inscribed into the body politic, those same individuals often maintain a heavy investment in those identities (see Higginbotham 1992).

This interrogation of the meaning of Blackness results in frequent references to W. E. B. Du Bois's twentieth-century-defining claim that "the problem of the twentieth century is the problem of the color line," as well as his idea of "double consciousness" and its foundational role as a trope in conceptualizing Blackness. As Adolph Reed argues, despite Du Bois's centrality in the study of African American life and culture, scholars have a tendency to analyze him reductively. In his essay "The 'Color Line' Then and Now: The Souls of Black Folk and the Changing Context of Black American Politics," Reed claims that scholars and artists use Du Bois's turn of the century text, and the central formulations that it contains—"the color line," "double consciousness," "the Veil"—transhistorically, expanding Du Bois's historically bounded "synecdoche," in which the experience of a mere part of the Black community stands in for it as a whole (Reed 2010, 253). The effect of this transhistoricism is to subsume the experiences of all people of African descent, in the past, present, and future, within Du Bois's concepts. Consequently, the effort to understand race in the African American literature of the twenty-first century requires a reconceptualization of this master narrative of double consciousness, making the work of twenty-first century African American literature an explicit project of building on and rearticulating Du Bois.

As I discuss at length in chapter 4, Alice Randall's 2009 novel *Rebel Yell* designates Barack Obama as an "unhyphenated" Black man, connecting the post era's redefinition of Du Bois with a vision of racial transcendence. Randall's is but one of the most explicit examples of how Barack Obama's presidency crystallizes the central question of citizenship within these identity discourses. As president, Obama centralized a contradictory Blackness within the American state. Not only was the backlash to his presidency explicitly racialized, his rise prompted valedictory declarations about the meaning and significance of this historical moment. Specifically, research by Catherine Squires (2014) reveals that the idea of a "post-racial America" circulated throughout the news media in the wake of Barack Obama's election most often as a way of reviving colorblind erasure of structural racism.[15] Furthermore, the conversation that played out in media, art, and within people's daily lives directly paralleled the post era's rhetorical situating of itself as explicitly coming after—post—the aesthetics of the late 1960s and early 1970s. In this vein, representations of Barack Obama are situated within attempts to position both his politics and his rise in the history of Black political discourse in the wake of the Civil Rights Movement. In popular terms, Obama stood as the culmination of the civil rights era dream. "Rosa Parks sat so Martin Luther King could walk. Martin Luther King walked so Obama could run. Obama ran so we could all fly," went one particularly uplifting version of this logic. Here, Obama's presidency serves as the end point of a long civil rights era and marks a decisive end to a specific history of struggle.[16]

The actual position of Obama with regard to the civil rights era Black political establishment is more complex, however, and better reflects the ambiguous transcendence of the post era. The gains of the Civil Rights Movement enabled broad-based political institutionalization within the Black community. Rogers Smith, Desmond King, and Philip Klinkner argue that the current era of racial politics, which they label "the third era," arose after a period of transition encompassing the tail end of the Civil Rights Movement that has "witnessed struggles between opposed 'color-blind' and 'race-conscious' alliances over race-targeted policies and programs" (Smith, King, and Klinkner 2011, 122). Akwasi Assensoh and Yvette Alex-Assensoh argue that the post–civil rights era has seen the growth of "Black political incorporation and incumbency" that led to the "waning efficiency" (Assensoh and Alex-Assensoh 2002, 194) of Black politics. Indeed, Barack Obama's rise serves as the culmination of a broader shift that Manning Marable named "postblack politics" (Marable 1993, 63) as early as the 1990s (see also Marable 1994; 1996).[17] Postblack politics aligns with the broader discourse of post-Blackness discussed earlier. The incorporation of Black politicians into the political power structure led Black elected officials to shift their appeals to a broader multiracial public and away from an explicit focus on the interests of the Black community. In practice, these appeals, and the policies they reflected, were "pragmatic" and generally colorblind or universal (Marable 2009, 6).[18] This shift from race-centered political alliances paralleled the rise of Barack Obama in Chicago and on the national stage.[19] In speeches such as "A More Perfect Union," Obama balanced appeals rooted in the particularity of his biography with universalist rhetoric focused on transcending past grievance and division (see Obama 2009).[20]

Likewise, the political scientist Frederick Harris quotes James Baldwin to label the process by which an explicitly racialized politics is erased as a condition of ascent as "the price of the ticket" (Harris 2012, 173).[21] Obama, in this sense, embodies a broader trend in American politics where the attainment of positions of power for Black people is contingent on distancing themselves from a politics rooted in a specific representation of the Black community. Indeed, while Smith, King, and Klinkner (2011) are right that the racial polarities of the current era in racial politics have become increasingly partisan, even Republican administrations have participated in the elevation of African Americans to high positions in government, implying that superficial diversity among positions of power may bear little relationship to liberation. Cathy Cohen, in her book *The Boundaries of Blackness*, describes such a period, in which the "symbolic opening of dominant society" requires that "marginal group members . . . police, both literally and figuratively, the most resource-poor and alienated of their communities," as a state of "advanced marginalization"(Cohen 1999, 63, 69). Cohen's argument accords with Smith, King, and Klinkner's claim that the backlash to race-conscious political organizing leads to forms of legitimacy contingent on the removal of race-based claims in mainstream politics (Smith, King, and Klinkner 2011, 121–35). Furthermore, as Imani Perry explains, "Access to privilege for minorities is often predicated upon their covering or masquerading critical expressions of identity" (Perry 2011, 135).

In its most pernicious form, post-black politics shepherds post-racialism. As Sumi Cho argues, post-racialism is an ideology that "represents a political retreat from race by redefining the terms for black politics" (Cho 2009, 1596). Though Cho argues that Critical Race theorists such as herself cannot ignore "how forging a national consensus of race-neutral universalism is so effective that post-racialism has become the presumed calling card of the first African American president," she also highlights the danger of post-racialism's appeal in its capacity to "form a type of cultural hegemony . . . [rooted in] presentist, 'yes we can' optimism" (Cho 2009, 1592). That Cho defines post-racialism using the relational term "retreat" highlights that while many who have written about race in the early twenty-first century would strongly dispute any argument that America has reached a post-racial era, they do argue for a retreat from determinative arguments about the relationship between extrinsic racial identification (how one is identified racially within society) and racial self-definition and self-expression (how one understands and performs one's own racial identity). The idea of a "retreat from race" also illustrates how the tension between optimism and pessimism manifests primarily in terms of ideas of temporality with the present constantly occupying the position of a transitional moment. The increasing primacy that Cho argues post-racialism holds assesses progress in the present specifically in terms of its relationship to a raceless future, narrowing definitions of what constitutes progress within the boundaries marked by colorblindness as an ideology.

The parallels between literary incorporation and political incorporation are no accident and generate the distinctiveness of post era discourse from superficially similar past eras. Obama's election lends weight to claims of progress and racial transcendence, while bolstering arguments that American society has undergone demonstrable shifts. Within that context, even the retrenchment of explicit racism in response to Obama's election can be cast as distinct from past instantiations because of the increased prominence and power of African Americans as a product of incorporation into dominant institutions. Consequently, the emphasis on individualism in the definition and performance of Black identity reflects how such processes of incorporation (within politics and cultural arenas) requires muting radical oppositional discourses and acceding to the growing neoliberal consensus within the post–civil rights era (see Spence 2015).

As a candidate, Barack Obama was accused at various points of being "too black" and "not black enough." The mixed-race son of a Kenyan immigrant student and a white mother, Obama's position within American racial hierarchies was in many ways stabilized through the figure of Michelle Obama. As Farah Jasmine Griffin argues, "Michelle Obama authenticated his blackness for many African Americans. He was not the descendent of enslaved ancestors; he had not grown up in a black community. But she was, and she had. The phrase, 'He married her,' was stated as proof that he made a conscious choice to identify with black people and to raise his children as African Americans" (Griffin 2011, 134). As Griffin explains, Michelle Obama stands in symbolically for a historical Black identity rooted in slavery and the Great Migration. While Obama's political rise occurred in tension with Black political institutions in Chicago, his wife's familial association with the city allowed him to draw on the history of Black Chicago as a core part of his identity. As First Lady, Michelle Obama was forced to confront intersecting constructions of race and gender identity that challenged any Black woman's right to be a "lady," let alone "first lady." Her defiant subversion of political fashion made Michelle Obama an icon even as she paradoxically performed respectability politics under the heightened gaze of the media. D. Soyini Madison explains that Michelle Obama, like her husband, models a kind of "postblack" identity by "destabilizing" "notions of blackness" through occupying positions of power (Madison 2009, 324). Even as right-wing media responded to the Obama family with racist dog whistles and white supremacist groups threatened them with violence, their presence in the White House modeled new constructions of Black identity and allowed for imaginings of different racial hierarchies.

Obama, then, parallels the broader cultural shifts encompassed by the post era, leading to his influential presence in African American literature. Obama's own skill as a writer and speaker only reinforces his status as a touchpoint for a cultural discourse that he himself participates in. On its own, the election of the first Black president would be an era-defining event because of its potential for synthesizing the progressive teleological narratives of American exceptionalism on the one hand, and towards freedom and full citizenship for the descendants of those whose enslavement was so fundamental to the foundations of the nation on the other. However, Obama's significance goes beyond just being the first Black president. Obama represents the dynamically shifting demographics of Black America, embracing diaspora, immigration, and globalization, as well as the growing importance of mixed-race identities in challenging monolithic definitions of Black identity rooted in a history of enslavement.[22] Furthermore, while they are cautious in declaring whether progress has already been made, political scientists such as Taeku Lee argue that Obama and his presidency have transformed the structures of race in the United States. Lee (2011) argues that "Barack Obama, irrespective of his preferences on the matter, stands as a metonym for race relations in the twenty-first century" (148), a point which Jarrett reinforces with regard to literary study by titling his book's conclusion "The Politics of African American Literature after Obama." In other words, any discussion of twenty-first century African American literature must account for the influence of not just Barack Obama himself but also the already ongoing shifts crystallized in Obama's symbolic presence across the first decade and a half of the early twenty-first century.

I centralize Obama's importance to this era with full awareness of Lauren Berlant's warning that "Obama is the distraction" (Berlant 2011, 241). In an essay on Obama's election's significance to the left, Berlant echoes a common argument that the mobilization of affect by the Obama campaign prevents the fundamental reorganization of society necessary to fulfill the promises made by the campaign. However, it is precisely because of Obama's broad appeal that his election highlights the key tension between progress and ongoing inequality. Berlant rightly highlights that a focus on Obama's election risks derailing left movements oriented towards collective liberation. Indeed, the success of the distraction that Barack Obama serves as concretizes those elements of the current racial discourse focused on individual expression rather than collective freedom.

Despite its emphasis on Barack Obama as an exceptionalist figure, the post era turn towards individualism does not accompany a shift away from centralizing the importance of racism to either individual authors or African American literature overall. Instead, it reflects an attempt to liberate the individual from both oppressive state violence and the existential violence of group policing through a discourse of authenticity. The murders of Trayvon Martin, Michael Brown, Rekia Boyd, Philando Castile, Freddie Gray, and so many others—and the movements that those murders prompted—do not refute any substantive investment in a transcendent present or future but instead reveal the continued power of past racial articulations, and the distance that still must be traveled towards liberation within the United States. In analyzing these complex articulations of American structures of domination, this book argues that twenty-first century African American fiction maps a shifting racial geography that moves away from conceptualizations of Blackness rooted in exclusion from full citizenship. Instead, texts of the post era illuminate structures that continue to marginalize Black people, but in new and different ways no longer sanctioned by the same legal regimes.

BLACK AND MORE THAN BLACK

In developing this book's arguments, I join substantial recent scholarship on contemporary African American literature. While, up until 2010, there were few book-length analyses of the period that went beyond discussing individual texts within more temporally broad studies, Christian Schmidt's book *Postblack Aesthetics: The Freedom to Be Black in Contemporary African American Fiction* (2017) is the first single-authored analysis of post-Blackness as a literary aesthetic (as opposed to edited collections that critique the concept, such as Simmons's and Baker's *The Trouble with Post-Blackness* (2015) and Derek Conrad Murray's *Queering Post-Black Art: Artists Transforming African-American Identity After Civil Rights* (2016), which focuses on visual art). Though our books share many of the same sources in defining post-Blackness, my work differs from Schmidt's in several key ways. Schmidt's book blankets work from the 1980s through the 2000s within his "postblack" aesthetics. Doing so conflates two related, but distinct, historical moments in which many Black authors centered the interrogation of Blackness as their subject. Indeed, this approach misses how the turn of the millennium accelerated the importance of such strains of African American literature in the context of a broader assessment of the meaning of Blackness and the position of Black people in American society. Furthermore, this longer time scale leads Schmidt to argue for post-Blackness as a specifically male aesthetic, potentially reproducing the sexist associations that writers such as Trey Ellis (whose 1988 novel *Platitudes* Schmidt analyzes) made between the mainstream and women writers.[23] Thus, while Schmidt's book serves as a useful entry in the growing literature on post-Blackness, it covers only a segment of post era thinking and it neglects the key twenty-first-century socio-historical context, most importantly the figure of Barack Obama, that I argue defines a broader post era link to the revision of double consciousness and political questions of progress.

In addition, the past few years has seen the publication of Salamishah Tillet's *Sites of Slavery: Citizenship and Racial Democracy in the Post–Civil*

Rights Imagination (2012), Brian Norman's *Neo-Segregation Narratives: Jim Crow in Post–Civil Rights American Literature* (2010), Anthony Reed's *Freedom Time: The Poetics and Politics of Black Experimental Writing* (2014), Robert J. Patterson's *Exodus Politics: Civil Rights and Leadership in African American Literature and Culture* (2013), and Aida Levy-Hussen's *How to Read African American Literature: Post–Civil Rights Fiction and the Task of Interpretation* (2016) among others. However, the dominant focus in the critical attention to the post–civil rights era remains its structural relationship to past instantiations of Black struggle. In particular, books like Tillet's and Levy-Hussen's join important studies such as Ashraf Rushdy's *Neo-Slave Narratives: Studies in the Social Logic of a Literary Form* (1999) and *Remembering Generations: Race and Family in Contemporary African American Fiction* (2001), Arlene Keizer's *Black Subjects: Identity Formation in the Contemporary Narrative of Slavery* (2004), and A. Timothy Spaulding's *Reforming the Past: History, The Fantastic, and the Postmodern Slave Narrative* (2005) in focusing on the legacies of slavery as an institution and the slave narrative as a literary form in contemporary fiction. Similarly, Norman and Patterson focus on the specific depiction of Jim Crow segregation and civil rights era leadership, respectively, in the post–civil rights era. Doing so, they join authors such as Erica Edwards, with her key study *Charisma and the Fictions of Black Leadership* (2012), in their attention to the evolution of Black political traditions into the present and their representation in African American literature.

Though less focused on the representation of history in the present, Reed's book's formalist attention to Black experimental writing, specifically on poetry and some drama, seeks to counter what he defines as "racialized reading" practices that "figure black writing as reactive rather than productive" (Reed 2014, 8). My own work shares Reed's focus on the ways in which "authors who self-identify as black take upon themselves the task of defining and redefining blackness for their own purposes" (Reed 2014, 3). However, while Reed's work is invested in "literature as a mode of *self-production*" (Reed 2014, 6, italics in original), I situate such a process within the landscape of twenty-first century racial discourse in the United States. In doing so, I avoid ascribing ontological weight to Blackness while examining the evolution of racial metalanguage during the first decade and a half of the new century. Consequently, in choosing representative texts, I generally avoid the more historically minded work that has been so ably analyzed by the books mentioned herein, and instead examine works that either explicitly or implicitly take racial identity in the new millennium as their aesthetic focus.

In choosing such works, I have limited myself to prose fiction, and novels specifically. I do this mindful of the fact that contemporary Black poetry

manifests many of the same tensions I describe in this book. Indeed, if anything, the negotiation of the relationship between newer forms of Black expression and the Black Arts Movement is heightened in poetry precisely because
the immediacy of the political themes of the movement lent itself to poetry as
a major genre for the period. The Black Took Collective's "Call for Dissonance,"
to take one example, lists the dominant stereotypes of Black writing in service
of questioning whether "these terms offer narratives that impede fresh considerations for another set of poetics?" (Harris, Lundy Martin, and Wilson 2001,
124). Reed's book strongly analyzes the tradition of revisiting and revising
Blackness within which it is necessary to situate the experimental poetics that
define the Black Took poets, such as Ronaldo Wilson, Dawn Lundy Martin,
and Duriel Harris. In a less experimental vein, poet Elizabeth Alexander, who
delivered a poem during Barack Obama's first inauguration, declares her own
poetic liberation in "Today's News":

> I didn't want to write a poem that said "blackness
> is," because we know better than anyone
> that we are not one or ten or ten thousand things
> Not one poem. (Alexander 2010, 36)

The "Call for Dissonance" and Alexander's poem reveal similar themes in contemporary Black poetry congruous to those, I argue, that define twenty-first
century African American fiction. Specifically, the celebration of heterogeneity
and the resistance to prescriptive aesthetics mirrors attempts to negotiate the
terms of individual liberation within a society structured by white supremacy.

However, because the novel contains "a certain semantic openendedness,
a living contact with unfinished, still-evolving contemporary reality (the
openended present)" (Bakhtin 1981, 7), it more explicitly engages with the larger
social discourse. Furthermore, with the current marginalization of poetry
publishing in the contemporary United States, these fiction narratives also cir-
culate, and thus participate, more widely in the public discourse on Blackness.
Accordingly, the texts on which I focus my analysis in this book are generally
bestsellers or by prominent authors who receive wide discussion in the media.
Within each chapter, I combine my close readings of the texts themselves with
a discussion of how they fit into the larger historical, social, and ideological
context of the shifting meanings of Blackness in the new century.

This book is structured around the conjunction between the post era and
the Obama presidency. Chapter 1 discusses the implications of labeling the
current era in African American literature aesthetically and overall. Focusing
on Golden's concept of "post-black art," as introduced earlier, I analyze the

expansion of the term post-Blackness to encompass the entire era in conjunction with an analysis of Colson Whitehead's novel *Sag Harbor* (2009). Whitehead's novel illustrates the tension in post-Blackness between a racial individualism that manifests the loosening bonds of group identification and the recognition of the still present meaning that race holds. Chapter 2 pushes against the implications of progress built into the categorization of "post-black art" by emphasizing the continuity between the representation of Hurricane Katrina in Jesmyn Ward's 2011 National Book Award-winning novel *Salvage the Bones* and Kiese Laymon's 2013 novel *Long Division* and tropes of orphaning and apocalyptic storms in African American literature and literary theory. Whereas the first chapter argues that Colson Whitehead's revision of the canonical "scene of instruction" in African American literature aligns with post-Blackness's emphasis on racial individualism, chapter 2 argues that representations of Hurricane Katrina reinscribe a racial group identification that resists such individualism. Framing my analysis through Rob Nixon's concept of "slow violence," I demonstrate how Ward and Laymon depict the precariousness of Black life to highlight how the margins become a site through which African Americans negotiate their vulnerability and survive in an anti-Black world.

In chapters 3, 4, and 5, I discuss how Obama's election provides a flashpoint through which some Black authors have envisioned the instantiation of new a racial order in dialogue with post era discourses. Specifically, chapter 3 analyzes Colson Whitehead's *Apex Hides the Hurt* (2006) and Paul Beatty's *Slumberland* (2008) through the lens of Charles Johnson's essay "The End of the Black American Narrative," published during Barack Obama's presidential run. Whitehead's and Beatty's novels represent attempts to imagine the dimensions of Johnson's call for "new, and better stories" (Johnson 2008, 42). Like Johnson, Whitehead and Beatty emphasize the provisionality of racial categories and labels to highlight their incapability of speaking to the diversity of Black experience in the present and future. Highlighting the commodification of Black identity and Black culture, Whitehead and Beatty interrogate the meaning of Blackness in the present as they trace attempts to evade capitalism's monetization of post–civil rights discourses of diversity and multiculturalism. Chapter 4, however, extends Johnson's reading of Barack Obama's election as an era-shifting moment by analyzing his representation as a character in Alice Randall's novel *Rebel Yell* (2009). Randall's novel addresses Obama's election directly through his inclusion in the story of Abel Jones III, the son of a prominent Civil Rights Movement attorney who becomes a spy and then a major figure in the war on terror under the Bush administration. Characterizing Obama as an "unhyphenated man" not burdened by Du Boisian double consciousness,

Randall narrates Obama's birth as a fairy tale at the end of her novel to imagine the incipience of a new era in which Obama replaces Abel—who kills himself in response to Obama's rise—as the bearer of the legacy of the civil rights era into a new century.

In the final chapter, I return to Obama's symbolic cosmopolitanism to analyze the implications of the recently expanding canon of literature by immigrant authors of color, particularly the African immigrants that Chimamanda Ngozi Adichie labels "Non-American blacks" in her 2013 novel *Americanah*. Through an analysis of Adichie's novel, I argue that the demographic changes of the post–civil rights era, enabled by the liberalizing of immigration law in the 1965 Hart-Celler Act, push against the assumption of a monolithic Black experience in the United States while also emphasizing the way in which Blackness continues to flatten the diverse experiences of people of color. To exemplify these shifts, Adichie's novel returns to the symbolic figure of Barack Obama, whose campaign hovers in the background of her protagonist Ifemelu's relationship with a Black Yale professor. Adichie's lens allows her to interrogate the structures of American racial dichotomies while constructing a diasporic Blackness that is at once derivative of such dichotomies yet also distinct.

ON THE BLACKNESS OF POST-BLACKNESS

Colson Whitehead and Racial Individualism

About halfway through Colson Whitehead's novel *Sag Harbor* (2009), his narrator, Benji, steals a six-pack of Coca-Cola from a friend's house. During the summer of 1985, in which the novel is set, Coca-Cola introduced New Coke, containing a supposedly improved formula and taste. Dedicated Coke drinkers such as Benji were not pleased, and there was a substantial backlash, leading the company to reissue the previous formula under the instantly nostalgic name of "Coca-Cola Classic." At this point in the novel, Benji has been hoarding Old Coke. Finding several six-packs of Old Coke at the house of his friend Karen, Benji finds himself in a dilemma over whether to steal them or not. A few pages earlier, thinking about whether to shoplift from a convenience store, Benji imagines the "crisp, familiar, and so-dignified" voice of Sidney Poitier saying, "They think we steal, and because they think we steal, we must not steal" (Whitehead 2009a, 101), leading him to pay for his Fruit Roll-Up. At Karen's house, however, he does decide to steal the Cokes, comically spilling them all over the floor as he attempts to make a stealthy exit. He reflects on the unique paralysis of his position: "Move. Don't move. Act. Don't act. The results were the same. This was my labyrinth" (Whitehead 2009a, 106). Benji's dilemma, framed as it is by Poitier's assertion of racial stereotypes, typifies the discursive tension over the definition of African American art in the twenty-first century. Much like Benji, the Black artist stands at the nexus of diverse racialized expectations about the relationship between an individual's racial identity and the form and content of their expression. Returning to the image of Benji, his crime exposed, I suggest one can read *Sag Harbor* as Whitehead's interrogation of a major post era dilemma: how do African American authors negotiate the ongoing attempt to define and label African American cultural expression in the twenty-first century?

In the wake of the substantive cultural and legal changes enabled by the long-term advocacy of African Americans during the civil rights and Black Power movements, the scope and nature of the opportunities available to African Americans has shifted, particularly for members of the growing Black middle and upper class. In response, African American literature has traced the consequences of these changes for African American identity. As the above scene in Whitehead's *Sag Harbor* illustrates, questions remain about the scope of the changes that have occurred during the post–civil rights era. Particularly, do economic gains among certain segments of the Black community simply mask the same stubborn structures of racial hierarchy and racial violence? *Sag Harbor*, rather than offering any definitive answer to the implications of the changing class structure of the Black community, hazards a tenuous portrait of racial power structures amid the transition. Specifically, this chapter analyzes Colson Whitehead's novel through the lens of Thelma Golden's concept of post-Blackness (Golden 2001) to argue that it typifies the term's evocation of a generational tension between the liberation of the individual African American subject and the recognition of the continued role that collective racial identities play in the larger society.

In assessing the implications of post-Blackness as a concept, Whitehead's fiction raises several key complications. First, in declaring *Sag Harbor* a "post-black story," the critic Touré, author of *Who's Afraid of Post-Blackness?*, cites its unwillingness to depict the "horror of being black" as one of the novel's defining features (Touré 2009). Touré's comments align post-Blackness with Charles Johnson's injunction in "The End of the Black American Narrative" to tell "new and better stories" that move beyond the simplistic narrative of struggle that has been at the heart of much of African American literature (Johnson 2008, 42). Both Johnson and Touré note that such an emphasis does not mean that society has wholly moved beyond the structures of racialized discrimination that gave rise to such struggles. However, as Touré's review also points out, it is precisely because of Whitehead's protagonist's "enormous class privilege" that he can write a story capable of being described as post-Black (Touré 2009). Though Touré highlights his association between class privilege and post-Blackness, Emily Lordi pointedly countered that Touré's assessment of "post-black" classism, in Whitehead's novel, relegates numerous already marginalized people to the position of being "still-black" (Lordi 2009).

Consequently, the issue of Whitehead's own class privilege, and the class privilege of the characters in his novels, calls into question the validity of analyzing his work as the basis for broader claims about the post–civil rights era. Whitehead's work underscores Henry Louis Gates Jr.'s argument that the central transformation of Blackness in the twenty-first century is specifically class-based, stating that "the fundamental problem for African Americans in the twenty-first century" is "how class differentials within 'the race' compound individual experiences of anti-black racism, and ever more profoundly shape what it means to be 'black' itself" (Gates 2012, x). Gates's decision to place "the race" and "black" in quotes highlights the broader indeterminacy emphasized by each attempt to characterize race in the new century. Gates's statement consciously borrows the form of Du Bois's famous turn of the twentieth century declaration that the "problem of the Twentieth Century is the problem of the color-line" to argue for the centrality of different class experiences in generating the transformation of African American identity in the twenty-first century (Du Bois [1903] 1999, 5). Furthermore, Gates is not the only one to document growing class cleavages within the Black community. Political scientists like Adolph Reed (2016) and Lester K. Spence (2015) have emphasized how intraracial inequality has transformed Black politics, incentivizing candidates that cater to the wealthy at the expense of a broad-based consideration of Black community interests.

In many ways, when Touré declares that "It's time for us to hear more post-black stories like [Benji's]" (Touré 2009), he expresses the common refrain that representations of Blackness in popular culture traffic in stereotypes focusing on crime and the urban underclass. Saying this, Touré argues that African American literature needs to properly reflect the shifting class demographics of the Black community. Writing only a few years after the summer of 1985 during which the novel is set, it is these class advantages that Trey Ellis described as defining what he called "the New Black Aesthetic." In that essay, Ellis discussed a generation of Black artists, most in their twenties at the time, who felt "misunderstood by both the black worlds and the white" (Ellis 1989, 234). As discussed in the introduction, Ellis defines "the New Black Aesthetic" widely, refusing to provide concrete characteristics to either restrict or clarify the qualities that unites the works of the artists he describes, from the California punk band Fishbone to filmmakers Spike Lee and Reginald Hudlin. Indeed, the characteristic that most unites the people he discusses is their shared class background, which he describes as "a minority's minority mushrooming with the current black bourgeoisie boom" (Ellis 1989, 234).

Touré's review of Whitehead's novel echoes Ellis's definition, arguing that what makes the novel a post-Black story, and what makes it both worthwhile and a model for future African American writing, is precisely because it tells a class story within the Black community that he presumes his reader has not heard before. Leaving aside the fact that stories of the Black bourgeoisie have been quite common and prominent throughout the African American literary tradition—stretching back at least as far as Charles Chesnutt's *The Wife of His*

Youth and Other Stories of the Color Line (1899) and *The Marrow of Tradition* (1901) and continuing through works by Jessie Fauset and others during the New Negro Renaissance—the depiction of the Black middle and upper class is one of the dominant characteristics of contemporary African American literature, with its parades of professors, doctors, lawyers, and, in Whitehead's fiction alone, a range of Black professionals, many of whom come directly from privileged backgrounds.

That so much contemporary African American fiction focuses on the experiences of the Black bourgeoisie, while also seemingly compelled to express the novelty of doing so, reflects several trends. First, the post–civil rights era has seen the expansion of the Black middle and upper class over the past half century. While overall income inequality between African Americans and whites remains substantial, a greater proportion of the Black population has seen not only income and wealth gains, but also entrance into institutions (up to and including the presidency) previously the exclusive province of whites (see Smith and King 2011).[1] Second, Whitehead's representation suggests that differential class experiences (particularly in the context of incorporation into the existing power structure) diminish what Michael Dawson called the sense of "linked fate"—the belief that the interests of the individual are directly connected to those of the race as a whole—among African Americans (Dawson 1995; see also Gay, Hochschild, and White 2016).[2]

This chapter does not dispute the centrality of changing class demographics in the Black community to the conceptualization of post-Blackness. As I show, however, Whitehead's novel reveals a post-Blackness less triumphal than Touré's review suggests. Though the novel highlights a specific class experience, it signals a broader post–civil rights uneasiness with a definition of Blackness as a collective linked to civil rights era struggle and the African American literary tradition. Whitehead's novel depicts a generation that is indebted to the struggles of their direct ancestors yet increasingly dissatisfied with the obligations that such a history seems to place on them based solely on their skin color. The remnants of Jim Crow's racialized order are still present; however, Benji and his friends chart individualized paths that are at once inherited from their parents and grandparents, yet distinct in their possibilities. Like the concept of post-Blackness itself, *Sag Harbor* imagines the possibility of change through the lens of irony, hazarding the possibility of liberation while qualifying its scope. Ultimately, Whitehead's novel emphasizes provisionality and anti-climax, promising revelation and consistently failing to deliver. The post-Blackness of Whitehead's writing mirrors the vacillation between optimism and pessimism in African American literature of the early twenty-first century, foregrounding the possibilities of a new era for African American art while highlighting the incompleteness of the liberation promised by the progress of the last half century.

CATEGORIZING AFRICAN AMERICAN CULTURAL PRODUCTION IN THE NEW MILLENNIUM: FROM POST-BLACK ART TO POST-BLACKNESS

Whitehead's fiction's emphasis on provisionality lies within the context of attempts to categorize the cultural production of the post era. In this chapter, I provide a genealogy of one of the key "post" terms: post-Blackness. While the term originated in the world of visual art, its circulation expanded with the release of Touré's book *Who's Afraid of Post-Blackness?* (2011). Though I only focus on one of the many "post" categories of the post era in this chapter, the conceptions of identity and politics and the category's relationship to the larger twenty-first century overlaps substantially with the various other terms. Consequently, my analysis of post-Blackness in this chapter can be read as largely applying to the full range of terms I have mentioned so far, with their subtle differences explained in my introduction. As the philosopher Paul C. Taylor has pointed out, despite the diversity of such terms, "there is considerable overlap between them" and they should be understood "as different names for the same complex reality" (Taylor 2007, 625).

As the scene with which I began this chapter illustrates, Whitehead is particularly attentive to the contradictory burdens felt by artists of color in the early twenty-first century. During a 1999 interview, Whitehead makes the connection between the post–civil rights era and the agency of the Black artist explicit. In response to a question about whether African American writers in the present "have more freedom than previous generations," he states, "Now I think there are a lot more of us writing and a lot more different areas we're exploring. It's not as polemicized. I'm dealing with serious race issues, but I'm not handling them in a way that people expect" (Whitehead 1999a). Instead of feeling obligated to address the importance of race in American society through the lens of a specific ideology, Whitehead describes an aesthetic freedom that is not about moving beyond race but is about redefining the relationship between racial identity and the individual artist.

The way Whitehead explains this redefined relationship makes his importance to critics seeking to define "post-" categories no surprise. Two book-length academic works, Derek Maus's *Understanding Colson Whitehead* (2014) and Kimberly Fain's *Colson Whitehead: The Postracial Voice of Contemporary Literature* (2015) analyze Whitehead through explicit "post" frameworks: "the postsoul condition" in Maus and "postracialism" in Fain. Maus situates

Whitehead within post-soul culture historically, linking his work to an "inter-generational tension" over Black identity (Maus 2014, 13). Fain goes further, positioning Whitehead as a prophetic figure in American literature and culture speaking to the "racial irrelevance" of "postracialism" in which "ethnicity remains an ancillary factor" for his characters or is able to be transcended (Fain 2015, xvii). Furthermore, Ramón Saldívar's article in *Narrative*, "The Second Elevation of the Novel: Race, Form, and the Postrace Aesthetic in Contemporary Narrative," uses Whitehead's novel *The Intuitionist* to define a new "postrace aesthetic" characterized by what he calls "speculative realism" (Saldívar 2013, 3). As Saldívar makes clear, Whitehead's novels typify how African American literature (and, according to Saldívar, American ethnic literatures in general) participates in a dialogical process by which racial identity and racial meaning are actively made and articulated. Literary works by authors of color have often served as radical critiques of American racial hierarchies. However, those very critiques have the potential to engender their own reified hierarchies, requiring still further, and distinct, interventions. Whitehead's interview illustrates this fact in relation to the orthodoxies of African American literature itself, arguing for the necessity of writing in different forms and dealing with distinct themes in a new historical context. As he points out later in the interview, it is not that what his interviewer labels as "the black intellectual novel" is actually a phenomenon unique to the present, it is that the determination of which forms are privileged, read, critiqued, and debated shifts over time to highlight what counts as "serious race issues" at any given moment (Whitehead 1999a).[3]

Whitehead's redefinition of what constitutes confronting "serious race issues" in the context of fiction mirrors attempts to define what Golden (2001) termed "post-black art." As introduced in the previous chapter, like Whitehead does with his own work, Golden specifically contrasts "post-black art" with the aesthetic principles of the Black Arts Movement to construct a generational term emphasizing individual artistic agency over the meaning of racial identity.[4] Post-Blackness underscores the simultaneous turn towards the privileging of individual agency over racial identity and expression and concurrent recognition of the continued centrality of race in contemporary American society. Golden's initial usage of "post-black" was modest, and she has repeatedly expressed surprise at its spread (including dismissing it in the exhibition volume for the *Freestyle* follow-up *Frequency* [2005]). The term, with its embedded reference to the Black Arts Movement (the "Black art" these young artists were supposedly post), however, was a way of hazarding a new aesthetic framework for understanding Black art in the twenty-first century. For this reason, Golden's short essay serves as the first major document of the post era, taking the turn of the century as an opportunity to rearticulate the meaning of Black identity and its relationship to the production of art.

With her use of "post," Golden suggests what Paul C. Taylor describes as "a sense of being in the wake of an important historical shift" (Taylor 2007, 625). Because of the dominance of the Civil Rights Movement in contemporary U.S. iconographies of race, current "post" categorizations are especially fraught. As Erica Edwards argues, the post–civil rights era has seen "the simultaneous upward and downward expansion of life chances for African-American communities," a disparity that has not only stalled "progress," but also potentially placed the interests of different segments of the Black community in conflict (Edwards 2013, 193). The Civil Rights Movement's dominant role in framing public discourse on race haunts the attempt to analyze African American art in the present precisely because it mirrors the tension between the triumphalism of many representations of the civil rights era and the incompleteness of the United States civil rights project. Thus, any attempt to argue that the current moment is "post" requires that an author negotiate this tension between the racialized structures of American society and the implications those structures hold for African American art.

To navigate this tension, Golden argues that the term refers to Black artists who are "adamant about not being labeled as black artists" even as they "[redefine] complex notions of blackness" (Golden 2001, 13). The looseness of Golden's definition mirrors her uneasiness with the prescriptions she associates with the concepts of "black art." In fact, Golden presents her original definition of "post-black art" ironically to preemptively deny the label's definitional power. Describing the term arising from her and Glenn Ligon's "shared love of absurd uses of language," Golden states she settled on the label based on "evidence of art and ideas that could only be labeled (both ironically and seriously) in this way—post-black" (Golden 2001, 13). Though her introduction is peppered with references to "the multicultural moment" in art, "the new paradigm in the recognition of heretofore often marginalized artistic practices," and a "new millennium" that "begged the inevitable question: 'after all of this, what's next?'" Golden seems reluctant to argue that "post-black art" is a definitive answer (Golden 2001, 13). Furthermore, Golden's apparent uneasiness with the frequency with which she is asked about the term during talks and interviews following her 2001 *Freestyle* introduction reflects her clear desire not to replace past aesthetic prescriptions for Black artists with new ones of her own.

Indeed, as Golden made clear during a 2009 talk at London's Tate Modern, she envisioned her initial use of "post-black art" as existing specifically within the particular history of African American visual art. Golden argues this approach to African American art becomes possible precisely because the generation of artists to which she refers relate to the civil rights era as "history" rather than through direct experience. The fact that these artists have heard about the civil rights and Black Power movements from parents and in schools and popular culture instead of having lived through it enables a simultaneous obsession with and distance from this history. Earlier in the talk, Golden explains the museum's 1968 founding was an expression of Black Arts Movement ideologies that argued for the evaluation of African American art based on its relationship to a definable Black experience. Consequently, upon taking over her position as curator, she describes her desire to initiate an idea of "what difference could mean within an institutional space organized, founded, and continuing to live within a definition of blackness" (Golden 2009).[5] As Golden's statement makes clear, her conceptualization of "post-black art" exists directly within a space that continues to be defined by Blackness. In other words, she saw herself as referring to post-"black art," rather than "post-black" art, based on the work of artists specifically resisting the prescriptive aesthetics of the Black Arts Movement. However, despite Golden's attempts to clarify her initial definition in her 2009 talk, "post-black" has circulated most commonly as a separate adjective (see Byrd 2002, 35). Though a usage that Golden repudiates, the adjective "post-black" and her initial definition share an attention to the meaning of Black art and identity in the wake of the civil rights and Black Power movements. Just as Golden emphasizes her desire to define the work of Black artists outside the normative frames of what constitutes authentic "black art" in the context of the African American struggle for civil rights, the application of the term as an adjective does not refer to being "post-black" in any totalizing way, but rather as an attempt to understand the meaning of Blackness in the present without being defined by previous normative definitions. Building on each of the authors I have cited here, Christian Schmidt offers a useful summing up of "postblackness" as a set of aesthetics that do "not present a new category of (black) identity but, instead, critically question and destabilize existing narratives of blackness" (Schmidt 2017, 64). Schmidt rightfully emphasizes that post-Blackness, whether in Golden's initial formulation or Touré's more expansive vision, does not speak to individual constructions of Black identity. Rather, it refers to a relation through which Black people and Black artists can evade a "narrow script of blackness" (Schmidt 2017, 28).

The popularity of the term suggests that "post-black" crystallizes something decisively different about the post–civil rights generation. In an essay in the exhibition volume for *Frequency* (the second of five "F series" exhibits at the Studio Museum, and the follow up to *Freestyle*), Malik Gaines argues that the liberation provided by "post-black art" resides in its ability to approach race in "multifarious" ways, allowing one to look at race in "a less structured" manner that gives "us African Americans the upper hand in dealing with the preposterous injuries of racism that inflict themselves across our culture" (Gaines 2005, 27). Instead of displacing either the history of struggle for civil rights or the present inequalities of race, Gaines sees this redefinition as enabling African Americans, particularly African American artists, to engage race through their own agency over the category, rather than submitting to definitions imposed either by historical constructs or present hierarchies. As Gaines points out, the aesthetic liberation conceptualized by "post-black art" occurs on the level of the individual rather than the entire race. Gaines's words recall how Golden's initial introduction of the term highlights the individual agency of contemporary Black artists in contrast to the collective aesthetics of the Black Arts Movement: "Their work, in all of its various forms, speaks to an individual freedom that is a result of the transitional moment in the quest to define ongoing changes in the evolution of African-American art and ultimately to ongoing redefinition of blackness in contemporary culture" (Golden 2001, 15). As the example of Gaines's celebration of the term illustrates, the popularity of the concept of "post-black art" arises directly from its implied restoration of the Black artist's capacity for self-definition, and, by extension, the Black individual's as well. Gaines's words find elaboration in Derek Conrad Murray's *Queering Post-Black Art*, which celebrates post-Blackness as both the product of queer artistic practice and a methodology for queering Black identity, "signalling a new blackness that was free of racial obligation and the burden of historical trauma" (Murray 2016, 19).

In contrast to the specific use of the term with regard to visual art and queer Black artists in particular, Touré's book *Who's Afraid of Post-Blackness?: What It Means to Be Black Now* (2011) uses the term post-Blackness in much more expansive ways, which he makes explicit by explaining that Golden does not necessarily endorse his redefinition. Though Touré defines post-Blackness in diverse ways throughout his book, he consistently emphasizes the fluidity of racial identity and the diversity of Blackness as its central characteristics. For example, he states, "We are in a post-Black era, which means simply that the definitions and boundaries of Blackness are expanding in forty million directions—or really, into infinity" (Touré 2011, 12). However, while he emphasizes that post-Blackness reflects an era of "rugged individualism," Touré does not argue for a definition of post-Blackness that imagines a Blackness detached entirely from the history and culture of African Americans (Touré 2011, 8). Instead, he argues that post-Blackness "means we are like Obama: rooted in but not restricted by Blackness" (Touré 2011, 12). Furthermore, as with Golden, Touré emphasizes that post-Blackness is not a descriptor of individual persons. Instead, he decisively argues for it as a generational term, referring to an "era when our identity options are limitless" (Touré 2011, 12).

It is Touré's expansion of the term in an attempt to designate a broader identity category that has prompted the most backlash. For example, the essays in the Houston Baker- and K. Merinda Simmons-edited *The Trouble with Post-Blackness* (2015) seek to rebut both the implicit optimism about racial progress they argue is embedded in his use of the term, and the distinction it claims among previous artistic expressions and those in the present. Indeed, the fact that Touré does not substantially revise the meaning of Blackness speaks to what Randall Kennedy, in a review of the book, calls the "fallacy" of his definition. Kennedy (2011) argues that the individualism that Touré emphasizes to rebut those "identity conservatives" who would police Blackness simultaneously undermines any capacity to designate the conditions of group membership (see Touré 2011, 23). However, as his book makes clear, Touré does not want to overturn Blackness as a group identity. The contradiction between the liberal concept of racial identity as the product of individual choice and the maintenance of an underlying conception of there being a common history and culture among African Americans which defines that racial identity illustrates a similar tension to Golden's incomplete definition. Ultimately, for both Golden and Touré, the idea of post-Blackness posits an incomplete liberation in which the normative Blackness each seeks to deconstruct remains implicitly present.

While Touré's book mirrors Golden's emphasis on moving beyond the political burden placed on African American artists, and individuals more broadly, his work also mirrors the self-help quality of Ytasha Womack's book *Post-Black: How a New Generation is Redefining African American Identity* (2010). Womack focuses on "post-blackness" as defined by the expansive opportunities available to a new generation of entrepreneurial African Americans with greater access to economic opportunities, elite educational institutions, and power in society. As with Touré's book, Womack centralizes the figure of Barack Obama as typical of these new opportunities, with his ultimate success as a model for other individuals to follow. In these texts, Obama is not merely emblematic of social change; his life, family, and success provide a template for the transcendence of social limitations based on race. Problematically, while these discussions of Obama note the forms of racism that linger in American society, they imagine the cumulative effects of a whole generation of primarily urban, young, educated, and successful Black men and women as capable of overcoming the ingrained structures of racism, further marginalizing racism in the American mainstream while underscoring the expansion of economic inequalities within Black communities. By envisioning a more meritocratic mainstream, in which white racism is envisioned as producing bumbling and clueless bureaucrats and middle managers who merely need to be negotiated with or tolerated, Womack, Touré, and others imagine a Blackness defined solely by those with access to certain forms of class privilege, neglecting the continued effects that structural racism has on the perpetuation of African American poverty. The emphasis on individual achievement aligns with a current focus on the success or failure of the individual rather than the group overall. Golden's artistic emphasis on the liberation of the individual creator from the proscriptions of Black Arts Movement era theorizing finds its larger expression in Toure's and Womack's more expansive discussions on the primary value of individual success, even within institutionally racist structures.

Despite such critiques, the movement of the term "post-black art" into the broader discourse on race highlights the attractiveness of the liberation it promises. Post-Blackness, whether in Golden's, Toure's, or Womack's usage, indexes the tension between the attempt to extend African American aesthetic traditions into the present and future absent the anxieties of influence that such traditions imply. On the most basic level, this is a tension between individual and collective identities. As Golden's initial definition of the term clarifies, post-Black art is not a "retreat from race" as subject matter (Cho 2009, 1596). Instead, it is an attempt to redefine what it means both to represent and individually perform racial identity. In this context, Whitehead's semi-autobiographical portrait of a distinct class segment of the post–civil rights generation undergoing a transition in how they understand their own racial identity typifies the tenuous and incomplete shift of "post-Black art." *Sag Harbor* attempts to rearticulate what it looks like for literary fiction to take on "serious race issues" without reinscribing monolithic labels that undermine individual agency.

COLSON WHITEHEAD'S REVISION OF TRADITION

In *Sag Harbor*, Whitehead animates the generational changes referenced in the foregoing intellectual history of post-Blackness in fictional memoir form. His novel depicts the coming-of-age of a generation of the relatively privileged children of the civil rights generation. Consequently, while the novel focuses on the semi-autobiographical character of Benji, the text functions as something of a generational origin story for the post-Black artist. As initial interviews and reviews pointed out, the story itself reproduces episodes from Whitehead's own youth, with details such as a BB gun accident leaving the protagonist with a pellet permanently embedded in his face drawn specifically from the author's childhood. As those early reviews also mention, *Sag Harbor* is an anomaly in Whitehead's oeuvre. Novels such as *The Intuitionist* (1999), *John Henry Days* (2001), *Apex Hides the Hurt* (2006)—which I analyze in detail in chapter 3—and *Zone One* (2011) simultaneously wear their genre influences on their sleeves while aspiring to high-concept postmodernist insight. Indeed, Whitehead's National Book Award and Pulitzer Prize Award-winning *The Underground Railroad* (2016) bears similarities to the neo-slave narrative form, but builds on the conceit that the Underground Railroad is a literal underground railroad. *Sag Harbor*, on the other hand, is deceptively slight. As Charles McGrath stated in the *New York Times*, "The closest 'Sag Harbor' comes to that kind of high concept [the nomenclature consulting of *Apex Hides the Hurt*] is a moment of crisis created by New Coke supplanting Coke" (McGrath 2009). As Derek Maus explains, however, Whitehead makes clear in interviews that he sees the realism of the coming-of-age story as simply another genre form to utilize and subvert (Maus 2014, 100). Whitehead's implicit resistance to any "climax" or "big revelation" repudiates not just the structure of the coming-of-age novel, but also the idea that a coming-of-age story by a Black writer should or would necessarily contain some conflict or struggle born of the protagonist's racial identity. Touré's review makes this explicit by comparing Whitehead's use of the memoir/coming-of-age form to Claude Brown's *Manchild in the Promised Land*, Richard Wright's *Black Boy*, Maya Angelou's *I Know Why the Caged Bird Sings*, and, more contemporaneously, Kody Scott's *Monster*, all of which "document the horror of being black and enslaved or segregated or impoverished or imprisoned" (Touré 2009). In this sense *Sag Harbor*'s focus on a new Black bourgeoisie forces a major question about post-Blackness as both aesthetic movement and identity construct. While there is no legitimate argument to be made that there are certain experiences or identity performances that are more authentically "black," does suggesting, therefore, that we have entered a "post-black" era, one defined by the diversity of Black experiences, neglect the still present role that race plays in determining social hierarchies, particularly around class? After all, as Stuart Hall famously argued, "Race is . . . the modality in which class is 'lived'" (Hall 1996, 55). While it is certainly legitimate to represent the success of members of the Black middle class, and to situate those experiences prominently within the African American cultural tradition, does such economic success imply the end of a definable racial tradition, as Kenneth Warren argues in *What Was African American Literature* (2011)? In other words, Whitehead's novel makes a point about African American literature more broadly. By resisting potential expectations, and denying the reader the anticipated conflicts, Whitehead diversifies what Black experiences can be described as "authentic" while undermining stereotypical associations between Blackness, poverty and crime.

In depicting this class experience, Whitehead makes Benji an archetypal "cultural mulatto." In "The New Black Aesthetic" (1989), Ellis positions cultural mulattism as liberatory, enabling the cultural mulatto figure to transgress cultural and racial boundaries with a minimum of fuss or hassle. The primary measure of this liberation is a sense of comfort. Unlike the classic literary tragic mulatto figure, Ellis seems to suggest that the cultural mulatto feels no inner existential conflict over whether their stack of Buzzcocks and Siouxie and the Banshees albums (to pick two of Benji's favorite bands) qualify their Blackness in any way. Furthermore, through the use of first-person narration, the text itself voices a cultural mulatto identity in which the references to early 1980s Black and white popular culture are flung widely, without regard for whether the reader will be aware of the references. The cultural literacy required by the reader necessitates an intimate familiarity with cultural touchstones racially coded as either Black or white. The focus on the cultural mulatto figure highlights the hybrid nature of American culture, troubling the segregated distinction between a specific tradition of African American art and mainstream American art. Just as the analysis of the mulatto archetype in American literature emphasizes how the boundary crossing of the tragic mulatto ultimately reifies the distinctions that their person would seem to challenge,[6] the cultural mulatto archetype depicts the post–civil rights generation as polyglot, able to navigate a range of cultural milieus and traditions without losing their Blackness.

For Whitehead, the doubleness of the cultural mulatto figure provides a template for imagining the irreconcilability of the different selves contained within the individual. Fundamentally, Whitehead's novel challenges any possible contours by which to delineate an authentic Blackness, while rejecting the idea that the lack of authenticity calls into question the meaning or value of race as an organizing concept. Expanding on Ellis's definition, Benji's, and *Sag Harbor*'s cultural mulattism does not merely trouble a nationalistic Blackness premised on the idea that there are more or less Black experiences, cultures, and identify formations. Instead, Whitehead's construction of Benji's double consciousness evidences little anxiety over his perception of his own racial identity. As with Thelma Golden's definition of post-Blackness, in embracing the fluidity of Blackness, these authors suggest that the flux is not a sense of a constantly shifting individual consciousness, but rather recognition that the categories themselves are constructed and shifting, and that the individual establishes a sense of self in relation to the shifting categories.

However, the desire present in Whitehead's novel to move beyond superficial overdeterminations of what constitutes Black art or Black experience—a desire mirrored in both Touré's and Thelma Golden's definitions of post-Blackness—forces a qualitative evaluation of what meaning race still holds in relation to the lives and experiences of the diverse members of the Black community.

After all, to acknowledge diversity, that there are as many ways to be Black as there are Black people, as Touré emphasizes at the opening of *Who's Afraid of Post-Blackness?* (2011, 5), is not to argue that race no longer plays a role in determining and shaping the diversity of individual Blackness. So, then what is the nature of that influence? Whitehead addresses this in describing the circumscribed limits of his characters' identity performance. In discussing the influences of stereotypes of Blackness on their experiences, Whitehead focuses on the example of whether one could walk down the street with a watermelon. "You didn't, for example, walk down Main Street with a watermelon under your arm. Even if you had a pretty good reason" (Whitehead 2009a, 88). Regardless of the specific circumstances within which one might come to walk down the street with a watermelon under your arm, one's behavior and sense of self is controlled not by the actual racist comments or perceptions of individual viewers of the action, but rather the perception of a gaze exerting social power. In a situation like this, mere perception is sufficient to determine one's actions.

Importantly, Whitehead emphasizes that one's actions are being externally determined regardless of whether one perceives oneself to be defying the presumed mandate by ostentatiously parading around deliberately with a watermelon:

> For argument's sake, let's say there was a brand of character who was able to say, Forget that, I'm going to walk up and down Main Street with a watermelon under each arm! And one between my legs! Big grin on my face! Peak o' rush hour! Such rebellion was inherently self-conscious and overly determined. It doth protest too much, described an inner conflict as big as that of the watermelon-avoiders. We were all of us stuck whether we wanted to admit it or not. We were people, not performance artists, all appearances to the contrary. (Whitehead 2009a, 88)

As Benji points out, one's actions are being overdetermined by racial stereotypes regardless of their content, suggesting both a perpetual and omnipresent quality to white supremacy. Benji's reference to the distinction between "people" and "performance artists" highlights the tension inherent in post-Blackness's turn towards individual agency with regard to racial identity. While arguments that there can be and should be no restrictions on how one performs one's Blackness appear liberating, they tend to focus on the idea of intraracial identity policing. Touré's expansion of Golden's term in *Who's Afraid of Post-Blackness?* specifically rebuts claims of inauthenticity within the Black community. Here, however, Whitehead reminds the reader that the exercise of power over how and in what ways racial identities are expressed is embedded in the larger society. The sense of being "stuck" signals the tension that Golden's and Touré's work intends to overturn, but even as a child, Benji is well aware of the restrictions that remain in place regardless of his individual desire.

RACIAL INSTRUCTION AND THE POST–CIVIL RIGHTS GENERATION

Other moments in Benji's childhood extend the power of the white gaze, but also challenge the degree to which it is determinative of his understanding of the meaning of his Blackness. Among the episodic summer experiences and flashback memories the novel recounts is a revised example of what Henry Louis Gates Jr. calls a "scene of instruction." As Gates informs Touré, such "scenes of instruction" are characteristic of the African American autobiographical tradition and are "[moments] where someone discovers they're Black and what that means—the societal limitations and the emotional assault that comes along with Blackness" (Touré 2011, 125). During classic examples of the trope,[7] the protagonist, usually at a very young age, is forced to recognize that the society at large considers their Blackness as a mark of deficiency, and that it will serve throughout their lives as a barrier to their success. The prominence of the "scene of instruction" in the African American literary tradition suggests its importance as a ritual moment of group identification. In other words, the "scene of instruction" emblematizes the precise moment at which the African American individual is forced to recognize their lack of agency over their self-definition of racial identity. By revising this particular trope, then, Whitehead specifically centers the restoration of individual agency over the meaning of Blackness within his generational portrait.

On a superficial level, the scene in Whitehead's text mirrors the trope. Whitehead's autobiographical narrator Benji is recounting his experience with fighting, recalling a moment during the fourth grade in which his father called him in to talk about an incident at school during which, his father says, "some boy called you a nigger" (Whitehead 2009a, 134). In response to these words, Benji attempts to correct his father's misconception. He denies his father's premise, saying simply, "He didn't say that" and describes how a young French boy, Tony Reese, "reached over to my face, dragged a finger down my cheek, and said, 'Look—it doesn't come off'" (Whitehead 2009a, 135). As with many African American literary scenes of instruction, the father here speaks from experience, instructing the child in the ways of society and the world. While Benji seems oblivious to the implications of what Tony's actions and statements imply about his race, the father emphasizes, "He was calling you a nigger. What did you think he was doing?" (Whitehead 2009a, 135.) Benji's father is infuriated that he did not punch the other boy, and through his own violence he underlines his disappointment with Benji by slapping him twice.[8] Benji's father is less concerned with the racist statement made by Tony than he is upset at Benji's failure to recognize the statement as racist and react suitably in response to it. With his slap, Benji's father is attempting to harden Benji against the hostility of a racist society. As both a member of the upper-middle class and the civil rights generation, Benji's father appears concerned that his son has been raised in relative privilege, and thus might mistake that privilege for the absence of continued structural racism. By slapping Benji, he illustrates an anxiety that his children may lack the same capability that he has had to succeed in the face of American racism. However, at the same time, Whitehead's treatment of the scene undermines its instructive capacity in the present racial context. Instead of remembering the flashback as definitional of his racial identity, Benji recalls the lesson as being about his father's power: "No one can hurt you more than I can" (Whitehead 2009a, 135). As Benji's perception of the lesson makes clear, whether the instruction with regard to race is appropriate or not to the moment, it does not stick.

Benji responds to the incident with his father by attacking Tony Reese at school the next day. In this context, the fact that Benji responds to his father's violence by punching Reece undermines the meaning of his actions as retaliation for his racism. Though he is not necessarily implying that responding to racism merely begets further violence (thereby calling for passivity on the part of Benji), Whitehead suggests that Benji's aggression towards Reece has become divorced from a concrete perception of how racial hierarchies operate. Furthermore, the schoolyard response to Tony's actions is mockery: "Everybody laughed at Tony Reese" (Whitehead 2009a, 135). Consequently, while the actions of the scene progress in the terms set by the father, with Tony's racism ultimately leading to Benji responding with violence—"the same end result, really" (Whitehead 2009a, 136), as Benji points out—Whitehead isolates Tony's racism from its societal context. Ultimately, the action is the product of an individual child and is not framed as a transformative moment within Benji's life as an African American boy. In this sense, while Colson Whitehead's novel contains a "scene of instruction," it is filtered through an individualistic lens that lends the story its "post-Blackness." By emphasizing the development of Benji's personal racial identity through this scene in a way that is divorced from the broader structural inequality that his Blackness might seem to signal, Whitehead characterizes his coming-of-age story as related to Benji's perception of his Blackness but not instructive of a normative external definition of its meaning.

The context of the scene suggests that Benji's class background enables him to more easily ignore the implications of Tony's racism. While Whitehead invokes what Robert Stepto calls a "schoolhouse episode" because of how often such scenes take place in the educational context, Benji's "schoolhouse" is an elite New York private school (Stepto 2010, 27). Furthermore, Tony Reese is an atypical antagonist as the son of "a bigwig at the French embassy" (Whitehead 2009a, 134). However, though economic privilege blunts the trauma of Benji's experience, Whitehead makes it clear that class status does not displace racism but only recontextualizes it. Instead, by centering this class experience, Whitehead demonstrates how the convergence between upward mobility enabled by civil rights era progress and contemporary forms of racial discrimination creates experiences among African Americans that are at once shared and sharply distinct. While Kenneth Warren has emphatically argued that such class differentials undermine the capacity to designate a coherent black community or specific "African American literature" (see Warren 2011, 139), Whitehead's representation undermines the decisiveness of this apparent shift. Even though Benji's experience is distinct from past articulations of the "scene of instruction" because of his class privilege, the presence of the scene echoes both continuing societal racism and the textual presence of recurring tropes that invoke rituals of group identification rooted in a racialized and segregated history that even such a revision recapitulates.

Ultimately, Whitehead's subtle revision of the "scene of instruction" illustrates that the redefinition of racial identity conceptualized by post-Blackness is more nuanced than the generation-defining term might initially suggest. Touré devotes a full chapter to the recounting of such scenes, and he asks each of his interview subjects "What is the most racist thing to ever happen to you? What was its impact on you?" (Touré 2011, 15.) The continued presence of the trope in Whitehead's novel and the prominence of the responses to the question related to encounters with racism in Touré's book highlight that post-Blackness does not imply the lack of the continuing presence of American racism. On the other hand, Whitehead's "scene of instruction" subverts the standard implication of the imposition of societal and psychological boundaries on the raced individual. The fact that Benji is confused by his father's actions does not elide the racism of Tony Reece. However, the fact that Benji recalls the flashback because of his father's violence towards him rather than to highlight the existential violence of Tony's racism deprivileges the deterministic structures of societal racism. In addition, by situating it within a flashback in the middle of the novel rather than as a formative moment early in it, Whitehead undermines the power of the white gaze. While Benji and his cohort are constantly aware of race and racism, the novel depicts their coming of age in terms that echo Touré's insistence on the liberation of the individual Black subject from the social and cultural expectations imposed by both the larger white society and

African American culture itself. If, as quoted earlier, these scenes instruct the individual African American on what Blackness "means" (Touré 2011, 125), then Whitehead's revision is a subtle suggestion that the scene instructs Benji about a more provisional sense of what Blackness *may mean* or *has meant*, thus distinguishing the present moment from the civil rights era past. [9]

Touré argues that Whitehead's fictional memoir is unique because it does not "document the horror of being black and enslaved or segregated or impoverished or imprisoned" (Touré 2009). As Whitehead's revision of the "scene of instruction" highlights, his novel, like "post-blackness" as a concept, does not deny the continued salience of the structural inequalities and oppressions that Touré lists in his review. However, in *Sag Harbor*, Whitehead, like Touré, raises the question of whether an emphasis on Blackness continually framed by the persistence of racism becomes itself a normative prescription of what it means to be Black and thus what constitutes authentic Black art. For example, on the map printed on the inside of the book's cover, Whitehead labels a house as "Truck with Confederate Flag." During the novel, Benji describes their reaction to the house in this way, "It also took us past the shabby green house where the pickup truck with the Confederate-flag bumper sticker parked, forcing us to say 'Fuckin' rednecks' whenever we passed it. Over the years, the 'Fuckin' rednecks' tally had really piled up. We were sick of saying it and sick of seeing the truck every summer" (Whitehead 2009a, 82). Benji's attitude towards the racism of the flag illustrates the continued power of structures that the flag represents even as it demonstrates the boys' frustration with how the act of responding to the flag has become obligatory. Whitehead is not excusing the truck owner; however, Benji and his friends' attitudes towards the truck illustrates a frustration as much with the presence of the bumper sticker as with the compulsory nature of their reaction. Therefore, we might ask, if post-Blackness and other post era categorizations are about the expansion of African American agency over the meaning of race, what are the dimensions of that agency, given the continuing presence of such markers of past racism as a Confederate Flag bumper sticker? Ultimately, the individual agency imagined by post-Blackness does not neglect the presence of institutional racism, but instead attempts to redefine the relationship between African Americans and such racism.

Whitehead's novel echoes the tension between the individual and the collective by framing the issue of agency in terms of the history of the Sag Harbor community and the position of the current generation in relation to that history. The novel emphasizes that Sag Harbor, as a community, is not an integrated, post-racial, or multicultural space. The characters repeat at various points that they are leaving their "black enclave" and "lighting out for the white side of the island" (Whitehead 2009a, 51), signaling the continued de facto segregation of Long Island. Whitehead depicts the casual segregation of the space as something ingrained in the space itself: "My mother used to say that the white people went to the ocean beaches in the morning, and the black people in the afternoon. I don't know how much of that was flat-out segregation or a matter of temperament—white people getting a jump on the day to do white-people things, and black people, well, getting there when they get there" (Whitehead 2009a, 51).

When describing a map of the area in *Guide to Sag Harbor: Landmarks, Homes & History*, Whitehead locates "the black part of town . . . off in the margins" (Whitehead 2009a, 18). Building on this sense of marginalization, Whitehead historicizes the founding of the community, specifically in terms of Jim Crow:

> The first generation came from Harlem, Brownstone Brooklyn, inland Jersey islands of the black community. They were doctors, lawyers, city workers, teachers by the dozen. Undertakers. Respectable professions of need, after Jim Crow's logic: white doctors won't lay a hand on us, we have to heal ourselves; white people won't deliver us to God, we must save ourselves; white people won't throw dirt on our graves, we must bury ourselves. Fill a need well, and you prospered. Prosper and you took what was yours. (Whitehead 2009a, 51)

As the sentences and clauses pile on top of each other, they depict a story of enterprising and exceptional individuals within the Black community responding to the racism of Jim Crow with entrepreneurial zeal. In this extension of Du Boisian "talented tenth" logic and Booker T. Washington-style Black capitalism, those within the community who filled the gaps created by white supremacy's disdain of the needs of the Black community do a service to that community and are, in turn, rewarded with their own elite institutions and spaces, such as the ability to vacation at Sag Harbor. The final words, "took what was yours," serve to reinforce the rightness of this economic logic, embracing a narrative in which the ancestors of Benji and his friends Reggie, Bobby, NP, and others, are merely reaping their just reward.

These founding generations are defined both in terms of their success within segregation and in terms of their relationship to the movement to overcome it. As the novel points out, not only are the characters the descendants of the Black elite under Jim Crow, they are also the children of many who were intimate participants in the civil rights struggle. The scene in which Benji's father hits him for his failure to retaliate against Tony Reece illustrates the burden being placed on the first generation to grow up without first-hand experience of the Civil Rights Movement, which Whitehead illustrates through their identity performance. Later in the novel, we learn that Benji and friends were, like Colson Whitehead himself, born between 1968 and 1972 (Whitehead 2009a, 49), positioning them squarely as what Mark Anthony Neal describes as "children of soul," those he defines as too young to have ever been adults during the civil rights era (Neal 2002, 3). Benji explains how his friend Bobby traces the "customary schedule for good middle-class boys and girls": "Underlining key passages in *The Autobiography of Malcolm X* and that passed-around paperback of *Black Skin, White Masks*. Organize a march or two to protest the lack of tenure for that controversial professor in the Department of Black Studies. It passed the time until business school" (Whitehead 2009a, 58). Whitehead's satirical tone demonstrates how the political beliefs of the previous generation have become fodder for the performance of a stereotype of Black identity, which he labels the "Militant." In contrast to an era in which such actions were part of large-scale transformational change, Benji describes Bobby and others of his generation as mere parrots of such revolutionary ideals. Instead of agitating for political change, the superficial adoption of nationalist politics reinforces their class privilege and does nothing to hamper their long-term individual success.

With his satire, Whitehead does not just undermine the implications of the performance itself but uses it as evidence of the breakdown of what political scientist Michael Dawson called the idea of "linked fate" among African Americans (Dawson 1995). Dawson argued that African Americans view themselves within a political context in which gains for any members of the community are seen as gains for the Black community as a whole. Dawson's data showed that while there certainly were class differentials within the Black community, members of that community understood their interests predominantly through the lens of race. Indeed, Dawson's research showed that feelings of "linked fate" increased along with education, meaning that the members of the middle and upper class in the Black community represented in *Sag Harbor* should show a particularly heightened sense of this collective fate (Dawson 1995, 81–82). However, Dawson's argument rested on data collected in the late 1980s, leaving open the question of whether the sense of "linked fate" he described continues to persist in the African American community and how it manifests itself in the larger culture.[10] While Whitehead's novel does not serve as a definitive data point overturning Dawson's thesis, his description of *Sag Harbor* evidences the breakdown in the relationship between individual and collective racial identity undergirding the linkages Dawson describes. Furthermore, Kenneth Warren cites Dawson's argument to claim that contemporary African American literature continues to grasp, with less and less legitimacy, onto its own political and social relevance (Warren 2011b,

136). Warren connects his discussion of the "indexical" and "instrumental" views of the political utility of African American literature to a sort of literary linked fate in which individual African American authors and characters are somehow representative of the whole race. However, while Warren is right to locate the anxious consideration of the significance of his actions and life in the protagonist's consciousness, what he sees as a "hyperbolic recrudescence" of the idea "that the welfare of the race as a whole depends on the success of Black writers and those who are depicted in their texts" is actually another version of *Sag Harbor*'s attempt to assess the implications of a loosening sense of linked fate (Warren 2011b, 139).

Additionally, Whitehead's text represents the transition towards an emphasis on racial individualism in terms that still echo the syntax of collective group identity. Far from representing a "hyperbolic recrudescence" of increasingly irrelevant beliefs in their own significance, his novel represents a satirical ambiguity in which the assumptions that underlie such logics are placed in dialogue with a vision of an increasingly atomized Black identity. Whitehead's novel depicts a generation that remains cognizant of a shared racial culture and common political interests, but for whom such bonds are weakening. Whitehead's portrait of Bobby emphasizes the simultaneously cursory and compulsory form that his engagement with the civil rights era takes. On the one hand, Benji's description of Bobby illustrates complacency on the part of his generation, as he performs a nationalistic Blackness right up until the point he is able to cash in within the society he is ostensibly fighting against. On the other hand, Whitehead implies that this "customary schedule" arises out of assumptions about which forms Blackness can or should take, specifically emphasizing the importance of the civil rights era in constructing such racial meaning.

While Whitehead suggests that previous generations saw themselves and their success as extensions of the broader African American community, the description of Benji's generation implies that the outward displays of representativeness have become mere performance. However, Whitehead's representation of Bobby illustrates how the centrality of the iconography of the Civil Rights Movement can over-determine the analysis of African American literature. By mentioning a text like *The Autobiography of Malcolm X*, Whitehead references the expectation that the reader might have that his book would focus on the experience of being African American in a racist society and thus contain scenes of revelation and epiphany in relation to racial identity. At various moments, the novel comments on these stereotypical expectations. As Benji puts it at one point, "According to the world, we were the definition of a paradox: black boys with beach houses. . . . What about the news, statistics, the great narrative of black pathology?" (Whitehead 2009a, 57.) Here, Whitehead emphasizes the power that such cultural narratives have to dictate the terms in which African American literature and experiences are understood, despite both the diverse experiences of African American individuals and the diverse aesthetic concerns of African American artists. Whitehead's decision to write *Sag Harbor* absent substantial racial conflict or epiphany is still dictated by the racial assumptions of writers, readers, and publishers alike. On the other hand, by playing with such assumptions, Whitehead's novel calls attention to their implications as a way of embracing this supposed paradox.

POST-BLACKNESS AND DOUBLE CONSCIOUSNESS

As Derek Maus points out, reviewers were quick to trumpet *Sag Harbor*'s sup-posed racial transcendence, focusing on its universal *bildungsroman* charac-teristics (Maus 2014, 99–100). The novel, however, is typical of the post era in its interrogation of double consciousness, which has served as a master trope of African American literature, undermining any claim as to an uncompli-cated universality (see Adell 1994).[11] While scholars such as Adolph Reed have critiqued the transhistoricization of Du Bois's concept because of its specific historical and class context (Reed 1997), Du Bois linked his description of the fractured individual consciousness specifically with the broader issues of racial uplift he addressed throughout both the rest of *The Souls of Black Folk* and contemporaneous essays such as "The Talented Tenth" (published in 1903, the same year as *Souls*) and "The Conservation of the Races" (published in 1897; the essay version of "Of Our Spiritual Strivings" titled "Strivings of the Negro People" was published in *The Atlantic* in 1897 as well). In such essays, Du Bois conceptualizes "double consciousness" as a gift, enabling insight into American society, and a curse, serving as a barrier to full citizenship in that same society, specifically aligned with the broader political goals of collective racial organiz-ing. With his emphasis on collective ideas of "uplift" and duty, as well as seeing African American cultural production as the contributions of "black folk" as a race, Du Bois specifically moves beyond seeing "double consciousness" as the mere province of individual psychology. However, the internal fragmentation conceptualized as "double consciousness" lends itself to a focus on wholeness within the self and suggests a therapeutic privileging of individual well-being in the face of claims of collective responsibility. It is in this context that Whitehead consistently addresses questions of doubling and fragmentation throughout *Sag Harbor*. While he is less concerned with the reconciliation of fragmented selves, Benji's struggles over his own sense of division, not the least from his position as a cultural mulatto figure, are consistently oriented towards questions of personal agency. Rather than rooting empowerment in the larger Black community, even within the exclusive bourgeois enclave he occupies, Whitehead focuses attention on the individual psyche.

In *Sag Harbor*, Colson Whitehead traces his protagonist's double consciousness to invoke the "unreconciled strivings" between race and nation defined by Du Bois in service of a positive irreconcilability. Indeed, Whitehead's novel documents the fracturing of the self as something with which one can feel fully comfortable. Whitehead's signals the irreverence of his meditation on identity doubling early in the novel by fully quoting Du Bois's famous formulation of "double consciousness." Whitehead's quoting of Du Bois locates his work within an African American literary tradition wherein Du Bois is a key ancestral figure. Whitehead frames his reference to Du Bois in several ways.[12] First, Sag Harbor is weighted by a legend that "DuBois [sic] came out to Sag once and ate there" at a local fish fry (Whitehead 2009a, 13). Second, while, as a teenager, Benji is mostly conscious of Du Bois as one of the "Famous Black People," the novel is written from an unspecified present, leading him to explain that "years later in college I'd read his most famous essay and be blown away" before quoting the famous description of double consciousness itself (Whitehead 2009a, 13).

Du Bois's presence here is critical in situating Benji's identity within African American literature. Quoting Du Bois's definition of double consciousness allows Whitehead to place Benji into a lineage of conflicted first person Black male narrators. On the other hand, by narrating the portion of Benji's life before he has read the essay, Du Bois is framed as a sort of distant ancestor, someone that Benji is conscious of, but not defined by. While Benji quotes Du Bois, the paragraph culminates in a joke tinged with youthful irreverence: "I thought to myself: The guy who wrote that was chowing fried fish behind my house" (Whitehead 2009a, 14). Though the reference highlights Benji's connection to an African American intellectual tradition, the joke establishes enough distance between Whitehead's protagonist and that same tradition to position it as something useable but not sacred. By setting the novel in 1985, yet maintaining a narrative voice speaking from an undefined present, Whitehead connects youthful irreverence with the defiance of tradition. Associating that revision with the narrator's teenage years uses the coming-of-age novel as a genre to perform the tone of simultaneous seriousness and sarcasm with which Thelma Golden coined "post-black art" in the first place. The narrator's reference to Du Bois undermines his authority as a theorist of the present, but it also implies a later maturity during which the narrator better understands his position in the lineage of African American literature and identity. This vacillation between a rejection of the sanctity of the Black culture and its reinscription mirrors post-Blackness's subtle revision of canonical concepts such as double consciousness.

By interrogating Du Bois's canonical formulation of double consciousness, Whitehead's text consistently reiterates the irreducibility of the doubled self. At various points, the narrator discusses his lack of consternation over the "two Greedos" in *Star Wars*,[13] ruminates over which of a friend's father's two simultaneous families is the "real" one ("One man, two houses. Two faces. Which house you lived in, kids, was the luck of the draw" [Whitehead 2009a, 122]), and the doubleness of aging, as younger selves give way to new selves. In each case, Whitehead focuses on the impossibility of resolving the doubles that he invokes. In displacing contradiction, Whitehead's narrator argues that the contradictory is a problem of signification rather than a lack of self. When he mentions that "according to the world, we were the definition of paradoxes: black boys with beach houses," it is in service of emphasizing that "what you call paradox, I call *myself*" (Whitehead 2009a, 57–58). Adopting similar phrasing, he emphasizes that with regard to the "two Greedos," "It's a simple thing to keep the two Greedos together in your head if you know how" (Whitehead 2009a, 157).

However, this irreconcilability is less a product of essential distinctions between individuals, and rather a consequence of the inadequacy of language. Whitehead's brief description of a firefly, late in the novel, highlights this point.

> A black bug secret in the night. Such a strange little guy. It materialized, visible to human eyes for brief moments, and then it disappeared. But it got its name from its fake time, people time, when in fact most of its business went on when people couldn't see it. Its true life was invisible to us but we called it firefly after its fractions. Knowable and fixed for a few seconds, sharing a short segment of its message before it continued on its real mission, unknowable in its true self and course, outside of reach. It was a bad name because it was incomplete—both parts were true, the bright and the dark, the one we could see and the other one we couldn't. It was both. (Whitehead 2009a, 153)

In this passage, Whitehead ruminates on the experience of being subject to the external social gaze to suggest the fallacy at the heart of naming. Labeling the bug a "firefly" defines its being only through the "fake time, people time" during which it is visible to others. By locating this meditation in terms of the natural world, Whitehead takes on the romantic quality of essentialism, questioning whether there really is some "true nature" to which names seek to refer. Whitehead's invocation of Du Bois's "unreconciled strivings" indexes how the conceptual labels and frameworks by which selves and ideas are made knowable limit one's capacity to understand the wholeness of that which is labeled. The firefly, named after only the briefest moments of its being, takes on a reality through that label that erases the rest of its being. However, as the quote makes clear, to say this is not to argue that the firefly should be properly named with reference to its "darkness" rather than its "light." Instead, Whitehead's celebration of the inherent incompleteness of naming mirrors Thelma Golden's attempt to document a shift away from a normative framework declaring that Blackness is knowable and definable towards an embrace of a more messy, fluid, and counter-normative present.

BEYOND OREOS: WHITEHEAD, POST-BLACKNESS AND THE PERPETUAL PROVISIONALITY OF NAMES

His engagement with the coming-of-age and memoir genres alongside his revision of Du Boisian double consciousness reveals Whitehead's attentiveness to a politics of naming epitomized in post era debates over how to categorize the post–civil rights era and its cultural production. Beyond seemingly esoteric questions of how to classify the art in a given exhibition, or what bookstore shelf on which to place particular works of literature, Whitehead's focus on the link between labeling and issues of authenticity reveals a tension between the desire for the continuation of a specifically racialized culture and the attempt to liberate the individual from the boundaries that any label necessarily erects.

The novel illustrates how, like Benji, Whitehead finds himself navigating a labyrinth of assumptions and imposed interpretations rooted in his Blackness. In a similar way as Touré's own stories of having his Blackness questioned because of lifestyle choices or tastes and Golden's descriptions of artists chafing under the expectation that they will follow Black Arts Movement aesthetics, Whitehead offers liberation in an individualism that resists societal expectations. As an interview subject for Touré's book, Whitehead speaks to this very topic. Referring to the use of the term "oreo" to denote an inauthentic Black person, Whitehead states, "Being called an oreo was stupid then and it's stupid now. People are just more aware that those categories are dumb. If you're an authentic person, true to who you are and how you're wired, then like what you like, whether its Led Zeppelin or 'Happy Days'" (quoted in Touré 2011, 56). Post-Blackness in general, and *Sag Harbor* in particular, reframe authenticity through the individual's expression of their own self-definition. Rather than privileging, as a metric, an abstract standard of what constitutes the Black experience, such expressions typify the post–civil rights perception of claims to collective identity as a vestigial burden of eras defined by more explicit cultural and political struggles.

As Kenneth Warren, citing Adolph Reed, points out, the turn towards privileging individual agency over identity mirrors the growing ubiquity of the memoir among "petit bourgeois" African American writers such as Whitehead. For Warren, the "infiltration" of "the style and sensibility of the personal narrative" into even non-memoir literary and critical forms illuminates the Black elite's investment in racialized identity as something that can be either claimed or disclaimed as desired (Warren 2011b, 122). Warren highlights the dominance of the memoir form to indict how a petit bourgeois insistence on the continued value and meaning of African American literature as a tradition obscures changing forms of inequality in the United States. In contrast, Whitehead interrogates the implications of the simultaneous investment in a racialized group identity and an individualism that would seem to defy the possibility of defining that group identity.

The subtle distinction between Warren's indictment and Whitehead's more tenuous exploration of the implications of post–civil rights African American identity formations marks the contrast between the cautious optimism conceptualized as post-Blackness and Warren's claim of it as a bourgeois fantasy. I share, to a degree, Warren's trepidation that an insistence on the maintenance of a racialized African American literature can mask the specific forms that racism and class inequality take in the present. However, to unilaterally declare that African American literature exists solely as a holdover from the response to Jim Crow fails to recognize that the continued investment in a racialized tradition is not merely "a marker of elevated status" absent a resistant political ideology (Reed 2016, 171). Instead, novels like *Sag Harbor* trace what Adolph Reed calls the "cultural ambivalence" of the Black petit bourgeoisie. The memoir genre and its fictional realist analogue allow authors and characters to negotiate the intersection of class-based and race-based interests through the question of how Blackness is defined, particularly in its cultural representation (Reed 2016, 169). However, while Reed views this ambivalence as masking a fundamental essentialism which maintains the centrality of racial identity while adopting the posture of liberation to claim the right to class privilege, Whitehead's novels reveal an ambiguity more in line with post-Blackness. Just as his revision of the scene of instruction in *Sag Harbor* demonstrates the continuing presence of rituals of collective identity while interrogating their ongoing meaning, Whitehead remains interested in what it means to write about "serious race issues" in the present while pushing against the prescriptive essentialism of definitions of Blackness rooted in past political struggles. In doing so, his novel, like the analytical category of post-Blackness, underscores the transitional nature of early twenty-first century African American aesthetics without specifically defining the outcomes of such a transition.

While the fact that the novel's structure mirrors the already ephemeral temporality of the summer months suggests transition, the final chapter underscores the broader theme of generational change. The chapter is set at an end of summer cookout and includes the familiar scene of an informal footrace. Public policy discourse has long used the metaphor of a race to evoke the limitations on opportunities that African Americans have in American society, and the policy prescriptions, such as affirmative action, that would address such limits.[14] Here, Benji gazes at the participants and contemplates the temporariness of each generation's experience: "Where was my replacement, then? Which boy was it, standing with the others at the starting line. Waiting for it to begin" (Whitehead 2009a, 262). With the novel's previous invocations of such luminaries as W. E. B. Du Bois, Benji's ruminations indicate that he might just as easily have replaced Du Bois in the way that one of these children will replace him. Wondering who that replacement will be, Benji locates a partial answer as he watches Barry David, who everybody thinks is someone else's cousin but to whom no one ultimately claims kinship, throw some patio furniture into a bonfire. As the patio furniture burns, Benji recognizes that just as his generation once represented change and the new, Barry David's generation will soon replace them. Barry David's willingness to violate the norms of the community and burn the patio furniture signals that what each generation builds can, and will, be torn down and replaced with something else. Conceptually, "post-black art" is born out of a similar generational shift, encompassing artists who feel restricted by what were once posited as forms of radical liberation. As the reaction of Randall Kennedy, among others, to Touré's book makes clear, post-Blackness carries its own fallacies and contradictions. In his book *The Grey Album*, dedicated to Whitehead, the poet Kevin Young dismisses post-Blackness, saying "blackness is not something I wish to be beyond or past; it is still ever-present and remains unavoidable, and more important pleasurable" (Young 2012, 283). However, despite his uneasiness with the term, on the next page, Young makes a nearly identical argument to Touré—"black art is whatever art is made by black folks" (Young 2012, 284)—suggesting that even if, as a term, post-Blackness causes uneasiness, the embrace of its aesthetic individualism is widespread.[15]

In the wake of the societal changes enabled by the popular Black movements of the long civil rights era, post-Blackness illustrates the post era focus on racial self-definition and individual identity performance. Consequently, post-Blackness does not emphasize decisive change in the present. Instead, the category is useful precisely because it speaks to the tensions within rearticulations of racial identity in the early twenty-first century. On the one hand, in emphasizing the agency of the individual over racial self-definition, post-Blackness underscores the problematic essentialism at the root of some arguments for cultural specificity, particularly within the discourse on what constitutes Black art. On the other hand, the emphasis on the individual is in tension with a racialized group experience rooted in a socio-historical continuity and aesthetic practices and traditions that each of the authors I have discussed strives to preserve. Furthermore, positioning all forms of collective racial identity as an overwhelming burden risks masking continuing forms of institutional racism; such structures may, in fact, remain intractable absent race-based anti-racist activism. Ultimately, rather than marking a decisive transformation, the debates and tensions prompted by the term's presence in post era critical discourse illuminates the early twenty-first century transitional period in African American literature and the complexity of seeking to define the meaning of racial identity in the present. Consequently, to return to Thelma Golden's question in the introduction to the *Freestyle* exhibition volume, post-Blackness serves not as a stable answer to the question of "what's next" for Black art in the new century, but as a provisional term speaking to the continual reimagining of what Blackness may mean in the post–civil rights era and the twenty-first century. In my next chapter, I take up the flip-side to the forward-looking optimism of Golden, Touré, and, though more limited, Whitehead. While each of these authors view the loosening bonds of racial expectations as at least somewhat liberating, their arguments reflect various levels of class privilege that displaces some forms of immediate vulnerability. As myriad events during the twenty-first century have demonstrated, class privilege is by no means enough to erase ongoing structures of white supremacy, a point which, somewhat disingenuously, authors like Touré acknowledge. However, class background certainly mitigates some aspects of the immediate forms of vulnerability that underlie what Saidiya Hartman defines, following Foucault, as racism: "the social distribution of death" (Hartman 2007, 129).

"KATRINA IS THE MOTHER WE WILL REMEMBER UNTIL THE NEXT MOTHER"

Apocalyptic Storms and the Slow Violence of Structural Racism

In his early post era essay, "Blue Men, Black Writing, and Southern Revisions," Houston Baker argues for "a new southern studies" (Baker 2002, 14). Seeking to counter the "major rewards for sycophancy, for solacing talk of 'race transcendence' by putatively new black 'Public Intellectuals'" (Baker 2002, 15), Baker roots his writing, and the broader Black creative project in a figurative and literal return to the South (Baker 2002). Given Baker's words, it is notable that the two major works that I argue provide a counternarrative to the progressive teleology of post-Blackness, Jesmyn Ward's *Salvage the Bones* (2011) and Kiese Laymon's *Long Division* (2013), are explicit products of the Black South. Indeed, both Ward and Laymon insist on the regionalism of their work, with their Southern heritage grounding their representations of Black life and motivating their responses to anti-Blackness. Baker's essay claims that the South is the foundational location of Black culture, and that only a return to the physical region of the South and the return of the South to the center of Black study will allow for a liberating response to ongoing white supremacy. It is no accident, then, that Ward and Laymon construct their representations of twenty-first century Black identity on the cultural foundations of Southern Blackness. Their work also provides a reminder that the post–civil rights era has seen a major demographic shift frequently described as the New Great Migration: a return of Black people from the West, Midwest, and Northeast to the South (Frey 2004).

Zandria Robinson (2014) argues for the necessity of centralizing region in any discussion of shifting Black identities in the post–civil rights era. "As the geographic and cognitive epicenter of American blackness shifts southward," she claims, Black southerners have constructed "new ways of being southern, being black, and being black southerners in the twenty-first century" (Robinson 2014, 7; 5). Connecting Baker's and Robinson's work, as I have done here, recognizes the complex intersection of the regional symbolism of the South between cultural rootedness and innovation. For authors like Ward and Laymon, their Southern Black identity provides the basis for situating themselves within a concrete cultural tradition, yet it also offers the opportunity to perform the "New Black" identities that Robinson proposes in her ethnographic research. As such, novels like *Salvage the Bones* and *Long Division* expose the tensions in post era writing between progressive emphases on the new and the longstanding communities out of which those claims arise.

The major post era idea that present forms of African American cultural production are distinct from past forms rests on the assumption that there have been decisive shifts in American cultures of race and politics. African Americans endured over three centuries of racialized slavery, followed by a hundred years of legally sanctioned segregation and second-class citizenship, prompting the legitimate question of whether that past can be left behind. As I have discussed, most of the essays that build the contours of the post era make several assumptions about the larger discourse on race in the United States. First, that it is overly focused on certain segments of the Black community, especially the so-called "underclass." These authors argue that there are legitimate ongoing issues related to entrenched poverty and lack of success within the Black community; however, they counter that there remains a statistically dominant segment of the Black population that does not reside either in poverty or any stereotypical "ghetto." The central concern aired in these essays is a legitimate one. The argument that African American communities propagate a "culture of pathology" has held enormous cultural influence ever since the 1965 report *The Negro Family* (better known as the Moynihan Report) (Office of Policy and Planning 1965). Furthermore, the images underlying and feeding into culture of pathology arguments—inner city crime, drug dealers on a corner, unwed mothers, welfare queens, hustlers, and pimps—still dominate the mainstream cultural imaginary of Blackness. From the rise of hip-hop to television crime shows and movies, the representation of African Americans often feeds into stereotypical assumptions that all African Americans fit a certain narrow range of stereotypes: poor, listening to hip-hop, playing basketball, violent. Second, these authors argue that the civil rights era—in this case, including Black Power Movements—dominates the historical iconography of Blackness in America. In particular, schools often focus on major movement leaders in teaching Black history, and thus tell a narrow story of the Black experience across history, if they discuss Black history at all. Third, because of the centrality of the political struggle for citizenship to African American history and the dominance of pathological images in the culture, these post era authors argue that cultural expression by African Americans is often only narrowly marketable, perpetuating certain cultural stereotypes and silencing alternative voices.

The post era, then, is defined by a push and pull between (1) racial optimism predicated on the entry of African Americans into unprecedented positions of power in the United States and the incorporation of previously radical discourses on race into mainstream institutions and (2) pessimism over the increasing class stratification in the Black community and the entrenched poverty and segregation that individual success masks. If *Sag Harbor*'s depiction of a well-heeled Black vacation community represents a qualified optimism around the expanding agency of the individual, then representations of Hurricane Katrina puncture this class-based fantasy of liberation. Images of those left behind to face the wrath of the hurricane and its aftermath, disproportionately of Black and brown people, underscored just how much of the optimism of the post era is speculative rather than real.[1] Writing in the wake of Katrina, post era African American literature that depicts the storm resuscitates longstanding tropes of the African American literary tradition and seeks a way to survive ongoing racialized state violence. *Salvage the Bones* and *Long Division* serve as signal examples of a post era counternarrative that specifically questions the idea of progress, finding refuge and strategies for survival in tropes drawn explicitly from the African American literary tradition.

AMERICA DOESN'T CARE ABOUT BLACK PEOPLE

The angry response to Katrina repudiates post era semiotic negotiations over labels and categories, perhaps most famously in Kanye West's nationally televised claim that "George Bush doesn't care about Black people."[2] In the face of Whitehead's irony, West's words are refreshingly direct, disputing the nuance others might desire in parsing the different class experiences and even national origins of segments of the Black community. Furthermore, while mainstream representations of the storm, such as HBO's television drama *Treme* (2010–2013), often acknowledge the entrenched segregation and racialized poverty found throughout the Gulf Coast (both before and after the storm), they also tend to assess the storm's effects evenhandedly, suggesting a universal impact that undermines what scholars such as Robert Bullard and Beverly Wright have found: the effects of both the storm and its aftermath were not felt equally by Black and white, rich and poor; instead, they were structured and reproduced by existing hierarchies (Bullard and Wright 2012).

Several of the major African American literary representations of the storm, however, push not only against the idea of the storm as either a natural disaster or something that caused general, universal suffering, but also against the valedictory optimism of the post era overall. In particular, Jesmyn Ward's *Salvage the Bones* and Kiese Laymon's *Long Division* explicitly situate the events of the storm within a long timeline that marks an ongoing and fundamental anti-Blackness in American society. Ward's novel incorporates images and explicit references to Zora Neale Hurston's *Their Eyes Were Watching God* to construct a tradition of apocalyptic storm narratives that serve to reveal and underscore institutional racism. Laymon enacts a similar relationship between present conditions and the past through time travel. His protagonist, City Coldson, displaced by the storm and out in the country with his grandmother, travels between 2013, 1985, and 1964, illuminating the persistence of the storm's aftermath. Each of these works dispute the exceptionalism of the hurricane to argue the need to understand the continuity between the period before and the ongoing aftereffects, which have only exacerbated neoliberalism's anti-Blackness.

Ward's and Laymon's novels center on the foundational trope of the loss of the parent. Esch, Ward's protagonist, has lost her mother during the birth of her younger brother, and the plot of the novel centers on her own impending motherhood. While the novel could fall into the trap of sensationalizing the image of the Black teen mother, it instead reflects on the attempt to live within the contours of what Orlando Patterson calls "social death" (Patterson 1982). The novel is set in the fictional Mississippi community of Bois Sauvage, whose name signals both its marginalization from the nation and the attitude of the rest of the nation towards the area and its residents. The novel traces the days leading up to the storm, as residents first live their daily lives and then prepare for and attempt to survive the storm. At the close of the text, Esch finds herself nearly alone, waiting on the return of China, her brother's prize dog, who has also recently given birth. The novel imagines salvage as a both obligatory and generative practice. While so much of the narrative about Hurricane Katrina centers on media narratives of survival and renewal (in its most egregious forms, politicians such as Arne Duncan have even celebrated the Hurricane for providing the impetus for large scale structural changes such as the privatization of the local public school system, see Anderson 2010), Ward's use of the term salvaging emphasizes the marginal and precarious position of her characters. As individuals whose struggles exist on the fringes of media narratives, if mentioned at all, Esch's family seeks a way to live within the space they define as home. While there are momentary suggestions of the potential for what might be viewed as opportunity—most prominently in the form of her brother's potential basketball scholarship—the novel largely traces how negligence of the concerns of the marginalized leads directly to their disproportionate vulnerability to what are framed as natural disasters. Because of the ignorance and neglect of the concerns of these populations, the novel's representation of Hurricane Katrina counters the sensationalism of the storm's immediate impact to highlight what Rob Nixon (2011) describes as "slow violence."

Importantly, Ward and Laymon center their narratives in Mississippi rather than New Orleans, which has dominated the cultural representations of the storm despite the eye of the Hurricane passing over the Mississippi Gulf Coast. Though the fact that New Orleans is a major population center explains some of this focus, the city's dominance of the discourse threatens to further marginalize already invisible populations struggling in the wake of the unnatural disaster. While Ward's novel documents the days leading up to the storm, Laymon's novel is more obliquely related to it. Laymon's protagonist City Coldson, from Jackson, finds himself staying with his grandmother in Melahatchie, a fictional town whose name evokes the Tallahatchie River from which Emmett Till's body was recovered. In Melahatchie, City hears about Baize Shephard, a local girl whose abduction is again haunted by the ghost of Till, but also the ghosts of more recent Black murder victims such as Trayvon Martin, who the book mentions. The time travel structure of the book both literalizes the presence of the past in the present and the present in the past while also providing a means of subverting it. When City travels back to 1985, and then 1964, through a hole in the woods, he discovers that Baize is not missing, but has instead traveled through time. However, the novel's central revelation is not only that City is Baize's father, with his friend Shalaya Crump as her mother, but that she is an orphan, her parents having died in Hurricane Katrina. Consequently, the novel is haunted by death, but subverts the finality of mortality to generate avenues for creative expression and agency. In particular, the novel repurposes the long standing African American literary trope of the underground to create a "black (w)hole"—to borrow Baker's critical formulation about these spaces—through which the absoluteness of differential Black vulnerability to violence and premature death can be, if not wholly evaded, at least combatted (Baker 1984, 139). The (w)hole, like the grammatical ellipses that provides the novel's other central image, constructs interstitial spaces in which anti-Blackness does not destroy possibility.

Befitting novels that emphasize recurrence, both *Long Division* and *Salvage the Bones* center on depictions of orphaning, a trope which stretches back to the earliest texts of the African American literary tradition and which links directly to questions of ancestry and reproduction. Frederick Douglass emphasizes slavery's destruction of the bond between parent and child. Describing the deliberate separation of him from his mother, he reflects on his indifference to her death: "Never having enjoyed, to any considerable extent, her soothing presence, her tender and watchful care, I received the tidings of her death with much the same emotions I should have probably felt at the death of a stranger" (Douglass 1993, 40). Coming alongside Douglass's declarations of birth and place, such a description reveals the enslaved individual as definitionally an orphan, a state that Orlando Patterson calls "natal alienation" (Patterson 1982, 5). Cut adrift from parentage before the narrative even starts, Douglass stands simultaneously as heroic individual who seeks and then attains his freedom and anonymous member of a collective defined by their marginalization from national citizenship.

In her seminal book, *Lose Your Mother*, Saidiya Hartman argues that slavery lives on through its "afterlife": "because black lives are still imperiled and devalued by a racial calculus and a political arithmetic that were entrenched centuries ago" (Hartman 2007, 6). Echoing a hauntology that finds literary expression throughout the gothic strains of African American literature (most famously Toni Morrison's *Beloved*), Hartman argues for an expansive understanding not just of slavery itself but its structuring logic. To explain this claim, she locates slavery's fundamental calculus in the loss of the mother, both in the literal sense and in the sense of the homeland. Because slavery necessitated the transformation of patrilineal inheritance laws, Hartman argues that "The mother's mark, not the father's name, determined your fate" (Hartman 2007, 80). Furthermore, because the enslaved exist legally as the property of their master, and do so even prior to their birth because of contracts that "[include] 'future increase'" (Hartman 2007, 80), they are fundamentally orphaned, removed from the lineage of the father, and tied only to the mother through the process of enslavement. For Hartman, the disruption of kinship is not a single break allowing for reparation on the other side. Instead, the orphaned slave remains adrift, incapable of suturing the historical disruption of the Middle Passage, yet also unable to be wholly of the New World. Hartman's book traces the failure of her journey to Ghana to provide the reparation or wholeness that she desires, with that failure standing in for the continued rupture, the open wound of displacement represented by the Transatlantic Slave Trade. Laymon's and Ward's novels similarly blur the line between life and death, suggesting an afterlife of trauma mirroring Hartman's arguments. Each novel is structured by different forms of loss. Esch has lost her mother during the birth of her brother. City finds himself staying with his grandmother, separated from his parents, and Baize has lost her parents in Hurricane Katrina. These novels echo Christina

Sharpe's claim that anti-Blackness functions as the "climate"—omnipresent and constant. In that context, the disasters emblematized in Laymon's and Ward's representations of Hurricane Katrina echo her claim that "the weather necessitates changeability and improvisation" (Sharpe 2016, 106). It is the imperative towards such improvisation that drives the narratives, even as both authors acknowledge the overriding force of structural racism within which the characters reside.

Both Laymon and Ward insist on situating the events surrounding Hurricane Katrina, and the racial ecology/environment they intervened within, along a continuum of ongoing marginalization experienced by Black people in the United States. The processes of othering and orphaning that they describe necessitate constructing new forms of agency within those same margins. Laymon's black (w)hole celebrates Black creativity as a means of resisting the ossification of state racism and the differential vulnerability to violence that it begets. If the progress marked by post era categories traces the gradual, and still incomplete but improving, incorporation of African Americans into the American state, then Laymon's and Ward's narratives resist that very metric.

The spaces in which Laymon and Ward locate survival contrast sharply with those emphasized by the dominant narratives of recovery from Hurricane Katrina. Those narratives, which focus primarily on New Orleans and its status as a great American city, highlight capitalist ingenuity and technological change in their depiction of thriving development, destruction of obsolescent neighborhoods and housing, and capital reinvestment. Barbara Bush's insistence during the immediate aftermath to the storm that many victims were better off in Houston considering the conditions in which they had previously lived finds echoes in portrayals of the Hurricane as opening the space for innovation and redemption (see *New York Times* 2005). The racist undertones of these representations of recovery justify the further privatization of already declining social services and profits accumulated through the replacement of longstanding Black neighborhoods with new development that prices residents out.[3] In contrast, both Ward and Laymon confront the persistent vulnerability of Black populations in America, but without sinking reductively into despair. Instead, their narratives document the slow violence of racism while embracing the spaces that African Americans have repurposed in search of a freedom still denied by the state. In doing so, they counter the valedictory optimism voiced by authors across the post era, for whom recognition by the state as full citizens remains the central marker of progress. In place of that recognition, these novels celebrate Black fugitivity in the face of a state they label as fundamentally hostile to the lives of Black people.

RACISM AS SLOW VIOLENCE

In *Slow Violence and the Environmentalism of the Poor*, Nixon defines "slow violence" as "a violence that occurs gradually and out of sight, a violence of delayed destruction that is dispersed across time and space, an attritional violence that is typically not viewed as violence at all" (Nixon 2011, 2). While Nixon defines the concept in relation to the long timescale of environmental change and destruction, his concept provides a framework by which to reveal the temporally and spatially segmented violence of Hurricane Katrina within a media landscape focused on spectacle. Indeed, it might seem strange to refer to the violence of Hurricane Katrina as occurring "gradually and out of sight" considering its prominence across media narratives. Furthermore, the public is well acquainted with the dominant images of the storm, from stranded individuals with signs on the roofs of houses asking for help, to those of people sleeping in the Superdome and on bridges in New Orleans, to the horrifying pictures of dead bodies amid the wreckage of the storm, and even to those people-less images of water, debris, and broken levees. The public is also likely aware that the violence of the storm did not affect all universally, but instead fell heaviest on the most vulnerable populations, especially poor Black and Latinx people. However, the very forces that made Hurricane Katrina anything but a natural disaster, such as the decades of investment in industry that weakened storm protection, the lack of investment in infrastructure to protect cities, the entrenched poverty, inequality, and lack of opportunity produced by a structurally racist education and economic system across the South and the United States as a whole, have all dictated the terms of recovery as well, requiring a broader lens through which to view the storm's effects across time and space (for detailed analysis of Katrina's aftermath see Johnson 2011).

In speaking of Katrina beyond simply a few days in August 2005, I follow Dylan Rodriguez, who argues that the "living time" of the Hurricane is "an ongoing material history of rigorously organized, state-facilitated, and militarized white racial domination" that extends in both directions—past and future—from the sensationalized spectacle of the storm (Rodriguez 2007, 133). Importantly, then, both Ward and Laymon insist on locating the specific events that provide the context of their narratives within a much longer lineage that stretches back through a history marked by Black struggle and Black death. In this sense, Katrina provides a signal example of Nixon's idea, in that the vulnerable populations most affected by the storm, and those at the heart of both these novels, became visible in late August 2005 only in the context of their differential vulnerability to the violence of the natural environment, and only then through the spectacle of their exclusion from the body politic of the larger state, symbolized both in the slow response to crisis and their representational portrayal as fundamentally other. The terms of this visibility, and its perpetuation of marginalization, only highlight how in the period leading up the storm, and in the period that followed it, these same people, spread across the nation in a diaspora that perpetrates its own violence, became invisible once again.

If "the tragedy of Katrina created a rupture in the racial-progress narrative that had all but erased the suffering of poor black people from the political landscape" (Harris and Carbado 2006, 92), then the consciousness of that rupture did not necessarily persist. Instead, narratives have most often turned to questions of how the Gulf Coast in general, and New Orleans in particular, could be revived. As John Valery White explains, such discussions necessarily "represent choices over who *should* return" (White 2006, 42) and, symbolically, choices about to whom the state is responsive. The decade plus since the storm has certainly seen a revival of New Orleans and related communities. Story after story in the *New York Times* and other national publications cite the city's revived culinary scene and vibrant rebuilt neighborhoods with available housing for the young and upwardly mobile (see, for example, Severson 2015). However, far from being the organic product of local democracy, the revival that these stories trumpet is the product of, as White explains, deliberate choices on the part of elite actors about whose lives matter, and whose priorities deserve to be heard. Hurricane Katrina then, as noted by Harris and Carbado, ruptured cherished narratives of racial progress, revealing images of poor Black people living in already difficult circumstances. Furthermore, as I discuss in subsequent chapters, such images continue to lie in tension with a racial progress narrative that was only revived following Hurricane Katrina with the candidacy and presidency of Barack Obama. Consequently, my analysis of Ward's and Laymon's novels situates them as narratives of anti-Blackness's "slow violence" to highlight the continued invisibility of the communities that the novels depict and to emphasize that when the novels do turn towards agency, they do so within the logic of those margins.[4] As Joy James explains, far from being powerless victims, "People were resourceful, found their loved ones, tended the traumatized, buried the dead, worked to rebuild lives and communities" (James 2007, 162, original in italics). Consequently, analyzing narratives of Black struggle against anti-Blackness during the post era reveals that the desire to tell more "post-black stories" of upwardly mobile Black professionals and their families risks rendering invisible the ongoing marginalization of the Black underclass.

"MAKE SURE YOU PRAY TO THE MOTHERS"

For an author whose work is suffused with death and violence, Ward projects a fierce optimism focused on survival. She boldly confronts what are so often stereotypes or caricatures—the Black male dog fighter, the sexually promiscuous teenage Black girl, the drug addicted mother—and forges narratives that insist on defiant love as the foundation of community. In her 2017 *Sing, Unburied, Sing*, Ward accompanies a young boy and his absent, yet still-alive, mother as they go to pick up his father from Parchman Farm Penitentiary. Ward avoids the stigmatization frequently imposed on young Black women, especially those who use drugs, to depict a resilient and resolute family facing the death of its matriarch, the young boy's grandmother. *Sing, Unburied, Sing*, like *Salvage the Bones*, offers Ward an opportunity to insist on the valuable ways in which those who live on the margins find ways to survive and support each other in the face of anti-Blackness and state violence. The later novel's injunction to "make sure you pray to the mothers" recognizes the trauma so frequently associated with the central trope of the loss of the mother while gesturing towards the collective practices that preserve the love of the parent-child relationship in the face of that loss (Ward 2017, 42). Across those depictions, the figure of the mother is at once anchor and scapegoat, symbol of love and monstrosity. By playing out the paradoxes attendant to both the representation of Black women and their lived experience in the United States, Ward traces what Erica Edwards argues, with reference to *Salvage the Bones*, is "an alternative epistemology of black freedom articulated through the unromantic depiction of black women's sex as a resource for collective preservation" (Edwards 2015, 156). Edwards's claim aligns with other critics in arguing that the collapse of boundaries between human and non-human, past and present, civilization and savagery in the novel provide an alternative foundation for care and protection outside of the state (see Hartnell 2016; Crownshaw 2016). Specifically, this alternative rejects post-Blackness's insistence on an atomized individualism in favor of a deeply rooted collectivism derived from the history of Black Southern life, what Edwards calls "the preservation of collectivity against singularity" (Edwards 2015, 158). The figure of the Black woman as sexual being and mother lies at the center of this preservation. The novel revisits the traditional trope of the loss of the mother to link the destruction of Katrina as (un)natural disaster with the forging of new bonds in the wake of loss.

In Hortense Spillers's canonical essay "Mama's Baby, Papa's Maybe" (1987), she attempts to construct an "American grammar book" out of the symbolic rupture of the transatlantic slave trade. In particular, she figures this rupture in specifically familial terms, arguing that the economy of slavery, paired with its legal architecture, makes African diaspora subjects orphans: "In effect, under conditions of captivity, the offspring of the female does not 'belong' to the Mother, nor is s/he 'related' to the 'owner,' though the latter 'possesses' it, and in the African-American instance, often fathered it, and, as often, without whatever benefit of patrimony" (Spillers 1987, 74). Spillers focuses on the pervasive narrative of absent fatherhood in sociological discourses of Black pathology, as her title reflects. *Salvage the Bones*, however, addresses the same themes of rupture, orphaning, and displacement through the lens of an absent motherhood. Ward constructs a history marked by tragedy but finds redemption in and survival amid love and community. In *Salvage the Bones*, time is marked by storms, tracing a history from 1969's Camille through 2005's Katrina and speculatively towards whatever future storm is coming. Connecting this hurricane-based temporality to the book's larger conception of history linked to the canonical staging of the loss of the mother, Ward seizes on the feminine names of the storms to describe them as versions of the mother-figure.

Spillers argues that the rupture experienced by members of the African diaspora creates an erasure of identity and selfhood that is filled in by stereotypical understandings of Black femininity and masculinity. In this way, stereotypes of Black selfhood construct a grammar by which white freedom, subjectivity and power are instantiated and perpetuated. The othering of the Black self, particularly the Black woman, denies a fully defined humanity or gender. Spillers posits this alienation (from gender, self, and nation) as foundational to Western civilization, positioning its anti-Blackness as inherent and unchanging. Discussing Frederick Douglass's *Narrative*, Spillers associates the consequences of this alienation with the foundational loss of the mother: "The destructive loss of the natural mother, whose biological/genetic relationship to the child remains unique and unambiguous, opens the enslaved young to social ambiguity and chaos: the ambiguity of his/her fatherhood and to a structure of other relational elements, now threatened, that would declare the young's connection to a genetic and historic future by way of their own siblings" (Spillers 1987, 76). As Spillers argues, and as Ward's novel affirms, the loss of the Black mother is not unique to enslavement, but instead a defining feature of modernity.

In *Salvage the Bones*, the loss of Esch's mother in childbirth is not represented directly but appears to be the product of the family's poverty and lack of adequate medical care. Indeed, the novel depicts the family as occupying a space still marked as "wild"—the town is called Bois Sauvage—standing on the boundaries between civilization and the natural world. While this is not to suggest that Ward primitivizes her characters, she does highlight their isolation from the central features of modernity, portraying them as largely self-sufficient, and only marginally in contact with the nation as a whole.[5] Ward's novel presents a setting in which the anxious consideration of authenticity is not a major question for the characters. Bois Sauvage is explicitly segregated—the novel is peppered with references to "the black Bois that we knew and into the white Bois that we didn't" and the city's "black heart" and its "pale arteries"—with desegregation efforts merely a history lesson rather than a lived reality (Ward 2011, 70; 97). Ward focalizes her representation of Hurricane Katrina through this fictional community, whose vulnerability is only exacerbated by their segregated marginalization in society.

Because of their unique ability to make visible the architecture of anti-Blackness, storms such as Katrina occupy a prominent role throughout African American culture. Ward's novel seizes on this tradition to envision a twenty-first century Blackness rooted in mythopoetical practices of the historical Black community in the South. Ward's novel, I argue, attempts to imagine motherhood liberated from "the regime of captivity" (Spillers 1987, 79). To enable this liberation, Hurricane Katrina serves as an eschatological cleansing and an image of the mother herself. The lives and bones that are "salvaged" provide the architecture for a racial selfhood that is derived from and the product of the distinctive juridical and cultural experience of African Americans in the United States. The narrative tradition of survival and struggle produced by this experience provides the template for envisioning a new self birthed by this trauma. As such, Ward's text, like Laymon's, emphasizes the continuity of a specifically racialized African American literary tradition in enabling the creation of new Blacknesses and thus repudiates attempts to argue for that tradition or Blackness itself as confining or limiting.

Ward represents Katrina as a particular chaotic vision of femininity. When the storm is named, Esch prophecies its danger: "The storm, it has a name now. Like the worst, she's a woman. Katrina" (Ward 2011, 124). The simplicity of the language here reduces the storm to its essence, aligning the naming of the storm with its status as a force of nature. Playing on the longstanding practice of naming, and gendering, storms, Ward transforms the abstract naturalism of the storm's power into a specifically feminized force.[6] Furthermore, that force is associated throughout the novel with a heightened sexuality. Describing her early sexual experience, the novel's young protagonist Esch imagines a storminess that foreshadows the hurricane: "I'd pulled the water with my hands, kicked it with my feet, let it push me forward. That was sex" (Ward 2011, 24). This imagery of water highlights its role as both giver of life and instrument of death that parallels Ward's complex presentation of motherhood throughout the novel. Not only does Esch's mother die giving birth to her younger brother, but the images of her brother Skeeter's dog China giving birth, and the specter of the death of several puppies during that act, suggests that motherhood should be understood not as the production of future generations, but as a chaotic and complex balancing of death and life more akin to the storm itself.

In concert with the metaphor of motherhood, the hurricane provides as much of an image of rebirth as it does of danger. Esch imagines the storm in eschatological terms directly connected to motherhood, "*Tomorrow*, I think, *everything will be washed clean*" (Ward 2011, 205). Esch suggests that this "washing clean" reveals truth. Casting herself as a modern Medea, another key reference in the text, Esch confronts Manny, the father of her unborn child, saying, "'The baby will tell,' I scream. 'It'll tell!'" (Ward 2011, 205). Paired together, these quotes suggest that the apocalypticism of the storm enables the destruction of the illusions concealing essential truths. While this process is prefigured throughout as violent, she also represents it as necessary and beautiful. The process of washing clean opens the possibility for new beings, a rebirth both for those already alive and for those yet to be born.

The storm allows Esch to fully comprehend the meaning of her role as mother. As she sits in the house listening to the pounding of the wind, she imagines her child.

> I lie awake and cannot see anything but that baby, the baby I have formed in my head, a black Athena, who reaches for me. Who gives me that name as if it is mine: *Mama*. I swallow salt. That voice, ringing in my head, is drowned out by a train letting out one long, high blast. And then it disappears, and there is only the sound of the wind like a snake big enough to swallow the world sliding against mountains. And then the wind like a train, again, and the house creaks. I curl into a ball. (Ward 2011, 219)

Those who experienced the storm describe its wind as destroying the possibility of thought.[7] In this moment, Esch seems almost beyond thought, fully immersed in her bodily state. In that state, she imagines herself as mother. In wondering who grants her that name, she considers a question that links her to the hurricane. While the National Hurricane Center named Katrina, the novel suggests that that appellation speaks to an essential truth. Similarly, Esch wonders here who gives her the name mother. Is it herself? Is the name hers? Esch's question here relates to the issue of self-ownership. Returning to Spillers, the orphaning of the Black subject was the product of a juridical structure that denied the possibility of selfhood. In this space, what is it that allows Esch to claim herself as mother—or, as the text ends, with her declaration "I am a mother" (Ward 2011, 258)? Critically, at this moment in the storm, Esch finds comfort and power in this self-identification. While the wind sounding like a train whistle echoes traditional symbols of flight—particularly the flight north from the Jim Crow South—such symbolic presences are dwarfed by the power of the storm. As she curls into a ball and the wind becomes the train, the traditional trope of deliverance, her selfhood is reduced to her body.

What Esch seeks is a space that combines home, love, and survival. While the hurricane ostensibly challenges the security implied in that formulation, it also enables a fuller realization of those same concepts. Following the terror of the storm, Esch awakes to a world ravaged by the wind, rain, and flooding. While the storm reinforces the sense of Black vulnerability, carrying many away to their deaths in its power, it also allows a paradoxical rebirth:

> I will tie the glass and stone with string, hang the shards above my bed, so that they will flash in the dark and tell the story of Katrina, the mother that swept into the Gulf and slaughtered. Her chariot was a storm so great and black the Greeks would say it was harnessed to dragons. She was the murderous mother who cut us to the bone but left us alive, left us naked and bewildered as wrinkled newborn babies, as blind puppies, as sun-starved newly hatched baby snakes. She left us dark Gulf and salt-burned land. She left us to learn to crawl. She left us to salvage. Katrina is the mother we will remember until the next mother with large, merciless hands, committed to blood, comes. (Ward 2011, 255)

This quote connects Katrina with Medea, who famously butchered her own children in retaliation for Jason's betrayal. However, while the demonization of Medea is easy, Ward suggests it misses the complexity of her role as mother. While Katrina "was the murderous mother," she is also the mother who brings them forth as "wrinkled newborn babies." The duality of death and birth generates a motherhood that does not ignore blood and embraces vulnerability. Indeed, it is precisely this vulnerability that elevates survival as something beyond a reaction to anti-Blackness. Instead, survival becomes the equivalent of mythic heroism, the structures of racism and structural oppression arrayed like the gods against the community. The shards of glass and stone that Esch collects on the beach symbolize survival. The way in which the actions of the storm erode the glass and rock recreates them in its image, but also therefore allows them to shine a light in the darkness. Like the shards, the people of the Gulf are battered and terrorized by the storm, but arise stronger, able to reflect on the effects of the storm. In this context, "to tell the story" is to construct a positive identity within survival and to embrace the love that allows for that same survival. In contrast to her earlier attempts to conceal her pregnancy, Esch finds triumph in it after the storm. When Big Henry tells Esch that "This baby got plenty daddies" he is not simply revealing his own feelings for Esch; instead, he elevates the community itself as familial model (Ward 2011, 255). While Esch's status as an unwed teen-age mother would seem to feed into stereotypes of Black female hypersexuality, and Manny's refusal of his child would seem to reinforce "the great narrative of black pathology," the storm allows for rearticulating familial status (Whitehead 2009, 57). Instead of simply seeking to find meaning in the structures of the liberal state, and the legal status of father and mother, Esch and her family find redemption outside the normative. In their case, Bois Sauvage is not so much a state of nature as it is another "hole" or ellipses, to foreground images present in Laymon's novel that I return to at length later in this chapter.

Providing a space for alternative identity formations, the storm, like the wood itself, washes away the structures of late capitalism, revealing the "dark Gulf and sun-burnt land" beneath. Ironically, rather than emphasizing vulnerability, such an explicit statement reframes Katrina as a site of comfort. In this context, what emerges after the violence of the storm is not merely the hard-fought resistance to a death that nature attempts to deliver to the helpless. Instead, it becomes a more complicated act of survival, in which the power of the storm reveals the fundamental complexity of life. Specifically, the equation of the storm with the act of childbirth, and the representation of Katrina as a surrogate mother that also allows Esch to embrace her own role as mother, locates life within death and death within life. In doing so, it reaffirms Black survival even within the seemingly totalizing forces of anti-Blackness. Instead of seeking redress in the form of inclusion within the state, as the liberal individualists discussed in the previous chapter did, Ward, like Laymon, finds strength in the margins, the holes, and the breaks. The end of the novel makes this sense of survival explicit, connecting Esch to the still lost, and possibly dead in the storm, China: "*China. She will return, standing tall and straight, the milk burned out of her. She will look down on the circle of light we have made in the Pit, and she will know that I have kept watch, that I have fought. China will bark and call me sister. In the star-suffocated sky, there is a great waiting silence. She will know that I am a mother*" (Ward 2011, 258). In this context, the affirmation of motherhood further connects Esch to Katrina. While the earlier statement that "Katrina is the mother we will remember until the next mother with large, merciless hands, committed to blood, comes" suggests time being marked by the sequence of storms, it also allows Esch to be the "next mother" who takes Katrina's place, both murderous and triumphant, like Medea. This affirmation of survival, and the courage and fighting that it requires, constructs a specifically gendered Black femininity not rooted in an investment in the national state, or compromised by such association. Instead, like Spillers argues at the end of "Mama's Baby," Ward "[claims] the monstrosity (of a female with the potential to 'name')" to "rewrite . . . a radically different text for a female empowerment" (Spillers 1987, 80).

A BARE-BULB PLACE

The monstrosity that Ward claims at the end of the text, and its capacity to name itself, is rooted in a specifically racialized tradition that rebuts the presumptions of its obsolescence in arguments such as the ones of Kenneth Warren (2011b) in *What Was African American Literature?* and Charles Johnson (2008) in "The End of the Black American Narrative." While, like Warren, Ward's text resists contemporary African American literature's ubiquitous obsession with access to power and post-structuralist questioning of authenticity, it also uses the idea of "salvaging" to emphasize the necessity of rooting oneself within the African American cultural tradition as the basis for the survival she celebrates. Ward builds this through-line with the inclusion of references to Zora Neale Hurston's canonical *Their Eyes Were Watching God*. As I have mentioned, the novel constructs the locality of the Gulf by marking time with the names of hurricanes. References to Hurricane Camille, and her parents' experiences of the storm, reveal the underlying architecture of the idea of Katrina as the mother who they will remember until the next mother comes along. In this logic, Katrina becomes another version of Camille, of Betsy, and of the 1928 Okeechobee hurricane that figures so prominently in Hurston's narrative.

Ward's references to the setting as a "bare-bulb place" associates Bois Sauvage with the idealized swamps of Hurston's novel in which Janie and Tea Cake experience a happiness disrupted by the storm (Ward 2011, 1). The monstrosity of Hurston's storm reinforces the hostility of nature and reveals the impossibility of a Black utopia in the face of white racism. Despite its burden, as with so many storms, falling heaviest on the Black community, Hurston's novel represents the historical reality of white bodies being given priority, buried in coffins by coerced Black hands as their community members rotted in the sun (Hurston [1937] 1990, 170–71). However, as with Ward's novel, while the storm disrupts Janie's happiness, and ultimately drives Tea Cake mad through the dog's bite, it affirms Janie's subjectivity through her survival. The fact that she has the ability to shoot Tea Cake, killing him to protect herself, using a skill taught within that swamp, valorizes Janie's capacity for independence and self-definition (Hurston [1937] 1990, 184).

However, Hurston's representation of self-definition and subjectivity does not devolve into a simplistic individualism. Instead, the structure of the novel, told through free indirect discourse as Janie speaks to her friend Phoeby on her porch, affirms the capacity for intersubjectivity that Ward references in Henry's statement of the child's many fathers. This idea gets its fullest expression in Phoeby's statement that "mah tongue is in mah friend's mouf" (Hurston [1937] 1990, 6). Similarly, in the midst of the storm, Esch tries to ventriloquize her mother: "I know the exact words she said, can see us sitting there by her lap, but all I can hear is my voice saying it, not hers" (Ward 2011, 221). Here, Esch is at once her mother and herself. She attempts, and fails, to speak in her mother's voice. But within that failure is the seed of her own voice, and her own self-hood as mother. Throughout the text, Esch's mother has stood as the carrier of tradition, and the carrier of narrative knowledge. Esch comes to occupy that role, supplanting her mother but not replacing her. Like a palimpsest, Esch is at once herself and the traces of her mother.

The land itself takes on a similar palimpsest-like quality. Esch describes the coming storm passing "slave galleys turned guesthouses," gesturing simultaneously to the images of progress and the scars that remain on the land (Ward 2011, 4). No amount of years can turn slave galleys fully into guesthouses, and the traces of that trauma, what Saidiya Hartman calls "the afterlife of slavery," will survive even if the guesthouses are destroyed in the flooding (Hartman 2007, 6). With its elevation of survival, Ward thus denies both the possibility and desirability of transcendence, choosing instead to locate subjectivity in a mode of survival similar to what Christina Sharpe terms "wake work": a way "to imagine new ways to live in the wake of slavery, in slavery's afterlives, to survive (and more) the afterlife of property" (Sharpe 2016, 18). Sharpe's words mirror Ward's location of agency within the governmentality of structural racism while resisting imperatives to subordinate either mourning or grievance as the terms of social inclusion.

Salvage, in this context, takes on several layers of meaning. In *Salvage Work: U.S. and Caribbean Literature Amid the Debris of Legal Personhood* (2015), Angela Naimou explains that "salvage is neither a full nor a failed recuperation; it is not a miracle of reanimation or resurrection; it is not part of the economy of recycling. It is not an inherently liberatory act and may be an exploitative one" (Naimou 2015, 9). Given this, salvage lacks any single moral imperative. Instead, it is a process of asking questions, an "aesthetics" in Naimou's terms, in which the encounter with "the ruined, junked, and trashed" requires the negotiation of both continuity and revision.[8] It takes the materials that are present, as damaged and harmful as some of them may be, and attempts to rebuild with and through them. However, this process of recuperation is not a simplistic attempt to revive or rebuild something into what it was in the past. Think, in this sense, of the glass and rock found on the beach. The scarring of the water, and the way in which it has hewn them into their new shapes, is irreversible. However, that same damage enables the reflection of light. Similarly, the rubble of the storm, as much as it is emblematic of neglect and terror, is also the ground for insight and survival. Surveying the scene at the coast, Esch asks a key question of the text: "There are only great piles of wood. . . . What could be salvaged? What hasn't been buried or swept back out to sea?" (Ward 2011, 252.) Here, the question takes on the tenor of the novel's engagement with eschatology, viewing destruction as both apocalypse and renewal. To salvage is a necessity for survival. However, that does not displace the issue of what should be salvaged and what left to destruction.

Furthermore, the sense of salvaging is inherently ambivalent in the context of the work to address the effects of Katrina. In the wake of the storm, much of the focus on rebuilding centered on New Orleans itself, with words such as *reconstruction*, *resurrection*, and *revival* all connoting the sense of a great American city reborn. However, not only does this framework neglect the experiences and lives of those like Esch and her family whose position outside the city of New Orleans grants them no telethon or platform through which to advocate for investment in their community, it also reinforces the conse-quence of disproportionate policies that poured federal and private money into the revival of predominantly white communities while neglecting the needs of predominantly Black ones. This is especially reflected in the very idea of return. Differential rates of investment and redevelopment have allowed the vast majority of whites to return to their homes while disenfranchising many Black residents: "The storm cut deeper for the city's African American households than for its white households; in 2006, nearly half (47 percent) of African Americans households lived someplace other than New Orleans, whereas only one-fifth (19 percent) of white households did so" (Bullard and Wright 2012, 84). Confining our understanding of the "disaster" to a sequence of days in August and September 2005 risks erasing the compounding effects of racially discriminatory policies both leading up to, and in the wake of, the storm. In this way, Katrina typifies Nixon's conception of slow violence, in which racism masks the long-term vulnerability of Black populations in the Gulf within the highly visible horror of the storm.

Colorblind neoliberal economic policies that dress up discriminatory out-comes in race-neutral language still perpetuate the differential vulnerability of racialized communities in the United States (see Ishiwata 2011). What remains so remarkable about Kanye West's statement that "George Bush doesn't care about black people" is its cathartic explicitness. In contrast to colorblind ideolo-gies and progressivist narratives of American history that demand qualifica-tions or calls for complexity, West's statement speaks directly in the grammar of racial logic. Ward's novel, like Laymon's, demands such grammar. To counter policies that continue to either make vulnerable racialized populations or to further victimize those already harmed, it is not enough to adopt the uto-pianism of racial transcendence, even in the particular racial individualism of post-Blackness or post-soul. Sometimes, to "trouble blackness," to borrow

Bertram Ashe's definition of post-soul aesthetics, only undermines the capacity to address continued racial injustice (Ashe 2007, 614). As Bullard and Wright argue, "What the New Orleans recovery process has showed is that policies intended to be race neutral can further devastate the most vulnerable populations, rather than alleviate the destruction caused by a disaster, if our policies are not race sensitive" (Bullard and Wright 2012, 95). The race sensitivity that they call for here finds its echo in Ward's representation of Katrina, which salvages a tradition that many post era critics argue belongs only to the past and deserves to be buried.

TIME TRAVEL AS AN ARGUMENT FOR A RACIALIZED TRADITION

Kiese Laymon's *Long Division* approaches similar themes to Ward by combining tropes of Black speculative fiction with the type of cultural satire found throughout post-soul African American literature (i.e. Trey Ellis's 1998 novel *Platitudes*, Paul Beatty's 1996 novel *The White Boy Shuffle*, and Darius James's 1992 novel *Negrophobia*). Laymon's stylistic innovations mirror Ward's depiction of the effects of Hurricane Katrina on marginal populations. However, while Ward's novel directly represents the storm itself, Laymon locates Katrina's aftereffects within a broader history of white supremacy. To do so, the novel repurposes time travel as both literal plot element and metafictional trope. Laymon intertwines two separate yet related novels, both of which feature a protagonist named City Coldson, constructing a form in which the novels speak to each other and intersect, suggesting a proliferation of narratives of which the novel is only one example. Furthermore, these two "novels" mirror the book's time travel conceit, with the 2013 City Coldson reading the novel *Long Division* featuring 1985's City Coldson, who later reads the version of *Long Division* starring 2013's City Coldson. The novel, set in Jackson and fictional Melahatchie, Mississippi, returns to events in 1964, implicitly referencing the kidnapping and murder of Michael Goodman, James Earl Chaney, and Andrew Schwerner, three visiting civil rights workers in Mississippi that same year. Like Octavia Butler's novel *Kindred* ([1979] 2004), in which a contemporary (1970s) interracial couple find themselves in the Antebellum South, the novel constructs a through-line between legal structures of racial apartheid (such as slavery and Jim Crow) and the more ambiguous present (see also Levecq 2000).[9] Opening with City's participation in a quasi-spelling bee in which youths use words given by judges in elaborate sentences, Laymon satirizes what President George W. Bush memorably called the "soft bigotry of low expectations" found in condescending forms of neoliberal multiculturalism that emphasize tokenism over actual engagement (see Bush 2000). Pairing satire with time travel, Laymon's novel focuses on the critical question of vulnerability through supposed racial progress. With the plot of the novel focusing on the disappearance of Baize Shephard, a young Black woman, in 2013, Laymon's intertwining texts collapse within each other around the core idea of Black survival in the past and present, and into the future.

Over the course of the novel, Baize's fate becomes simultaneously clearer and more ambiguous. Within the copy of *Long Division* that the 2013 version of City Coldson is reading, 1985 City encounters Baize sitting on her porch after traveling into the future and steals her laptop computer and cellular phone. After losing the laptop in an encounter with the KKK in 1964, City returns to 2013 to bring Baize back in time to help him, his crush Shalaya Crump, and Evan Altshuler, a Jewish boy from 1964. Thus, the 1985 version of *Long Division* appears to solve the disappearance of Baize Shephard in 2013 by suggesting that she has traveled through time to help the 1985 version of City Coldson. In contrast, 2013 City Coldson believes that Pot Belly, an older white man, has done something to Baize. Two major plot developments complicate matters. First, Pot Belly explains to City that he was the young white boy that City's grandfather died saving from drowning. Second, Baize reveals to 1985 City that her parents are City and Shalaya, and that they died in Hurricane Katrina.

The reference to Hurricane Katrina provides the novel with its most robust image of Black vulnerability. Gazing at the Gulf of Mexico in 1964, Baize tells City about how her parents dropped her off in Jackson before returning to Melahatchie, where they disappeared. Describing her anger, she declares a desire to "kill the sky" (Laymon 2013, 221). Baize's description links her parents' disappearance with her own. Going beyond a discussion of their death, Baize describes them as simply vanishing. This idea of disappearing, whether in the context of Baize's parents or Baize herself, highlights vulnerability. There is conclusiveness to simple death that disappearance denies. Baize's anger at the sky derives from her sense of powerlessness. By labeling an abstract entity like the sky as having agency in their deaths, it provides Baize with both a target for her anger and a sense of how she can confront the unjust seeming arbitrariness of the storm.

Furthermore, the idea of disappearing speaks simultaneously to different registers of vulnerability for African Americans. First, the word disappearance suggests an inexplicability and suddenness, as in something that is there and then immediately gone. Second, it introduces an overtone of silence that renders forms of Black death unspoken and unspeakable. While the novel describes the media reports that proliferate in the wake of Baize's disappearance, their presence speaks to this same silence. Baize's disappearance fuels a mass media business that requires content, but which lacks the capability of speaking to either the depth of Baize's experience or the true tragedy of her disappearance. In addition, such a media firestorm only further highlights the glaring widespread silence that attends the daily experience of Black death in American life. By highlighting such silences, Laymon suggests that the illusion of engaging with past forms of violence and discrimination in the present only further silences the actuality of that history. The death of Lerthon Coldson in 1964 occupies the same black hole as Baize's death. Whatever publicity it may have generated only reinforces existing structures, not offering City and his peers any avenue for new imaginings.

In the novel, Hurricane Katrina becomes an instrument of such disappearances, underscoring continued Black vulnerability and questioning the extent of racial progress. Katrina haunts Laymon's novel from the beginning, as references to dislocated Gulf residents and rebuilt houses culminate in Baize's discussion of her parents. As a focal point, the storm typifies the sense of being subject to an uncontrollable power. Furthermore, by not representing the storm, it functions as a black hole of its own, into which City and Shalaya disappear even as they remain present on the page, and into which Baize ultimately seems to disappear as the City and Shalaya on the page diverge from the paths they seem destined to take by not falling for each other. At the end of the novel, in a scene of City talking with his grandmother, who appears like an apparition in the 2013 of the 1985 *Long Division*, Laymon ruminates on the meaning of disappearing. "People disappear, City. . . . We live, we wonder, we love, we lie, and we disappear. Close the book" (Laymon 2013, 258). However, despite the implied passivity, Mama Lara suggests an avenue for City's agency: "Sometimes, when folks disappear, they come back, don't they?" (Laymon 2013, 259.) As Mama Lara attempts to get City to answer what makes people disappear, she interrogates him until he answers "People," and then turns the question around: "And everything that makes people disappear can make people what? . . . Reappear?" (Laymon 2013, 260.) Mama Lara's and City's dialogue provides a roadmap for the agency City might exert, even within the "hole" that allows for both travel through time and disappearance. Here, Mama Lara suggests that City has all the tools necessary to transcend the apparent limitations of time to enable not just the imagining of a different future, but also the ability to transform the past. However, as the time-travel structure suggests, those tools are fundamentally tied to that very past and require its engagement. In other words, Laymon does not imagine City as transcending a racialized past, but instead generating agency from and through that past, an agency that he describes in terms of reading and writing, thus tying the text to the oldest traditions in African American letters.

In this way, Laymon's novel resuscitates core tropes in the African American literary tradition as the means of continuing to liberate the African American self in the present. In contrast to the various post concepts discussed in the introduction and chapter 1, Laymon maintains the centrality of that racialized tradition as the only means by which young African Americans can continue to survive in America. To construct the through-line in this tradition, Laymon connects time travel to the practices of reading and writing, extending agency to the individual through the process of revision. As City reads the copy of *Long Division*, he is transported into the past (first 1985 and then 1964) both figuratively (by reading about it) and literally (as the character City who travels backwards and forwards to 2013 and 1964). Furthermore, Laymon resists a simplistic backwards-looking timeline in which 2013 City's narrative is privileged. As 1985 City reads his own copy of *Long Division*, the narrative is filled in as the reader is reading it. As he notes when nearing the end of the novel, his copy of the text has only blank pages instead of an ending, indicating that the narrative the reader is reading (the frame narrative in 2013) is ongoing, with an ending that remains unwritten.

Discussing time travel in Octavia Butler's *Kindred*, scholars have emphasized the role it plays in making the past recoverable as well as troubling distinctions between the present and a past defined by slavery—by literally bringing the past into the present and the present into the past.[10] However, Laymon's time travel is of a slightly different character. While the narrative pivots on "recovering" a history that is hidden—namely the circumstances at the Shephard house involving City's and Shalaya's grandfathers—it constructs a metafictional simultaneity in which the events within each "novel" are going on at the same time, and affect each other in real time. The metafictional quality of Laymon's time travel—it is a novel about stories being written as they are occurring—connects directly to the novel's investment in reading and writing as revolutionary tools. In this sense, the novel is quite traditional, returning to master tropes that lie at the core of the African American literary tradition (see Stepto 1979).

In his attention to temporality, Laymon chooses his dates very deliberately. Initially, the "present" of the outer frame, in 2013, signals the idea of racial progress satirically. As City's friend and nemesis LeVander Peeler wins the national Can You Use that Word in a Sentence competition (before elaborating and costing himself the win), the announcer says, "LaVander Peeler, you have done the unbelievable! Times are a-changing and you, you exceptional young Mississippian, are a symbol of the American Progress. The past is the past and today can be tomorrow" (Laymon 2013, 43). Laymon highlights the common post-racialist fantasy of racial progress, in which the racism of the past can be declared definitively dead allowing for a new and progressive future. Laymon further gives the 2013 frame a sense of the unreal by narrating its characteristics within the 1985 novel:

> "Like what if there's this huge flood that kills people? Or if the water in the Gulf turn black? Or if we have a black president and . . ."
> "A black president?" I asked her. She threw me off with that one. "And black water? And you say I'm crazy?" (Laymon 2013, 54)

Here, those elements of the 2013 present that are definitional become near-future science fiction, in which the ascendance of a Black man to the White House is unthinkable nearly three decades earlier. While the references to Obama suggest progress, the insertion of Katrina anchors this vision of the future, making it clear that their meanings are fundamentally interconnected.

The setting of the inner novel in 1985 suggests the same youthful innocence as that captured in Colson Whitehead's *Sag Harbor*, set during the same summer. Like Whitehead, Laymon signposts his characters' youthful naivete with pop cultural references. When they travel to 2013, they approach technological advances like encounters with aliens. While the exchange quoted here highlights coming changes, Laymon positions the temporality of 1985 as liminal, between the more defined sense of 2013 and 1964. It is notable that the characters spend the least time in 1985 itself, using it as a launching point into the future and past. In characterizing 1985 in this way, Laymon emphasizes the same sense of transition that animated early post formulations by Trey Ellis (1989) and Greg Tate (1992), which argued that there was something different going on in African American culture but without fully articulating the nature of this difference.

In contrast, 1964 Mississippi is weighted down with heavy symbolism through its association with Freedom Summer, and most concretely, with the murder of civil rights workers Goodman, Chaney, and Schwerner near Philadelphia, Mississippi. With the character of Evan Altshuler, Laymon references the collaboration of northern Jews and African American activists throughout Freedom Summer. The house that Lerthon Coldson dies in, which becomes the Shephard house, is a Freedom School dedicated to helping students "begin to question" (Laymon 2013, 214). The teaching handbook for the Freedom School emphasizes the already present stores of knowledge among those that the school claims to teach: "All of them will have knowledge far beyond their years. This knowledge is the knowledge of how to survive in a society that is out to destroy you" (Laymon 2013, 214). As with City's rumination, the handbook links knowledge explicitly with survival within conditions of vulnerability.

As the characters travel from year to year, Laymon challenges the underlying linearity that often structures time travel narratives. While he gestures towards causation that argues if one changes the past then it necessarily changes the future, he also connects the process of storytelling with temporality. In other words, the timelines occur both in linear relation to each other even as they also occur simultaneously. Because of this, Laymon allows space for agency in how his characters interact within the freedom imagined through time travel. Instead of forcing them to adapt to concrete external rules, time travel becomes an allegory for reading and writing. At the end of the novel, Laymon constructs a dialogue between reality and fiction:

> "What does Jesus say is the difference between the fiction in your head and the real life you live? You know what I mean? It's like there's two of everybody, the one in fiction and the one in real life. But what's the difference?"
>
> "Really, it ain't no difference, City . . . Because unless you use both of them the right way, they just as bad or just as good as you want them to be. But you lead both of them." (Laymon 2013, 265)

Laymon emphasizes that the process by which the self is constructed is a process of writing, in which the individual is not merely subject to external forces that they are largely unable to explain. Instead, the "fiction in your head" and the "real life you live" are versions of each other, endlessly permeable and fluid. More than simply writing, by building and rebuilding, the boundaries between truth and fiction, past and present and future, self and other, all collapse. City's liberation from the powers that be happens with his embrace of his own voice. Instead of speaking on command, in the way that the Can You Use the Word in a Sentence competition demands, the writing process that the novel models and develops enables a non-contingent agency. If words, and people using words, make people disappear, then people using words can enable their reappearance. Here, the boundaries between the (fictional?) Baize and (real?) Baize blur, and her disappearance in each version of Long Division becomes a form of paradoxical presence.

The final image of the novel brings together its themes of love, survival, and agency through literacy. In contrast to their somewhat friendly rivalry at the beginning of the text, the end finds City and LeVander united in a way that emphasizes their love for each other.

> In that hole, right in that second, I felt as far away from Melahatchie and I felt as close to a real character as I had ever felt. And the craziest thing is that I wasn't sure if that was a good, bad, or sad thing. With LaVander Peeler's head on my

shoulder, we started rereading *Long Division* from the beginning, knowing that all we needed to know about how to survive, how to live, and how to love in Mississippi was in our hands. The sentences had always been there [ends mid-sentence]. (Laymon 2013, 267)

Here, Laymon elides distinctions between reader and writer, positioning LeVander and City in the hole that allows for travel through and across time. In doing so, he suggests the metanarrative meaning of time travel as a form of liberation that is possible within the "hole." However, in contrast to canonical narratives of Black (w)holeness such as Ralph Ellison's *Invisible Man* (1952) and Richard Wright's "The Man Who Lived Underground" (1945), City is not left alone in the liminal space.

By including LeVander in the hole with City, Laymon explodes the presumption of the isolated self. As Robert Stepto argued, in analyzing *Invisible Man*, Ellison's narrator provides a synthesis of two dominant narratives in African American literature: "ascent" and "immersion" (Stepto 1979, 167). In imagining the return of the narrator from the wholeness enabled through his plunge into the liminality of his hole, Stepto argues for an enlightened literacy drawn from a parade of models (i.e. Booker T. Washington, Frederick Douglass, etc.) the narrator encounters throughout the novel in service of a new kind of narrative self. Relatedly, Houston Baker Jr. analyzes Richard Wright's well-known story "The Man Who Lived Underground" to outline what he calls "Black (W)hole Rites" or "Rites of the Underground" (Baker 1984, 156). He delineates a process by which the Black subject attains the wholeness necessary to compose a new society: "To be *Black* and *(W)hole* is to escape incarcerating restraints of a white world (i.e. a *black hole*) and to engage the concentrated, underground singularity of experience that results in a blues desire's expressive fullness" (Baker 1984, 151–52). Baker's theory of a "rite of passage" oriented towards Black expressive wholeness resonates strongly with Laymon's novel, which, after all, charts the coming of age of its teenaged protagonist. As I have explained, the novel culminates with the intersection of the various narratives contained within the book, positing City as both composer and consumer of the text. As City retreats to the "hole" that has provided the means of time travel, he seeks a space of expressive wholeness in which he is author of his own experience. In doing so, Laymon links together the "black hole" in the woods with City's (Black) (w)holeness.

In line with Baker's outline in *Blues, Ideology, and Afro-American Literature* (1984), City's initial entry into the hole precipitates a consciousness of the structural anti-Blackness that is, at once, the topography of his and his friends' experience and their inheritance. The time travel conceit, then, ties together past events with the name-checked events of the present—the election of President Obama, the murder of Trayvon Martin, the events surrounding Hurricane Katrina—within a lineage of marginalization and precarity. The "kidnapping" of Baize Shephard, therefore, recalls and reenacts past tragedies, both those within the memory of the novel's characters and those outside of their consciousness. By resolving Shephard's kidnapping in the context of her orphaning during Hurricane Katrina, Laymon establishes his text as an incomplete and ongoing narrative. The narrative, however, continues multi-directionally, into the past and present as much as the future. Importantly, then, Laymon situates City and LeVander in the "hole" at the end of the text to revise the failed narratives of ascent that Baker analyzes. With regard to Wright, Ellison, and others, the ascent and its concomitant structural societal transformation—what Baker labels as the "idealized rite of aggregation," but which he also tags as "the impossibility of reintegration" (Baker 1984, 156)—fails due to isolation. In contrast, Laymon's already communitarian image of City and LeVander constructs an imaginative community in which new narratives and new forms of love are possible precisely because of their location within the hole.

Laymon challenges both the isolation of the individual within the structure of the narratives of either ascent or immersion and the location of the hole as marginal, a temporary stop on the way. The hole here encapsulates the indeterminacy that generates both fear and sadness, but also hope and love. In that context, the turn to reread *Long Division* supplements the image of LeVander's head tenderly resting on City's shoulder. To reread is not to return to a single static narrative but to actively engage in the process of rewriting and redefining, to make the past, present, and future reappear. In doing so, City and LeVander insert their own voices and agency among that which has been and continues to be. Fred Moten argues, in reference to the music and literature of the Black radical tradition, that liberation lies "in the break," the space between lines or notes within the narrative that cannot fully be voiced or explained or defined, even when those lines or notes imply an apparently static essentialist conception of Blackness (Moten 2003). Similarly, Laymon gestures towards the privileging of a static past in which the "sentences had always been there," but he makes clear that the fact that they have always been there does not mean that their form is either simple or unchanging. Instead, the implied ellipses at the end of the final sentence, which connects to the ellipses printed on the page preceding the first page of the text (and contained in the dots on the "i"'s in the novel's title), opens the possibility for not only City's agency, but also the reader being in the hole as well. Moten, returning to the black (w)hole of Ellison's *Invisible Man*, argues that the "refusal of closure" that Laymon's novel typifies, "is not a rejection but an ongoing and reconstructive improvisation of ensemble" in which the seemingly transitional, the space between, becomes generative (Moten 2003, 85). In line with Moten's argument, Laymon finds a space for radical change even among what appears to be static.

The ellipses, which the novel adopts as one of its key tropes, directly relates to Katrina's narrative role as both instrument of violent absence and creator of new spaces for creativity. After stealing Baize's laptop in 2013, City finds a series of "storm rhymes" in her Microsoft Word "recent documents" menu. Opening "Storm Rhyme #4," City is struck by the power of Baize's voice. He particularly finds himself drawn to the words as if they were written for a reader who "could be like me" (Laymon 2013, 75). Addressing the question of readership, City emphasizes the presence of ellipses in the rhyme: "I knew no Honors English teacher or librarian was 'the reader' for 'Storm Rhyme #4.' And it wasn't just because of the cussing or rhymes. It was mainly because of those dots she used. She used dot-dot-dot to start the rhyme, and she used dot-dot-dot in the middle of the rhyme, and she used dot-dot-dot at the end of the rhyme" (Laymon 2013, 76). I argue, as noted earlier, that the ellipses signify the spaces within which new imaginings are made possible—like Moten's "breaks." In this case, it is those same ellipses that extend the scope of the rhyme. Much like the argument of Black Arts Movement poets that the written text of any poem was limiting because it only reflected one of a theoretically infinite number of performances, Baize's ellipses open up permutations within the rhymes themselves.[11] These spaces, like the hole used for time travel, expand the scope of the poem to encompass the active participation of the reader. As City comes to understand later, by recognizing his own interactive authorship in the act of reading and writing, and thus rewriting, survival is predicated on learning to understand the sentences that are already present, and which you may have even authored yourself. Here, Katrina becomes a fertile symbolic ground on which Baize erects a new edifice. In this sense, her rhymes, which in this case narrate displacement and loss in the face of the storm, make her parents, including City himself, reappear, not just in the fanciful sense of the time travel that allows him to read his daughter's expressions, but also through the participatory authorship of being her reader.

The fact that the rhymes speak in a voice undecipherable to the "librarian" or "Honors English teacher" locates authenticity outside institutional authority. For Baize, City, Esch, and the others who populate these works, survival is predicated on the claiming of a self that cannot be dependent on institutions rooted in the denial of one's humanity and legitimacy. Instead, the fact of Black vulnerability, and the expressions that it engenders—what Houston Baker calls the "mythicohistorical archive of black incarceration in the Americas" (Baker 2002, 11)—provides the basis for claiming a self-ownership oriented around the process by which the Black community has, and continues to, survive in the United States. City's statement that the authenticity of Baize's voice meant that "I could still hear Baize saying the words to 'Storm Rhyme #4' in my head" validates a Black oral tradition that remains present in the literary works I have discussed so far (Laymon 2013, 75).

The SNCC volunteers who went to Mississippi to start Freedom Schools emphasized that all the necessary knowledge and strategy already existed in the consciousnesses of those subjected to the structural logic of Jim Crow. The role of the Freedom Schools that Laymon depicts was not to provide external knowledge that those in the state lacked but rather to enable a process of expression by which the knowledge that was already present—Laymon's "sentences [that] had always been there"—could be mobilized.[12] Similarly, Baize informs City, "The ellipsis always knows something more came before it and something more is coming after it" (Laymon 2013, 245). In other words, the ellipses are a simultaneous gesture of both connection and disconnection. They tie together past, present, and future, while also allowing for survival within that timeline. The novel prefaces the sense of Black vulnerability early on.

> In the backdrop of us walking were old images of folks in New Orleans, knee deep in toxic water. Those pictures shifted to shots of Trayvon Martin in a loose football uniform, then oil off the coast drowning ignorant ducks. Then they finally replayed that footage of James Anderson being run over by those white boys over off Ellis Avenue. The last shots were black-and-whites of dusty-looking teenagers from the Student Nonviolent Coordinating Committee holding up picket signs that said "Freedom Schools Now" and "Black is not a vice. Nor is segregation a virtue." (Laymon 2013, 9)

Here, the images of Katrina (or it could be Camille, Betsy, or the 1927 flood, reinforcing Ward's depiction of time marked by storms), Trayvon Martin, James Anderson, and SNCC construct a narrative of Black vulnerability across time, creating equivalence between the still present danger to young African Americans and the conditions of the past. Among these images, the ellipses that structure their time shifts signify time passing without change. However, as the arc of the novel makes clear, while this narrative of suffering is present, it is not the only narrative the can possibly be constructed out of such images. Instead, Laymon elevates survival as an act of courageous liberation instead of merely a pessimistic response to a hostile society that relies on Black vulnerability to perpetuate itself. That this survival, for Laymon, is rooted in love might make some readers view the text as hopelessly naïve. However, Laymon's understanding of love, and the creative engagement it fosters, emphasizes that the community meanings embedded in labels such as "Black people" are not meant to be either confining or totalizing, as post-Blackness would have it. Instead, they offer the base for creativity, opening spaces signified by the text's recurring ellipses. In the version of *Long Division* that 2013 City reads, 1985 City is fated to disappear, along with Shalaya Crump, in Hurricane Katrina, stranding their daughter Baize. The novel refuses, however, to grant the black hole of the storm the sucking power it so often acquires in cultural representations. Instead, while the storm reveals the ongoing vulnerability of Black bodies in the United States, it also opens the possibility for rebuilding, as both City's grandmother's rebuilding of her shotgun shack in the wake of the storm and the fact that City and Shalaya don't end up together typify. In other words, even the story is always evolving and changing, despite its static appearance.

Likewise, in representing the long and slow violence of Katrina, both of the authors I have discussed have sought literary forms that seek to provide an avenue for expression for that which was already present. To do this requires the salvaging of the themes and structures in order to fuel the agency of each subsequent generation in their subject formation. By emphasizing the incompleteness of narrative and ending with reflections that highlight the labor that will be necessary to either continue the process of revision and rereading (in *Long Division*) or salvaging and survival (in *Salvaging the Bones*), both authors refuse to differentiate the current moment from those of the past and those to come in the future. As I discussed in chapter 1, texts such as Touré's *Who's Afraid of Post-Blackness* premise their arguments for racial progress and the shift towards racial individualism on the increased access of people of color to economic and political power. Such arguments buttress the association of individual subjectivity with liberal capitalism, focalizing political demands for equality on issues of access rather than on transforming the structures of society in any fundamental way. This shift attempts to assert the centrality of what Edwards calls "the black normal": "the constellation of narratives, images, and state discourses that tie black freedom to the nation-to-empire-building project through images and imaginaries of everyday black empowerment within state institutions" (Edwards 2015, 143). The literature of post-Blackness, as I have argued, consequently focuses on members of this relative global elite, such as the doctors and lawyers and their children in Whitehead's *Sag Harbor*, Long Island. In doing so, contemporary African American fiction frequently highlights the post–civil rights era expansion of the Black middle and upper class by either rejecting depictions of the Black poor as either popular cultural stereotypes or by joining in and pathologizing marginalized communities.[13] In contrast, Ward and Laymon insist that even if some things have changed, they have not changed so sharply as to transform the fundamental anti-Blackness of the American state. Both authors construct through-lines, both thematically and formally, between the struggles of the past and the twenty-first century that reveals the relationship between the various permutations of white supremacy.

Notably, as post era authors linking their texts to the African American literary tradition, both Ward and Laymon call back to earlier reference points—Hurston, the underground of Ellison and Wright—rather than the Black Arts Movement. They do not link the explicit political content of their works with a definable movement, as authors did during BAM. Instead, they seek the reconstitution of a collective Blackness through the revision of canonical tropes. In doing so, they reject post-Blackness's emphasis on the individual at odds with the identity policing of the collective while still rejecting injunctions to collectivize Blackness in essentialist terms. By linking the process of writing, especially revision, with loving resistance and the practice of survival amid anti-Blackness, they reassert the need to acknowledge the power of anti-Blackness while resisting the dominant "therapeutic" or "prohibitive" readings identified by Levy-Hussen (2016). Focusing on Hurricane Katrina allows Ward and Laymon to deepen the representation of an event that turned the neglect of Black populations into headlines even as it failed to make visible the slow violence of racism of which the few days in August and early September 2005 were only an especially violent example. With their structural incorporation of references to past texts in the African American literary tradition and signal events in Black political traditions, Ward and Laymon construct a twenty-first century extension of those traditions that militates against valedictory declarations of transcendence.

"NEW AND BETTER STORIES"

Crafting a Literature to Fit a Barack Obama World

With his rapid rise from a little-known state senator who gave the keynote address at the 2004 Democratic National Convention to the junior senator from Illinois to the first African American major party presidential nominee to the first Black president, Barack Obama has become the principal referent for popular and scholarly discourses on race. Consequently, it is no accident that Charles Johnson's 2008 essay "The End of the Black American Narrative," connecting questions of individual liberation from racial prescription with ideas of belonging and citizenship, was the cover story for an issue of *The American Scholar* depicting the then-candidate Barack Obama. Addressing the headline's claim, "Black Americans Need a New Story: The Old One No Longer Fits a Barack Obama World," Johnson collapses post–civil rights economic and demographic changes into the symbolic implications of the first Black president to argue that a narrative of "pervasive victimization" no longer fits a Barack Obama world (Johnson 2008, 38). In the present, Johnson seems to claim, the ambiguous and fragmentary relationship between Blackness and belonging, Blackness and citizenship, no longer need be contested. Notably, unlike Kenneth Warren in *What Was African American Literature?*, Johnson does not turn from a focus on race to one on class as the major dividing line of the twenty-first century. Instead, much like other post era theorists, he empha-sizes how focusing on Black identity in the present through the lenses of the past erases the individual. While Johnson echoes theorists of post-racialism and post-Blackness in affirming that racism is still present in American society, both structurally and interpersonally, he emphasizes the transcendence of those same things to urge the writing of "new stories" and the creation of new identities to instantiate and mirror the new world he sees.

In this sense, the election of the nation's first Black president serves as a flashpoint for a larger imagined shift towards a new era of Blackness in the

United States. Consequently, "a Barack Obama world" is not contingent on any specific reading or understanding of Obama's political actions or policy or the actuality of his election or presidency. Instead, "Barack Obama" names a broader conceptual shift towards a race-free Blackness. The next two chapters address two ways of analyzing this "Barack Obama world." In chapter 3, I use Johnson's essay as a conceptual center around which to examine the penumbras of Obama's election. In doing so, I hazard a tentative answer to a question his essay prompts: what might the "new and better stories, new concepts, and new vocabularies and grammar based not on the past but on the dangerous, exciting, and unexplored present" look like in twenty-first century African American literature (Johnson 2008, 42)? In chapter 4, I analyze Alice Randall's 2009 novel *Rebel Yell* as a representative example of several Black and white authors who have already fictionalized Barack Obama as a character or reference point in imagining the transitioning present. Across these two chapters, I trace how the figure of Barack Obama anchors the attempt to imagine new meanings for Blackness that go beyond previous conceptions defined by a history of struggling against institutional oppression. For this chapter, specifically, I focus on how authors such as Paul Beatty and Colson Whitehead buttress Charles Johnson's call for new ways of conceptualizing Black writing that do not hinge on claims to a specific or definable Black experience.

THE CANONICAL BLACK AMERICAN NARRATIVE

Charles Johnson rose to fame during the late 1970s and early 1980s. He started his writing career as a cartoonist, taking inspiration from the vibrant Black Arts Movement-influenced scene in Chicago, and from writers such as Amiri Baraka. Coming of age in the late 1960s, Johnson belongs to a generation that precedes the "children of soul," such as Whitehead and Beatty, who were born during the Civil Rights Movement and so did not experience the movement as adults. Inspired by Buddhism and his academic studies of continental philosophy (he received a Ph.D. in the subject from Stony Brook University in 1988 and published his dissertation, a phenomenological approach to African American literature called *Being and Race*, that same year), Johnson's fiction explicitly rejects Black Arts Movement-style nationalism in favor of a philosophically-minded embrace of anti-essentialism and flux. As part of a tradition that an early Whitehead interviewer problematically called "the black intellectual novel" (Whitehead 1999a), Johnson, alongside writers such as Clarence Major and Ishmael Reed, inspired the postmodern play and poststructuralist interrogation of meaning celebrated by Trey Ellis's "The New Black Aesthetic"

(1989). Johnson's work, then, represents a strain of post–civil rights African American literature from the 1980s that presaged many of the themes that blossomed during the post era.

Writing in 2008 as a tenured professor and canonical author, "The End of the Black American Narrative" maps out a territory for African American writing that Johnson imagines is freed from the burden of "victimization" (Johnson 2008, 38). Johnson portrays what he labels "the Black American Narrative" as a useful epistemological framework that has endured centuries prior to becoming obsolete. As he explains, this narrative "is a tool we use, consciously or unconsciously, to interpret or make sense of everything that has happened to black people in this country since the arrival of the first 20 Africans at the Jamestown colony in 1619" (Johnson 2008, 33). Elucidating the long history of racial violence and dehumanization in the United States, Johnson suggests that the tool has been useful for much of its history, providing a central organizing principal for Black politics and writing, and serving as a "starting point," an "agreed-upon premise" in confronting not just the political, economic and cultural problems of the colonies and, in turn, the United States, but also as the basis for self-fashioning. However, it is this latter element that prompts Johnson's interrogation. Building on his own philosophical training in Buddhism and phenomenology, Johnson decries the overdetermination of the Black American Narrative on ideas of the self and nation. He argues that the dominance of this narrative colors every aspect of American life, especially that of African American individuals: "This unique black American narrative, which emphasizes the experience of victimization, is quietly in the background of every conversation we have about black people, even when it is not fully articulated and expressed" (Johnson 2008, 33).

So, if the Black American narrative is a "tool" that "has an epistemological mission: namely, to show us something," why does it fail to "have the qualities of coherence, consistency, and completeness" in the present (Johnson 2008, 33–34)? To make his argument, Johnson turns to a central quote from W. E. B. Du Bois's address "The Criteria of Negro Art" in which Du Bois asks what the goal of full citizenship is: "We want to be Americans, full-fledged Americans, with all the rights of American citizens. But is that all? Do we want simply to be Americans?" (Du Bois 1926). Claiming that "we who are dark can see America in a way that white Americans cannot," Du Bois decries the petty consumerism and materialism of the United States to argue that full citizenship and participation are meaningless if they are wedded to an exploitative capitalist apparatus that continues to oppress and destroy virtue. Johnson uses Du Bois's quote as a metric of racial progress, noting that the various superficial achievements that Du Bois fears have been accomplished, from monetary success to fame, celebrity, and even power. Johnson argues that this history climaxes with the accomplishments of Barack Obama, at that moment predicting "the possibility that he may be selected as the Democratic Party's first biracial, black American candidate for president" (Johnson 2008, 37).[1] Johnson aligns himself with Du Bois to question whether these successes constitute genuine progress, but he argues that they have, at a minimum, shifted the Black American narrative.

Johnson is particularly concerned that allegiance to the canonical Black American narrative constitutes its own kind of enslavement. He explicitly equates legal racialism with the narrative's cultural persistence, saying that to argue "that the essence of black American life is racial victimization and disenfranchisement, a curse and a condemnation, a destiny based on color in which the meaning of one's life is thinghood, created even before one is born . . . is not something we can assume" anymore (Johnson 2008, 37). Arguing that "the specific conflict of this narrative reached its dramatic climax" at the height of the civil rights era, Johnson presages Kenneth Warren's argument that African American literature is defined by its specific response to Jim Crow segregation by two years (and at least one year prior to his Du Bois lectures at Harvard that became the book) (see Warren 2011b). Arguing that present day inequalities are more reflective of class hierarchies than racial discrimination, Johnson celebrates a return to "the thing itself," quoting Husserl (Johnson 2008, 39). Unlike Warren, who makes a similar point, Johnson's essay argues that to return to "the thing itself" is to focus on the individual, which, for Johnson, means the transcendence of limitations imposed by both an adherence to the Black American narrative and its dominance of our reading and interpretive practices. Johnson casts this development as a broader liberation for African Americans, who will no longer be limited by "an intellectual construct" that "is often more appealing and perfect (in a Platonic sense)" than the "ambiguous and messy" reality (Johnson 2008, 39).

Johnson defines this liberation in two principal ways. First, he argues that the transcendence of the Black American narrative constitutes a freeing of the individual from the yoke of the group. While Johnson celebrates the collective Black experience and history, and does not deny either its influence or its meaningfulness, he quotes Martin Luther King Jr.'s famous passage from the "I Have a Dream" speech that has so often been appropriated in service of colorblind racism to urge the writing of "narratives of individuals, not groups" (Johnson 2008, 42). Furthermore, given Johnson's authorship of *Dreamer* (1998), a complicated philosophical novel about King, his appropriation of King's words cannot be dismissed as easily as they can when used by authors much less versed in his thought. Second, Johnson argues that the philosophical error of the Black American narrative lies in its inability to either reflect or respond to the messy complexity of reality. In Johnson's conception, the Black American narrative serves a utilitarian purpose oriented towards Black political struggle (much like Du Bois argued in "The Criteria of Negro Art") but fails as a claim to truth. Because of changes to the structural reality of race, according to Johnson, the persistence of this narrative only perpetuates the problematic aspects of that stasis without allowing for the freedom to engage with "the dangerous, exciting, and unexplored present" (Johnson 2008, 42). The product of this freedom, for Johnson, will be "a provisional reading of reality," "a tentative thesis" that "[does] not claim to absolute truth" (Johnson 2008, 42). In other words, Johnson's argument here elaborates on one of the key themes of his fiction: flux.[2] In this context, the importance of the provisional is heightened. Rather than standing as an obstacle to truth, it becomes the truth itself, with the racial lens serving as the obstacle to our understanding. And it is this racial lens that Johnson desires to render obsolete.

Johnson views the Black American Narrative as a product of market forces and intraracial aesthetic limitations. "New and better" narratives, then, will challenge the power of structures and forces external to the African American artists themselves to define the contours of Black cultural expression. The fiction I analyze in this chapter traces the tentative construction of these new narratives through the interrogation of Blackness itself as a market category. Attacking capitalism's incorporation of Blackness and Black culture through the mechanisms of the market—principally, in the form of "diversity" rhetoric and superficial multiculturalism, which conceal a fundamental identity essentialism—Whitehead and Beatty privilege fugitive gestures that seek to evade, however temporarily, such incorporation.

In chapter 1, I argue that Colson Whitehead's novel *Sag Harbor* (2009) constitutes a post-Black story in which the prescriptive meaning of Blackness becomes fodder for the elective identity performance choices of a certain class segment of the Black community, thus loosening the bonds of linked fate. Here, I turn to another of Whitehead's novels, *Apex Hides the Hurt* (2006), wherein he interrogates the meaning of naming. Following a Black nomenclature consultant hired to rename a town, Whitehead reflects on the burden of history and the mystical significance read into classifications so often used to enact racial prescriptions. Culminating in an ambiguous and clichéd choice of "Struggle" as the name for the town, the novel, like Johnson, emphasizes that labels can only ever be provisional. Equally satirical in tone, Paul Beatty's novel *Slumberland* (2008) follows the crate-digging DJ Darky as he journeys to Berlin in search of the perfect beat. Seeking the legendary lost musician Charles Stone, known as the Schwa, Beatty imagines a renewed Blackness through the destruction of its nationalistic baggage. Both novels confront an intractable paradox in which Blackness's cultural value exists simultaneously as a commodity to be fetishized within the market and as the historical foundation for struggle and resistance. Answering Johnson's call for new narratives that reject the search for absolute truths, both authors do not seek to resolve such a paradox but instead negotiate its temporary evasion. Unlike chapter 4, the works I discuss in this chapter do not specifically address Barack Obama and largely precede even his campaign for the presidency; however, their attempts to imagine what a provisional Blackness might look like complement Johnson's essay's attempt to construct a new Black American narrative that fits an Obama world.

HOW CAN ONE NAME A CITY, LET ALONE A GENERATION?

Unlike *Sag Harbor* (2009a), *Apex Hides the Hurt* (2006) fits squarely within Colson Whitehead's more conceptual oeuvre. In the novel, an unnamed nomenclature consultant is called upon to decide on a name for a town founded by the formerly enslaved in the Midwest. Initially named Freedom, the town had been renamed Winthrop upon the arrival of a white industrialist, whose barbed-wire factory led to the town's incorporation.[3] With burgeoning growth spurred on by the establishment of Aberdeen Software in the town, CEO Lucky Aberdeen hires the protagonist's old employer to generate a new name for the town, rigging the game in favor of his preference, New Prospera. As even this bare summary makes clear, Whitehead consciously eschews subtlety with his choice of names. Indeed, he calls attention to their allegorical nature, saying at one point of Freedom, "must have been a bitch to travel all that way only to realize that they forgot to pack the subtlety" (Whitehead 2006, 76). Within this allegorical structure, Whitehead stages the compelling and passionate discourse over the proper naming of African American cultural practices to emphasize the provisionality of both the labels themselves and what they claim to represent.

Each of the labels plays out a discourse on power and American history. Consequently, the nomenclature consultant's process of choosing between the names interrogates narratives of national identity and belonging. Winthrop, the current name of the town, draws on two principal sources to construct the narrative of mainstream industrial capitalism. First, Winthrop's connotation of a New England elite is cemented by the discussion of the protagonist having gone to Quincy, a thinly veiled fictional version of Harvard University (Whitehead's own alma mater). Indeed, one of Harvard University's residential colleges is named Winthrop House after John Winthrop, which aligns the name with the second important referent: Winthrop's famous "city upon a hill" speech. In that speech, titled "A Modell of Christian Charity," Winthrop, one of the first governors of the Massachusetts Bay Colony, casts the colonist's project as endowed by God (Winthrop [1630] 1838). Aligning with similar idealizations of the newly colonized continent as a kind of return to the Garden of Eden—John Locke, for example, famously said, "Thus in the beginning all the World was *America*" (Locke 1689, §49)—Whitehead's invocation of the speech refers to a historical imaginary in which America serves as a virgin land tamed to enable power and prosperity.

The town's original name of Freedom, unofficially selected prior to legal incorporation, speaks to one of the principal structures underlying the narrative Winthrop connotes: slavery. Freedom, which is supported by the town's Mayor, Regina Goode, a descendent of one of two early town patriarchs, emphasizes a respect for the agency of the formerly enslaved. Whitehead specifically isolates the name from the narrator's corporatist task by declaring that "Freedom was so defiantly unimaginative as to approach a kind of moral weakness" (Whitehead 2006, 83). Freedom in this context is both commemorative and aspirational for a people newly freed from slavery. Just as many enslaved individuals changed their names in registering with the Freedman's Bureau to claim agency over both their identities and to codify their new status, the town name of Freedom makes both a declarative claim to freedom, while implying that the very structure of the community itself is both illustrative and constitutive of that freedom. Whitehead addresses this history directly near the end of the novel, aligning naming with subjectivity: "What did a slave know that we didn't? To give yourself a name is power. They will try to give you a name and tell you who you are and try to make you into something else, and that is slavery. And to say, I Am This—that was freedom" (Whitehead 2006, 206). But what then would it mean to return to this name in the ambiguous present of the novel? The African American individuals in the town are now descendants of those who had been enslaved, with one of those descendants in the highest position of power as Mayor, one of three equal voices on the voting body tasked with making this decision. Whitehead forces the reader to recognize that while the choice of Freedom has a superficial attractiveness for several reasons (i.e. it was first; it demonstrates a respect for the specific history of the town; it implies the restoration of a potentially lost history of the town that has been somewhat forgotten in the century plus period of being called Winthrop), the name, despite its lack of subtlety, conceals as much as it reveals about that history.

In advocating for the name, Goode frames the change to Winthrop as a divestment of agency born of the particular economic and political reality of the period:

Winthrop comes to town, he has the resources to build that thing. Most important, he's white. What are Goode and Field going to say? They didn't have a
choice, did they? Back then. What could they do? They lose this land, this land
is what they are at that point. They lose that, they lose themselves. He's not
threatening them, Winthrop. But he wouldn't have to say it. They did what they
had to do. Give up their name for their lives—was that a little thing or a big
thing after all they'd been through? . . . Well, I have a choice. And I choose the
truth. (Whitehead 2006, 116)

Goode's reference to the "truth" suggests that she sees the name as something
other than an arbitrary signifier. Indeed, she links the act of naming with the
selves of the town's residents, arguing for a kind of essentialism, in which the
town's "true name" must necessarily derive from and be expressive of some
fundamental truth embodied by the town's founders (Whitehead 2006, 127).
Goode argues that Freedom was not simply a contextual expression by the
newly free. Instead, she views the name as tapping into some fundamental
reality that was only displaced by structures of power over which the town
founders had little to no control. Without the political influence of Winthrop,
their town would fail to gain recognition in the law. Interestingly, nowhere in
the novel does Whitehead imply that this early naming battle was a product
of deliberate racism on the part of Winthrop. Whitehead goes so far as to
establish power for both Goode and Field within the early council, giving
them two seats to Winthrop's one, implying that any decision to change the
name had to have been made through some version of the agency of the two
Black patriarchs. In this context, Regina Goode is arguing that recognizing
the broader power structures forces the acknowledgement that despite their
numerical superiority on the council, Goode and Field were never truly free
to decide on the name they desired, driven by both economic necessity and
the racial politics of the era. Consequently, her argument in favor of renaming
that town Freedom is that this would not be a renaming, but rather a form
of reparative justice. However, by terming Freedom the town's "true name,"
Goode goes beyond merely supporting the restoration in property terms to
suggest a pre-lapsarian state prior to the initial renaming not unlike the Edenic
imagery conjured by the reference to Winthrop. In doing so, she implies that
the initial name has a greater authenticity than either Winthrop or the other
option of New Prospera, not merely because of its primacy, but because it is
the expression of the town's initial founders.

By associating Freedom with Goode's explicit choice of an authenticity discourse, Whitehead directly connects his novel with post-Black Arts Movement
debates over the politics of authenticity. Goode's claim that Freedom is the

town's "true name" mirrors arguments by Black Arts Movement scholars that the quality of Blackness in a piece of literature or art could simply be known to the point of near quantification. For example, in his book *Understanding the New Black Poetry*, Stephen Henderson discusses what he calls "saturation," arguing that African American art can be analyzed in terms of its "fidelity to the observed and intuited truth of the Black Experience" (Henderson 1973, 62). In other words, Goode's position here mirrors the more caricatured versions of the Black Arts Movement that insist on the definability of Black identity and experience (see Crawford 2017; Avilez 2016).

Each of these claims to authenticity dispute post-structuralist arguments for the arbitrariness of signifiers. In contrast, the various post era attempts to crystallize the meaning of racial identities that I discuss throughout this book call attention to the social constructed-ness of labels, attempting to carve out space for individual liberation while recognizing the power that such labels hold. The arguments that Whitehead voices through Goode underline the romanticism of racial essentialism, and the appeal it derives from its truth claims. However, Whitehead highlights the danger in such claims. In line with Whitehead's choice to root Winthrop's wealth in barbed wire, arguments for authenticity cause injury in their erection of specific boundaries. The "identity policing" that Touré (2011) refers to, for example, may enable the construction of a definable collective for political action, but it risks marginalizing individuals and groups that do not fit into specific definitions of what constitutes Blackness, such as the African immigrant communities whose fiction I discuss in chapter 5. On the other hand, as the patina of alienation that hovers over *Apex* (and Whitehead's other novels) makes clear, recognizing the untenability of such truth claims risks atomizing communities, leaving them open to the neoliberal multiculturalism of a company like Aberdeen Software, which seeks to update the privatization of the town naming.

In this sense, the battle over the town name becomes a proxy for the more abstract question of the stakes of labeling, and indeed language itself. Representing the topography of the battle as a racialized terrain, Whitehead emphasizes that, as Evelyn Higginbotham argues, race is fundamentally a "metalanguage" that connects individual identities to broader issues of justice, nationalism, and progress (see Higginbotham 1992). Just as Goode's advocacy for Freedom represents a narrative of restoration that was unjustly taken from the town's original African American inhabitants, Winthrop and New Prospera speak to alternate narratives making similar claims to authenticity. Framed as it is through the explicit reference to John Winthrop's "city upon a hill" speech, Winthrop signifies a deracinated narrative of American progress, a representation of traditional American values. The argument for Winthrop relies on the idea that the recognition of the government signifies the true origin of the town and that prior to that moment it was merely a surreptitious "settlement" (Whitehead 2006, 76). This framing suggests that the economic paternalism of the Winthrop family is the true driver of both the history and meaning of the town. Whitehead questions this paternalism, preserved in Albie Winthrop's continual insistence that he is everyone in the town's "uncle," through the emptiness of Winthrop's ancestral home. While it remains on a tract of land still worthy of being called an "estate," the house itself contains almost nothing, leaving the symbolic site of the family's value an empty shell and relying on the implied narrative of the town in the name alone, thereby preserving a sustained illusion of power.

This representation does not, however, suggest that names such as Winthrop, and the white supremacy it invokes, have been wholly divested of power. Whitehead directly connects the protagonist's access to the renaming contract with the Winthrop name through the thinly veiled representation of a Harvard-like university that both Albie and the narrator attended. Through this connection, Whitehead simultaneously suggests how such names are still "keys" even as their power relies more and more on the superficial (Whitehead 2006, 69). The fact that the narrator attended Quincy situates him within the power hierarchies established and perpetuated by the Winthrops of the world. Much like Regina Goode's status as mayor, Whitehead's narrator is not a marginal outsider, but rather a specifically groomed representative of powerful institutions.

Critically, it is only through his discussion of his admission to Quincy that we find out that the narrator is African American: "He had filled out a form the previous summer at the African American Leaders of Tomorrow conference . . . Quincy believed in diversity" (Whitehead 2006, 70). Inserting such a remark so late in a short novel, Whitehead, as an African American novelist, subverts the audience's presumption of the narrator's race before ultimately confirming it. Furthermore, marking the protagonist's racial identity in this way aligns racial designation with the practice of exclusion, showing that even the inclusion of the narrator re-inscribes the forms of exclusion that generated racial categorizations in the first place. In addition, by displacing the racial identifier away from any bare description of the physical body of the protagonist, whose major physical characteristic in the novel is a limp, Whitehead addresses the issue of racial identity in the absence of the question of its existential meaning to the protagonist himself. Race becomes removed from the individual and associated with the broader social question of the meaning of diversity.[4]

The characterization of Quincy as an elite university also highlights Whitehead's interrogation of how naming practices abet the neo-liberalization of diversity as a concept. The last choice for the town's name, New Prospera, highlights the corporatization of multiculturalism, and the illusion of progress resting on the expansion of neoliberal capitalism. Whitehead's description of the firm reinforces a portrait of the university in which "official anti-racisms have disconnected race from material conditions, even as they have fatally limited the horizon of social possibility for overcoming racism to U.S.-led global capitalism" (Melamed 2011, xvii). As Whitehead's depiction of Aberdeen Software demonstrates, this movement of anti-racism away from movement advocacy towards official policy leads multinational corporations to adopt the language and optics of human rights and liberation as good publicity. Describing the Aberdeen Software conference occurring during his time in the town, the narrator notices, "They were a pretty mixed group, Lucky's future business partners and incipient flunkies—put a picture of Sterling Winthrop's laborers next to a picture of Lucky's multiculti crew and caption it CHANGING TIMES" (Whitehead 2006, 83). As the narrator gazes on this group, the reader is forced to question what actually has changed. While the demographics of the labor force are different, what does that signify? Is it merely representative of a new business cultural buzzword like "multiculti," or does the embrace of multiculturalism go beyond surface level inclusion and tokenism to reorder access to power, and through the power, force a redefinition of identity categories? In the context of this description, the firm's initial proposal of the name New Prospera reflects neoliberalism's privatization of even anti-racist activism. Whereas Winthrop evokes paternalistic company-town capitalism, New Prospera imagines the corporation itself as a synecdoche of the larger nation and world, absent burdensome questions of redistributive justice.

By distracting from systemic questions of governing and justice to focus on the signification of the town name, the prominence of the Winthrop and Aberdeen Software corporations in the novel raises the potential that the discourse of naming practices could itself conceal the perpetuation of capitalist exploitation and inequality. However, *Apex Hides the Hurt* suggests that Whitehead is highly sensitive to this possible reading, providing something of a preemptive critique of it. On the one hand, the naming of the town certainly is indicted in the same structures of power that necessitated the change from Freedom to Winthrop in the first place. Despite the narrator being positioned outside of the firm for which he used to work (for reasons that remain murky throughout the novel), there is an explicit promise from his former boss that if he chooses New Prospera (created by the firm), he could have his old office back, as well as the clear implication that without his institutional pedigree, he would not be in a position of judgment in the first place.

On the other hand, the novel's titular ad campaign, and the protagonist's role in it, makes clear that Whitehead sees the issue of naming as central to, rather than a distraction from, the larger anti-capitalist critique. The narrator's greatest triumph as a nomenclaturist was his development of the name for a brand of Band-Aid competitors seeking to market flesh colored bandages to the demographically diverse market.[5] On a certain level, the "Apex hides the hurt" campaign that the protagonist develops is Whitehead's most pointed satire of racial egalitarianism concealing economic exploitation, with individual consumers as its agents: "The product moved. The boxes didn't say Sri Lankan, Latino, or Viking. The packages spoke for themselves. The people chose themselves and, in that way, perhaps he had named a mirror. In pharmacies you started to see *that motion*—folks placing their hands against the box to see if the shade in the little window matched their skin" (Whitehead 2006, 109). As Whitehead describes, in this context, racial progress becomes a means of profit and the "solution" an illusion of justice. While the symbolic displacement of the market's assignation of whiteness as the origin of the "flesh" color would seem to indicate the removal of their market privilege, Whitehead implies that regardless of any potential symbolism, the displacement is merely the product of a multi-national corporation seeing a gap in the market and seeking to fill it.

With the images of consumers placing their literal skin next to the boxes to determine the appropriate numbered skin-tone, Whitehead shows how the labels constructed by society become determinative of individual identity. Such widening of options is progress of a sort, as with changing racial categorizations, yet one still must align oneself with something. Much like an individual filling out a census form, seeking to decide whether to label themselves as white, Black, or, more recently, choosing multiple categories, the illusion of choice masks a continued racialization that suggests a collective enterprise. Like an updated version of Benedict Anderson's "imagined communities" (1983), national, cosmopolitan and particular identities are all enacted by the simple act of purchasing bandages: "In the advertising, multicultural children skinned knees, revealing the blood beneath, the commonality of the wound, they were all brothers now, and multicultural bandages were affixed to red boo-boos. United in polychromatic harmony, in injury, with our individual differences respected, eventually all healed beneath Apex" (Whitehead 2006, 109). Echoing Rey Chow's critique of the simultaneous universalism and particularism of the idea of ethnicity,[6] Whitehead provides the reader with a utopian vision of consumers brought together into a universal humanity through their simple capacity to bleed (thus echoing facile clichés of how underneath the skin, our blood is all the same) while affirming difference through the acknowledgement that each person does have a different "flesh" color. The agency that Whitehead's protagonist frames as allowing "people [to choose] themselves" thus conceals capitalization on both difference and its proliferation. One can easily imagine a science fiction version of the novel in which social categories of race such as Black and white have been replaced by groupings by Apex numbers (white = #A12, for example), resulting in harmony and social order.

In addition, Apex's product highlights the illusion of individual agency over "choosing" the racial self. The superficial appearance of choice enables the accumulation of further capital, relying on society's racial divisions to expand the customer base for supposedly flesh colored band-aids. However, instead of pivoting from his critique of individual agency over racial categorization towards a return to the collective, Whitehead, as he does in *Sag Harbor*, locates possibilities in the recognition of the arbitrariness of the act of signification itself. After all, the return to the collective, which would be most directly signified by the re-adoption of the name Freedom, in opposition to either Winthrop or New Prospera, would embrace the discourse of authenticity's essentialism. Instead, Whitehead turns from his critique of individual agency towards the embrace of a temporary answer that recognizes both the power that language holds but also its capacity for change.

Confronting the romantic essentialism that appears to elevate Freedom over either the crass corporatism of New Prospera or the ossified white supremacy of Winthrop, Whitehead's protagonist asks whether a new name "[changes] the character of the place? . . . [Does it] cover up history?" (Whitehead 2006, 129.) Analogizing the naming to the literal Apex bandages, Whitehead suggests a contradictory answer. On the one hand, Whitehead seems to affirm the integrity of his protagonist while simultaneously suggesting the impossibility of his task:

> A name that got to the heart of the thing—that would be miraculous. But he never got to the heart of the thing, he just slapped a bandage on it to keep the pus in. What is the word, he asked himself for that elusive thing? It was on the tip of his tongue. What is the name for that which is always beyond our grasp? What do you call *that which escapes*? (Whitehead 2006, 183, emphasis in original)

This passage speaks to several of Whitehead's most persistent themes. Each of Whitehead's novels are defined by the search for some meaning, either historical or definitional. In *The Intuitionist* (1999b), Lila Mae Watson is investigating the failure of an elevator she inspected through an Intuitionist method. In *John Henry Days* (2001), J. Sutter is covering the launch of the John Henry stamp and attempting to understand the meaning of his profession along with the event. Despite *Sag Harbor*'s superficial difference from Whitehead's other novels, it is centered on the elusive profundity of an adolescent summer, with its promise of monumental changes and individual revelations (see chapter 1). In *Zone One* (2011), Mark Spitz implicitly seeks the meaning of the plague that has led to the post-apocalyptic world in which he lives while *The Underground Railroad* (2016) questions the meaning of freedom. However, as illustrated in this passage from *Apex*, Whitehead's postmodernism militates against this search, suggesting that its object is elusive, even ultimately impossible. In each novel, while the reader is left with an answer to the central questions of the text, Whitehead always emphasizes that it is merely one answer, and not a definitive one. Consequently, while this passage seems to affirm the protagonist's integrity by suggesting that he is not merely seeking a name for the town to satisfy either his individual career ambitions or any particular constituents, but rather is seeking some idea of the "true name" to which Regina Goode refers, he remains frustrated in that search precisely because of an instability as to what a name really means.

At the novel's conclusion, Whitehead's protagonist departs from the three names proposed throughout the novel to settle on the name that Field had initially proffered for the town, Struggle. On the one hand, the choice implies the broader historical project of restoration, going even further than Freedom would have, to reveal a history even more concealed than that of the choice voted on by the formerly enslaved. It also serves as a sort of alternate or shadow history of the town, with the consequent implication that not only should they possibly have chosen the other path in the past, but that it might be more accurate to both that past and the present. However, as the novel makes clear throughout, no naming choice is ever merely the expression of individual agency. Even leaving aside the hidden alternative of Struggle, the initial choice of Freedom gains its meaning through the explicit contrast to slavery contained in the name, thus the product of a political context contingent on racialized slavery. In investigating this history, the protagonist suggests that "if they had created a law to change the name of the town, that meant there must have been a name to change it from" (Whitehead 2006, 61). The novel argues for an expansion of this principle to suggest that not only does the act of renaming imply a prior name, but that there is no act of naming other than renaming, and no identifiable origin, or "true name," to fully restore.

So, if naming oneself is never a full expression of either individual or collective agency, what does the protagonist's choice suggest? Is it a "good name" that was "[waiting] for its intended" as "Apex" was for the bandages (Whitehead 2006, 4)? As with Lila Mae's search for the truth in *The Intuitionist*, the act of naming in *Apex* takes on a quasi-spiritual quality throughout the novel, providing the ending with the patina of spiritual resolution or catharsis. However, in each case, Whitehead suggests that the spiritual quality is more an expression of our desire for meaning than actual meaning. As he puts it in *The Intuitionist*, meanings "just need the need of others" (Whitehead 1999b, 241). In choosing Struggle, Whitehead's protagonist locates its rightness in the reorientation from outcome to process:

> Given the choice between Freedom, and his contribution, how could their flock not go with Goode's beautiful bauble? Field's area of expertise wasn't human nature, but the human condition. He understood the rules of the game, had learned them through the barb on the whip, and was not afraid to name them. Let lesser men try to tame the world by giving it a name that might cover the wound, or camouflage it. Hide the badness from view. The prophet's work was of a different sort. (Whitehead 2006, 210)

The movement from "nature" to "condition" not only addresses the desire to conceal "the badness" of both life and history, it also pivots from the search for essences or truths towards arbitrary signifiers. With this description, Whitehead aligns Field, and, by extension, his protagonist, with his other pseudo-prophetic figures, such as Fulton and Lila Mae in *The Intuitionist*, J. and John Henry himself in *John Henry Days*. Field takes on the role of truth teller, choosing a name that speaks to the reality of the ex-slave experience in a way that Freedom only seeks to conceal. In this context, the act of naming could be viewed as a transgressive act of truth-telling, one that the town was unwilling to listen to in the past and continues to be unwilling to do so in present. Jesse Cohn reads the protagonist's novel-closing choice as an injunction, "a promise to struggle, to fight, at the cost of gratification" (Cohn 2009, 20). Extending Cohn's reading would imply that Whitehead sees struggle as a perpetual narrative of African American life, a truth that forces aside the obfuscations of late capitalism's diversity rhetoric. The protagonist's words here imply that Struggle does not conceal the wound but instead reveals it, suggesting that the name removes the bandage, rather than putting it in place. In this way, Whitehead suggests that Struggle is the repudiation of the act embodied in the naming of the Apex bandages: "he had to admit that Struggle got to the point with more finesse and wit. Was Struggle the highest point of human achievement? No. But it was the point past which we could not progress, and a summit in that way. Exactly the *anti-apex*, that peak we could never conquer, that defeated our ambitions despite the best routes, the heartiest guides, the right equipment" (Whitehead 2006, 210–11, emphasis added).

However, despite the quasi-spiritual tone of this passage, Whitehead's insertion of a requirement that the town keep the name for at least one year suggests that one should read the final decision as a form of abdication, a perverse joke on the protagonist's part to punish the town, for reasons that remain unclear. To be the anti-apex in this context would be to remove illusions rather than impose them; not necessarily to determine the town's true name but to approach it, to reach "a summit in that way," even if the final peak remains inherently elusive. In that sense, my argument here aligns with Stephanie Li's discussion of the novel in her book *Signifying without Specifying* (2012). However, where Li, like Cohn, reads "Struggle" as a kind of truth-telling, connecting the choice with Barack Obama's insistence on maintaining the teleological push for a "more perfect union," I see Whitehead as emphasizing the provisionality of the label not in service of a teleological progress, but to parody the very idea of naming (see Li 2012, 68–99; see also Maus 2014, 88). In other words, Whitehead's protagonist attempts a kind of "fugitive" gesture here (Whitehead 2006, 171). He is trapped in an impossible situation. Despite his role as a nomenclature consultant and his book-long insistence on the quasi-sacred quality of names, there is no proper name for the town that avoids entrapment in the neoliberal branding exercise that structures the text. In the face of this impossibility, then, Whitehead's protagonist refuses his task, choosing a name that he knows will dissatisfy all stake-holders. Doing so embraces the temporariness of the name, resisting the essentialism of the "true name." "Struggle," then, allows the book's protagonist to make a joke of capitalism's capture. That the town's contracts require it to maintain the name of his choosing for one year only cements his determination within the terms of his own compromised position.

The choice here of Struggle is particularly instructive in the context of Johnson's "The End of the Black American Narrative" (2008). Johnson's essay prompts the question of whether Whitehead's ending serves to reify the traditional narrative of Black struggle, tracing a teleology from slavery through freedom, the struggle for civil rights up through a progress signified by a Black mayor and the access of a young African American man to a fictional stand-in for Harvard and a Madison Avenue advertising firm. However, such a reading misunderstands the temporary nature of any conclusions in Whitehead's work. In the novel, Struggle is provisional not just because it might merely push the tension over naming into the next year, but because it is not a true name at all. Despite the desires for specific narratives of authenticity embodied in each of the names, none of them can lay claim to being authentic. With the last lines of the novel, Whitehead denies the healing implied by the naming of trauma to suggest the perpetuation of the wound: "As the weeks went on and he settled into his new life, he had to admit that actually, his foot hurt more than ever" (Whitehead 2006, 212).

At the end of the novel, the narrator's choice of "Struggle" is an act of neither recuperation of a lost past nor a description of the present. Instead, the name serves as a placeholder. Indeed, the novel frames the contestation that it contains in terms of branding, implying that the fight is not about authenticity in the first place, but rather the fetishistic quality of the names themselves. Yet, if the name is a placeholder, then what is it a placeholder for? Does it enable the space for further racialized political agitation? Does it mask the ultimate bankruptcy of the discourse itself? In attempting to answer these questions, it is necessary to note how each of Whitehead's novels ends in process. In each case, the reader is left only with a suggestion of meaning, rather than any stable coherence. As mentioned earlier, the final line of the book signals a continued festering underneath the Apex bandage on the narrator's injured toe. Consequently, if Whitehead leaves the reader in process, the novel marks such a process as one of concealment, undermining whatever redemptive quality the narrator's choice may seem to summon. The inadequacy of Struggle as a name instructs the reader to recognize how even makeshift terms enable the reader to see beneath their surface. After rhapsodizing throughout about the spiritual dimension of naming, and the search for something's true name, Whitehead provides a name that would have fit as the righteous and powerful climax of a novel from the height of the civil rights or Black Power movements. In doing so, he reframes the analytical lens that Johnson decries to emphasize provisionality, echoing Charles Johnson's call for "a tentative thesis" that does "not claim to absolute truth" (Johnson 2008, 42). Rather than serving as the spiritual climax in which the revelation of the town's true name charts a path towards a more righteous future, the name merely fulfills a contractual obligation, with its ultimate future unresolved.

In his deliberate choice of a term that mirrors a facile reproduction of civil rights era rhetoric, Whitehead generates a placeholder that remains necessary not because it speaks to some abstractly authentic African American experience. Instead, the term demarcates the contours of experiences and expression that are lived within continued racialization while highlighting the necessity of its continual provisionality. Whitehead's novel suggests that the issue is not about determining what can be labeled authentic. Instead, in serving as a placeholder for a larger discourse that is both more complex and more diverse than any term can possibly encompass, Struggle traces the continued presence and influence of structures and institutions still defined in racial terms, however inadequate they are. In doing so, the placeholder does not serve as a prescriptive discourse but rather as a marker for the presence of the racialized discursive structure itself. In doing this, Whitehead seeks to negotiate the tension between the liberation of the individual Black subject and the centrality of race in American cultural discourse that I have been describing. He uses the word to stand in for the structures within and against which he as a Black author is writing even as he undermines the definitive-ness of the name, suggesting the concurrent resistance that necessarily always accompanies such an acknowledgment.

BLACKNESS AS PASSÉ

Paul Beatty's novel *Slumberland* (2008) opens with the following question: "I mean, don't they know that after fourteen hundred years the charade of blackness is over?" (Beatty 2008, 3.) Labeling Blackness as a charade, Beatty's novel mirrors Charles Johnson's attempt to reframe race in terms of the indi-vidual as a means of liberation. Throughout this book, I have shown how the turn towards the individual mirrors the broader optimism over racial progress, which imagines a teleological path towards liberation by detaching questions of rights and citizenship within the political and social realm from those of racial identity. One must make a distinction, as I've discussed in relation to Whitehead's work, between valedictory declarations that a post-racial utopia has been reached and the liberation asserted by authors such as Beatty, Johnson, and Whitehead. Instead of trafficking in facile narratives of superficial progress, Beatty, like Johnson and Whitehead, highlights how Blackness functions as a marketing category or commodity, limiting aesthetic possibilities rather than expanding them. Consequently, in contrast to the conclusive declarations of the much-mocked idea of post-racialism, to assert that Blackness is "passé," as Beatty does throughout his novel, is not to celebrate the reaching of some end point where racism has been overcome. Nor is it to completely embrace the class-based arguments of Warren and scholars such as Adolph Reed. Instead, the assertion of the pastness of Blackness claims the right of redefinition rooted in individual liberation. In this way, *Slumberland* is the chronicle of seeking out "who they really are" underneath the narratives written onto Black people's skin (Beatty 2008, 3). Beatty's ultimate satirical target is essentialism, and the claims of authenticity that it engenders. Taking music as his subject, Beatty explores the commodification of Black identity and Black culture through the most popularly consumed African American cultural form. Delving into the world of crate-diggers and jazz heads, he exposes how subcultures abet the broader capitalist structure in transform-ing Blackness into a marker of cool.

The overall plot of the novel is ultimately quite simple. DJ Darky, a Black music collector and DJ from Los Angeles, builds what he thinks may be "the perfect beat," but which is lacking one thing: Charles Stone playing over it. Charles Stone, whose designation as the Schwa positions him as occupying an indeterminate or liminal position, is a recluse who has not been seen in decades.[7] After receiving a tape of a man having sex with a chicken sound-tracked by music that DJ Darky instantly recognizes as the Schwa, he decamps from Los Angeles to Berlin to work in the bar from which the package was sent, hoping to find him. Following the fall of the Berlin Wall, DJ Darky does eventually encounter Stone, who was trapped behind the Wall after its quick erection. After collaborating, they decide to erect a new Berlin Wall of sound by playing Darky's perfect beat, a performance which is explicitly linked to the end of Blackness.

Ultimately, the strongest objects of satire in the novel are those individuals who most buy into myths of racial authenticity. For example, Lars, a German music journalist, asks DJ Darky "What's it like listening to jazz with no white people around?" reflecting a genuine belief in the "mystique and exclusivity of Negro expression" (Beatty 2008, 92). Fetishists like Lars imagine that the cultural cache of Black expression derives from some mystical coolness, alter-nately denied to and appropriated by whites. Lars himself attempts to deal in this cultural currency even as he recognizes it only as an object of worship by speaking in a quasi-Black dialect and hanging out with DJ Darky. Existing within the milieu of crate-digging DJs, Beatty characterizes Lars in this way to reveal the orthodoxy lurking within the attempt to find those hidden gems and perfect beats. Lars is only able to conceive of Black artists as Black artists, finding himself attracted to their expression as a means of transgressing his own whiteness. This is neither a new phenomenon nor a new critique, as Beatty makes clear with his references to Mezz Mezzrow, Alan Lomax, and other canonical white figures in Black music. As a variety of cultural critics have argued, the very process of crate digging carries undertones of objectification. Prioritizing exclusivity and rarity, DJs frequently capitalize on songs and beats for which their creators have received little compensation (see Tucker 2010).[8] As with writers like Mezzrow, Lomax, and Mailer, subcultures that emphasize such rarity construct a stereotypical narrative of coolness and authenticity through Blackness as a way of imagining their own liberation from white supremacist thinking. However, for Beatty, his point goes beyond describ-ing the fetishization that underlies Norman Mailer's characterization of the "White Negro" (Mailer 1957). Instead, Beatty aligns such fetishization with market forces that commodify Black culture and Black people and a broader essentialism that he sees as confining African Americans, artists and otherwise.

For example, in line with post-Blackness, Beatty critiques how the African American literary publishing industry plays into stereotypical representations of Black people. Beatty specifically satirizes his fellow Black novelists who exploit this system for their own enrichment. Mirroring Colson Whitehead's genealogy of a Black intellectual literary tradition (see chapter 1), Beatty elevates an avant-garde tradition in opposition to static representations of race. The character of Tyrus, a playwright whose last name Maverick signals the commodification of supposedly risqué Black art within the mainstream, links the narrative to African American literary production. Beatty satirizes the industry that Tyrus inhabits, describing his reading practices as follows:

> He kept up with contemporary African-American male literature. That night he was reading a trade-paperback tome entitled *Want Some, Get Some. Bad Enough, Take Some.* Like everything else he read, it invariably bore a series of blurbs comparing the author's biting satire to Ralph Ellison and Richard Wright, a comparison that I never understood because Richard Wright isn't funny. (Beatty 2008, 103)

For Darky, and Beatty, the literature that Tyrus consumes, and feeds into through his own work, reduces Blackness to a static narrative, wherein "brilliant, underappreciated men . . . [ground] their fragile blackness" through the guidance of an earthy, impossibly understanding "brown-skinned" woman (Beatty 2008, 103-104). For Beatty, such a narrative has fallen into cliché, elevating the concerns of a particular blackened version of a mainstream white bourgeois figure, whose Blackness becomes a site of contestation because of its association with both stereotypically white settings and concerns. In highlighting this mainstream narrative, Beatty assaults the fetishization of the Black middle class and the claims of their marginalization within the mainstream construction of Blackness. As Darky's engagement with Tyrus reflects, the middle-class Black experience has been at the center of twenty-first century representations of Black identity. However, despite inverting post-Blackness's critique of publishing by arguing that Black middle- and upper-class characters are currently over-represented, Beatty maintains its broader distrust of how incorporation into mainstream cultural industries risks essentializing Blackness.

Ultimately, it is not just the static racialization of such narratives that is problematic, but the entire ecology within which the process occurs. As his portrait of Tyrus makes clear, Beatty envisions African American literature as a kind of hustle, one in which Tyrus's self-identification as "performance artist slash poet slash playwright slash filmmaker slash activist" reveals a culture industry predicated on reductive understandings of Black identity and Black expression (Beatty 2008, 102). The biting comment that critics hail each subsequent novel by an African American male author as the new Ralph Ellison or Richard Wright, deliberately eliding both the distinctions (and substantial interpersonal conflict) between those two figures, and misreading their work to do so, builds on Johnson's insight that the expectations of racial writing act as a lens through which reading is conducted, foreclosing both productive new interpretations and distorting even the new and innovative expressions that already exist.[9]

Where Beatty goes further than post-Blackness in his critique of how Blackness has become a static marketing category, however, is in constructing a framework by which to imagine what this new Black expression will look like. Throughout the novel, Beatty plays out various examples of racial thinking, which he links to music, finding each of them problematic. For example, chapter 6 of Part III, titled "The Souls of Black Volk" as a riff on Du Bois and his work's German inspiration, compares competing models of racial thinking during two of DJ Darky's gigs. In the first one, DJ Darky plays a neo-Nazi rally. Engaging with Thorsten, who hired him, DJ Darky expresses confusion over the presence of mixed-race white supremacists. Thorsten replies that he is "not so stupid as to believe in racial purity. . . . It's the hate that's important" (Beatty 2008, 175). Here, Thorsten represents an oddly sympathetic white supremacy, reinforced by his later presence at the performance meant to raise a sonic Berlin Wall. When he argues that "it doesn't matter who does the hating, but who you hate" (Beatty 2008, 175), Thorsten recognizes the instability of the very boundaries that mark out the contours of that hate. Mixing a deeply held essentialism with recognition of the social construction of identity, Thorsten sees race as a social organizing principal, a way of making sense of the society around him, locating himself within it. Recognizing that the narrative the he constructs is both unstable and impermanent, he finds space within his community for Gerhard, the mixed-race Nazi. Building on this insight, Thorsten punctures the very foundations of his ideology, arguing "There are no 'Aryans,' it's a fake race, a marketing tool. It's ethnic branding" (Beatty 2008, 177). Thorsten's words here echo not just DJ Darky, who opens the novel by speculating on replacing race with a system based on SPF sunscreen numbers (a near mirror image of Colson Whitehead's *Apex* meditation on labeling races with band-aid batch numbers), but expands on the insight to recognize race's positioning within a larger capitalist apparatus: "One day there will be no races, no ethnicities, only brands. People will be Nikes or Adidas. Microsoft or Macintosh. Coke or Pepsi" (Beatty 2008, 177).

Hovering over the entire scene is the meaning of "volk." Thorsten distinguishes his hatred between DJ Darky himself and Black people by saying, "I don't have a beef with you, just your people" (Beatty 2008, 177). Referring to Beatty's Du Bois referencing section title, Thorsten recognizes that race is a myth even as he constructs a foundation of social exclusion and violence on it. In "The Conservation of the Races," Du Bois insists on the contributions to world culture that each race is capable of making and will make (Du Bois 1897). As Beatty appears to reference, Du Bois specifically expands this idea in the final section of *The Souls of Black Folk* through the medium of music to argue that "the sorrow songs" are such a contribution. Here, however, Beatty situates Thorsten's recapitulation of the division between the individual and the "volk" within a site of musical performance to position music itself as a pathway out of static ideologies of race.

In a subsequent gig, DJ Darky performs for an ideologically inverted version of the mixed-race neo-Nazi Gerhard: an "annual Afro-German get-together" (Beatty 2008, 177). In contrast to Gerhard's self-hate, and the admittedly false essentialism of the neo-Nazis, Beatty describes the Afro-Germans as the apotheosis of Blackness:

> Du Bois's Talented Tenth come to life. They're almost a Stepford race. Unified as only an invisible people without a proximate community to turn one's back on can be. Human museli, they're multilingual and multikulti, exceedingly well mannered and groomed, and, though most show the telltale sign of biracial-ity—the prominent shiny forehead—on the whole they're a stunningly hand-some and intelligent people. (Beatty 2008, 177–78)

Here, mixed-race identity stands for a larger cosmopolitan turn in world culture, celebrating hybridity and intersection and decrying the rigidity of Nazi race-science. Their handsomeness and intelligence stands as prima facie evidence of their rightfulness for a new postmodern world. The fetishization of buzzwords like multikulti and mixed-race playing out as the character-ization of a new racialization for a new world. DJ Darky describes how his girlfriend Klaudia, who is Afro-German, "dragged me to countless workshops, lectures, and films where I'd watch and listen to a people construct an identity from historical scratch" (Beatty 2008, 178–79). Beatty portrays the liminality of the Afro-Germans as producing a skewed version of their Blackness and Germanness, respectively. Comparing these workshops to porn sets, Darky locates the commonality between them in their "forced sterility" that distances them from the messy reality. Lest the reader think that DJ Darky's own music, liberated from such gigs, offers a musical form that transcends the commodi-fication of Blackness, Beatty closes this part of the book with a performance at "the Free University" where Darky plays an inspired set for an audience of one, the janitor. Beatty mocks the artist's desire for cult stardom through a transcendent concert that rebuts the cultural meaning and power that Darky seeks through his quest to find the Schwa. Whereas, in the first two scenes, DJ Darky positions himself as an enlightened observer able to understand the underlying structures he encounters, this final concert definitively encompasses the protagonist within Beatty's satire. His own pretensions about his music's value confront a world indifferent to his innovations.

In these settings, DJ Darky sees others, and then himself, seeking a pathway towards meaning, and through that meaning towards liberation. Within the novel, such a pathway is guided by the music of Charles Stone, the Schwa. Ultimately, the music that the novel champions is at once racial and non-racial, culminating in the novel's climactic staging of DJ Darky performing with the Schwa to construct a new Berlin Wall of sound. In this scene, Beatty begins the process of constructing "the new Black American narrative" that Johnson urges. Specifically, Beatty imagines this narrative as ambiguous, temporary, and still related to race, but in such a way as to slip the bonds of the narrative of struggle. Through performance, DJ Darky transitions from his simplistic insistence that Blackness is passé to a more complex understanding of what that means. As the Schwa begins playing, DJ Darky imagines the end of Blackness: "With the Schwa's band tearing a hole in the space-time-music continuum, I felt like calling the time right then and there. Press the receiver to my ear so I could hear her say, 'At the sound of the tone the American Negro will be passé, and I for one couldn't be happier'" (Beatty 2008, 225). His language here is notable. As Kenneth Warren agreed, during an interview with Henry Louis Gates Jr., his 2011 book *What Was African American Literature?* should have likely been titled *What Was Negro Literature?* because the Jim Crow-responding aesthetic he traces was defined in those now-defunct racial terms (Warren 2011a). Beatty's insistence throughout the novel on using the term Negro links his racialisms with Warren's and suggests that the passé attitude that he notes is not to the racial concept as a whole, but rather to its obsolete versions.

In the context of this performance, the Schwa serves as the "paterfamilias" (Beatty 2008, 227). He does not so much represent a static Blackness within his self-performance as he represents a previous generation linked to DJ Darky's father, which he describes as "fiercely independent, brilliant, and slightly touched, they were the type who'd represent themselves in court—and win. Children of the civil rights movement, they were the first generation of African-Americans with the freedom to fail without having to suffer serious consequences. They're the Negronauts the black race sent off into the unexplored vastness of manumission" (Beatty 2008, 162). Exploring how these men sought out, and were inspired by the Schwa, Darky links them to a vanguard racial politics that points towards the liberation he seeks in his music. Consequently, when the Schwa "[leaps] on the track," he brings the accumulated weight of his knowledge and experience to bear on the process of transcendence (Beatty 2008, 227). In doing so, he creates a counterpoint to Darky's beat, rather than any reader-anticipated harmony or consonance. This counterpoint comes to a head as the Schwa plays the most canonical twentieth century African American melody, James Weldon Johnson's "Lift Every Voice and Sing," also known as the Negro National Anthem.

> He was switching up the tempo. Segueing from a frenzied fortissimo to a languid legato by quoting from "Lift Every Voice and Sing," the Negro national anthem. It's a beautiful yet trepidatious song, and especially so in his hands. Musical mason that he was, the Schwa erected a series of African-American landmarks upon the foundation I had laid down. The contrapuntal effect of our discordant architectural styles meshed together wonderfully. One moment the beat was a towering black obelisk, the next it was an ebony-walled Taj Mahal. The music was so uniquely majestic I felt like stepping outside of the song. A disembodied DJ floating out into the audience, putting a proud arm around his unborn child, and saying, "See that song? Hear that music? Daddy helped build that." (Beatty 2008, 228)

As DJ Darky notes, Johnson's melody serves as a "landmark" of the canonical narrative. The Schwa's intervention marks even a passé Blackness as originating in a past whose monuments still stand. The references throughout this passage to architectural features grants Blackness a material presence rather than just a metaphysical one. As the book makes clear, Johnson's "black American narrative" is not simply a story but is instead a built architecture that provides an edifice, however "trepidatious," for the advancement of African Americans. In elevating such material references, Beatty properly frames the weight of the seemingly trivial argumentation over when and how Blackness has become obsolete or "post." To declare an end to Blackness, however qualified the terms, is to destroy not just the monuments themselves but also the tradition of struggle and triumph that they symbolize. The final line of the quote furthers the stakes. DJ Darky finds himself seduced by the Schwa's use of Johnson's melody and imagines himself as one who extends the old narrative, claiming his own patrimony. Here, Beatty notes how the "black American narrative," however potentially unsuited to the present and future, provides a source of pride, and constructs a tradition in which to invest.

However, just as the music imagines the transition beyond racialization as "the American Negro," they construct a new anthem, and a new architecture, through the old one's deconstruction:

> Forced to relent to my racial and turntable obstinacy, the Schwa deconstructed "Lift Every Voice and Sing" by laying out like a suicidal Acapulco cliff diver who

could give a fuck about timing the tide. He paused, then took a deep breath and cannonballed into his own tune, unleashing a voluminous splashing salvo of triplets that shattered and scattered the song into a wave of quarter, half, whole notes that fluttered to the floor in wet, black, globular droplets. (Beatty 2008, 229)

In this moment, Beatty's use of "Lift Every Voice and Sing" echoes Shana Redmond's argument about anthems generally in African diasporic culture: "the songs carried alternative theorizations and practices of blackness, becoming representations that were sought out, not stumbled upon" (Redmond 2013, 2). Such songs are not static, but are instead both methods and products of political agency, the revision of which enables the construction of new publics and new movements. The conflict and collaboration between the Schwa and DJ Darky is generational and allows for the construction of a new Blackness. As the Schwa inserts "Lift Every Voice and Sing," whose words and melody speak to an imagined Black nation, DJ Darky resists his out-of-body experience to push back against that nationalism. In doing so, he demands that the Schwa transform the melody to fit a world in which "blackness" is "passé." However, the conflict does not simply move the Schwa towards DJ Darky's new architecture. Instead, both are forced to transform their aesthetics in response to each other. DJ Darky begins by further quoting from Black musical traditions, from hip-hop to doo wop, attempting to drag Johnson's canonical melody into a new future. In response, the Schwa's "voluminous splashing salvo of triplets" explodes "Lift Every Voice and Sing"'s melody and rips it to pieces. In this struggle between DJ Darky and the Schwa—present and past generations of Black artists—Beatty illustrates the complexity of what it means to imagine Blackness as no longer relevant. The presence of the masonry of Blackness throughout the song belies the assertion of its transcendence. However, the process by which that Blackness is approached destroys any sense of its sacredness, demanding its simultaneous deconstruction and reconstruction within new terms instantiated through the performance.

By linking racial identity with the Berlin Wall that the music seeks to replace, Beatty accords Black nationalism landmark status while still tearing it down. The scene itself echoes an oft-cited biblical scene in African American music and literature: the Israelites and the Walls of Jericho. In that story, the Israelites, under the command of Joshua, have returned to Canaan after being exiled as slaves. Facing the walls of Jericho, the first city in Canaan they conquer, the Israelites circle the city for several days, ultimately playing trumpets and singing to bring down the walls. Like the broader story of the Israelites, this episode resonates with the experience of racial slavery, promising a process of exodus, or return, and the ultimate restoration of birthright. In Beatty's retelling, Blackness itself becomes the walls, the material edifice that must be brought down to provide restoration. Consequently, the performance models something that DJ Darky notes early in the novel: "playing with the knowledge that the search for identity and a sense of place is both process and result, and the trick is to fool the audience into thinking you know exactly where you're going" (Beatty 2008, 22). By elevating the process of the search for identity, the exodus itself, rather than the end of diaspora in the restored homeland, Beatty emphasizes what Johnson describes as a story that is "at best, a provisional reading of reality" (Johnson 2008, 42). The contrapuntal interplay between the Schwa's deconstruction of "Lift Every Voice and Sing" and DJ Darky's sampling aesthetic enables a "freedom" that the Schwa describes as a state in which "You can do what you want. No demands. No expectations" (Beatty 2008, 230). The removal of expectations and demands liberates African Americans from the script of the "black American narrative." When DJ Darky encounters Tyrus and ironically craves "a gratuitous, multigenerational tale of colored-people woe that would assure the white reader and the aspiring-to-be white reader that everything would be okay despite the preponderance of evidence that nothing is ever okay" he ironically reveals that "Shit is no longer okay, but that's a good thing" (Beatty 2008, 231). Similar to Johnson, Beatty sees the narrative of struggle as an ironic source of comfort, with its simplistic linear teleology of overcoming and progress. As a soporific that masks the ongoing structures of oppression, along various axes including race, such narratives flatter the reader into a complacent fog perpetuated by such cultural touchstones as mainstream contemporary African American literature and the music of Wynton Marsalis.[10]

The work of the DJ constructs what DJ Spooky describes as "the self as 'subject-in-synchronization'" (Miller 2004, 84). If any and everything is "available for the mix" and "you can never play a record the same way for the same crowd," then the DJ stands as a vanguard of the perpetual remixing and reconfiguration of identity (Miller 2004, 64; 114). Much as Charles Johnson speaks of the need for "new vocabularies, new syntaxes" of Black identity, Beatty's DJ Darky operates within a dynamic and fluid milieu in which the cultural material of the past—from fascist and racist iconography to racial nationalism—becomes a storehouse of creativity, allowing him to generate perpetually "new [ways] of pronouncing the ancient syntaxes that we inherit from history and evolution" (Miller 2004, 75). Framed in relation to Blackness, such a sampling aesthetic sees Johnson's canonical "Black American Narrative" as an artistic trap that can become the pandering hustle of a character like Tyrus unless transmuted through continual remixing. As with the similar traps that Colson Whitehead's nomenclature consultant seeks to evade with his provisional selection of "Struggle," the avoidance of stasis requires the kind of push and pull enacted through DJ Darky and the Schwa's final performance, cyclically deconstructing and reconstructing the traditions and narratives underlying racial identity to avoid its ossification in Marsalis-style fetishization of tradition. In her analysis of *Slumberland*, L. H. Stallings reads the text as a repudiation of Beatty's association with post-soul and post-Black aesthetics. She uses the framework of "funk" to argue that the novel interrogates the question of the end of Blackness only to finally return to its reification: "as funk suggests, blackness never really went anywhere" (Stallings 2013, 210). Stallings is certainly correct to note the revived instantiation of Blackness at the novel's end, and thus the failure of its putative ending. What her reading misses, however, is that, like *Apex Hides the Hurt* and Johnson's essay, the end of Beatty's novel points to a new and provisional meaning for Blackness rather than either its ending or its maintenance. As much as Beatty, like Whitehead and others, expresses discomfort with post-soul, post-Black, and other post era labels, it is this revived and ambivalent Blackness that they label rather than any definitive transcendence of the past.

AFRICAN AMERICAN LITERATURE FOR A BARACK OBAMA WORLD

The texts analyzed in this chapter offer tentative answers to the question of what the literary representation of Black identity and the Black experience will look like in the twenty-first century, in "a Barack Obama world" (Johnson 2008). As I said earlier, however, the reference to "Barack Obama" here serves as a proxy for the claim that the twenty-first century has seen sufficient change to require a rearticulation of the meaning of racial identity. With *Apex Hides the Hurt* and *Slumberland*, Whitehead and Beatty militate against the assumption that Blackness encompasses a definable or specific experience in the present. In doing so, they seek a racial topography that can simultaneously attend to the persistent monuments of Black struggle without allowing those same monuments to foreclose the possibility of a more substantive freedom. To do so, they target the commodification of Blackness and its reduction into a marker of style. Much as Obama himself would later be critiqued for indulging a politics of celebrity and capitalizing on his associations with Black cultural figures such as Jay-Z and Beyoncé as a way to perform a certain coolness, Whitehead and Beatty interrogate whether Blackness can cut through the late capitalist institutions into which it has been incorporated (see Walker 2012, xiv-xvi; Kellner 2009). The provisional answers they put forward presage the ambiguity of Obama's candidacy and presidency, in which Obama himself became a blank slate for different constituencies to construct narratives of (inter)nationalism and racial identity. In this sense, the presence of Barack Obama as a cultural figure crystallizes a central strand of post era argumentation that holds that post–civil rights shifts require revising American racialisms to account for the diversity of experiences encompassed by the label "Black."

At the end of his novel *The Sellout* (2015b), Beatty parodies the optimism surrounding the election of a thinly-veiled stand-in for Barack Obama, who he labels "the black dude" (Beatty 2015b, 289), emphasizing his narrator's rejection of either collective burdens or celebrations rooted in race. Interviews following the novel winning the prestigious Man Booker Prize make clear that the brief scene represents Beatty's own reaction to his peers. The presence of such a brief coda underscores the cultural ubiquity of Obama's election as a twenty-first century touchstone for any discussion of Black identity. The subtle, but important, distinction that Beatty maintains between "the black dude" and the unnamed Obama extends *The American Scholar*'s cover reference to "a Barack Obama world" in making it clear that any such touchstone is less about Obama as a person than "Barack Obama" as the locus for diverse narratives read into his person and biography.

As I have mentioned before, the tradition of African American political advocacy has largely oriented around the need for and possibility of forcing America to live up to its stated ideals. Because personhood, rights, and citizen-ship were conceptualized and legally codified specifically exempting Black people as inhuman, a post-racial future requires the removal of the distinc-tion between the position of whites and Blacks within the law. As Karla FC Holloway puts it, "Citizenship is the way in which the law recognizes—or does not recognize persons. And it does so with a peculiarity of language that points to the origins of our considerations that divided humans into different classes by race" (Holloway 2014, 53). It is no accident that, in considering the status of African Americans within the legal structures of the state, the figure of the first Black president symbolizes the possibility of a new conceptualization of citizenship. As Johnson's essay demands, the gap between the kind of progress symbolized by Obama's ascent and the ongoing inequalities it does nothing to address necessitates a new Black American narrative to explain its complex-ity. *Apex Hides the Hurt* and *Slumberland* stand as early literary attempts to interrogate the confluence of narratives that would be put in dialogue during the Obama years, and which are taken up, this time with explicit reference to Obama himself in Alice Randall's *Rebel Yell* and Chimamanda Ngozi Adichie's *Americanah*, the subjects of the next two chapters.

THE AUDACITY OF HOPE JONES

Alice Randall's *Rebel Yell* and the Idealization of Barack Obama

Barack Obama's first campaign for the presidency relied heavily on ideas of transcendence, primarily emphasizing a hope that was positioned as audacious rather than naïve.[1] In political terms, this made sense. Obama was campaigning on a platform of unifying and moving forward from a Bush presidency defined by military quagmires, legal abuses in foreign policy, and, right before the 2008 election, a huge financial crisis, all of which led to plunging approval ratings for the then-president. On the other hand, there was an abstraction to the campaign's optimism reflected less in the actuality of Obama's policies or experience and more in the sense of Obama as an embodiment of change. Obama was clearly conscious of this possibility. While, in the introduction to his policy oriented *The Audacity of Hope* (2006), Obama describes himself as "the prisoner of my own biography," he goes on to suggest the incompleteness of that statement: "but that is not all that I am" (Obama 2006, 14).

This sense of both the moment's and Obama's singular possibility prompted Toni Morrison to issue her first public endorsement of a presidential candidate, an especially notable action given that Obama's primary opponent was the wife of the man that Morrison had famously mustered demographic trends and cultural stereotypes to declare the nation's first Black president over a decade earlier. Morrison's endorsement is notable for its embrace of Obama as embodying a transformative change through which she imagines the full realization of American multiracial democracy. In a letter to the candidate, Morrison refers to 2008 as "one of those singular moments that nations ignore at their peril" and states that she is "convinced" that Obama is the person to "capture" the "opportunity for a national evolution (even revolution)" which "will not come again soon" (McGeveran 2008). Morrison's language mirrors the orientation of the campaign, emphasizing positive transformation while implying the historic nature of the moment. Critically, Morrison explicitly distinguishes the momentous singularity she invokes from the fact of Obama's race, which she claims would not be sufficient by itself for her support (nor would Hillary Clinton's gender, she notes).

Morrison's references to her belief in Obama's ability "to help America realize the virtues it fancies about itself" signals the underlying teleological implications she reads into the then-candidate's importance. Paired with Morrison's claim of Obama's ineffable but clear "authenticity," her statements imagine his election itself as a symbolic event by which America is made definably different (McGeveran 2008). While Morrison's letter to Obama specifically undercuts the assumption that her endorsement is somehow rooted in the mere fact of Obama's Blackness, the "authenticity" that it posits cannot be detached from Obama's racialization. Morrison's phrasing particularly concretizes this definable difference as a convergence point imagined throughout African American political thought between American ideals and American realities in the nation's treatment of its African American citizens. As Michael Dawson has argued, "A central theme within Black political thought has been . . . to insist that the question of *racial* injustice is a central problematic in *American* political thought and practice, not a minor problem that can be dismissed in parentheses or footnotes" (Dawson 2003, 14). Through protest and resistance, African American politics has long highlighted the question of whether there was a substantive reality lying behind nationalist bromides of liberty and equality. While many strains of Black political thought have reflected substantial doubt as to the presence of a progressive telos directed towards making American ideals a reality, Dawson notes that "historically, the majority of black activists have argued that the just demands of African Americans are fully consistent with the broad principles of American democracy" (Dawson 2003, 247). Within this logic, Morrison argues that Obama's election represents a signal moment within both the long tradition of Black political organizing and the realization of mythic American values.

Morrison's argument that Obama's election is broadly symbolic reflects the wider reaction to his candidacy and his election. Various works of American literature have embraced the symbolism of Obama's candidacy to conceptualize the implications of this generational shift. Michael Chabon's *Telegraph Avenue* (2012) contains a scene in which his main characters perform at a fundraiser for John Kerry during the 2004 presidential campaign that features a speech by the then-state senator Obama. The scene speaks to the utopian impulse of Chabon's novel, which imagines a dynamic, if occasionally combative, multiracial democracy. Consequently, Obama's function in the novel is to stand in for the embodiment of that dream, leading Chabon to indulge in a similar idealization of Obama as a national figure as Morrison does, and, as I will argue, Randall does as well (see Chabon 2012, 158–63). Similarly, the plot of postmodern experimental novelist Steve Erickson's *These Dreams of You* (2012) spirals out of its opening depiction of election night 2008. Erickson's main character Zan views Obama's election as miraculous, "the sort of history that puts novelists out of business" (Erickson 2012, 12). Erickson goes further than Chabon to link Obama with Robert F. Kennedy, and the social movements of the 1960s, and the increasingly globalized present invoked through Zan's adopted Ethiopian daughter.[2] In the case of each of these novels, both by white authors, Obama stands as an idealized representation of American democracy itself, with his election implicitly valorizing the broader national history.

However, among the texts that have most directly engaged with Obama as either historical figure or symbol, none has done so as immediately and directly as Alice Randall's novel *Rebel Yell* (2009b). Because of this, an analysis of Randall's novel provides insight into the specific nature of the future that is being imagined through Obama, and its relationship to American history, in general, and the Civil Rights Movement, specifically. The novel was one of the first to fictionalize Obama as a character, situating him specifically within discourses of racial identity to imagine the transcendence of Du Boisian "double consciousness." Randall's representation of Obama expands on Morrison's endorsement letter to allow for a deeper understanding of the twinned meaning of the concepts of "hope" and "change" attached to the Obama campaign. Ultimately, not only is Randall's novel the most sustained representation of Barack Obama in contemporary African American fiction, it also provides the fullest articulation of a post era vision of Blackness as a specific revision of double consciousness and allows for an epochal movement beyond both the Civil Rights Movement and the post–civil rights era. Randall describes Obama as "an unhyphenated man," unburdened by the "two-ness" W. E. B. Du Bois defined as the product of "always looking at one's self through the eyes of others, of measuring one's soul by the tape of a world that looks on in amused contempt and pity" (Du Bois [1903] 1999, 11). In positing Obama as the vanguard of a unified Blackness and Americanness lacking the fragmentation that Du Bois's famous formulation centralizes as the defining gift and curse of the African American population, Randall locates liberation in a post-racialism defined by the removal of the primacy of the white gaze.

With its portrayal of Abel's central role in the War on Terror, some critics have focused on Randall's representation of the changing landscapes of the post-9/11 security state. In her article, "Of Cain and Abel: African American Literature and the Problem of Inheritance After 9/11" (2013), Erica Edwards argues that Randall's novel depicts the diversification of power structures defined by a

newly fragmented double consciousness in African American cultural production. She delineates this double consciousness as being marked on one side
by "allegiance to a post-segregation US state that demands complicity with
racialized state terror," and, on the other side, "by nostalgia for a black cultural
past identified by its very distance from canonical national knowledge and
cultural production" (Edwards 2013, 191). Given her focus on Randall's novel,
Edwards correctly analyzes Abel's characterization in terms of this fragmentation to highlight his complicity in the reconfiguration of racialized state terror.
However, by focusing on Abel, Edwards explicates only one aspect of the novel's
engagement with state power. In contrast to its portrayal of Abel's participation
in the post-9/11 War on Terror, the novel idealizes Barack Obama as a figure
capable of healing these myriad divisions. In this regard, the novel reveals how
what Edwards describes as the "language of fracture" is wedded in the novel to
re-conceptualizations of Blackness that imagine reparation (Edwards 2013, 191).

My argument in this chapter, then, does not dispute Edwards's characterization of post-9/11 African American fiction as much as it argues that her claim
is incomplete without recognizing how the idealization of Barack Obama as a
post-racial figure connects the reimagining of Blackness in the present with the
broader "complicity with racialized state terror" that Edwards describes. While
Obama appears, without speaking, in only two scenes in the novel, Randall
directly associates the characters of her novel with elements of his biography, and
attributes Abel Jones III's acceptance of his death directly to Obama's ascendance
as a politician. By the end of the novel, Obama takes Abel's place as father to his
son and proper inheritor of his civil rights legacy. Ultimately, through watching Obama's 2004 Democratic National Convention speech and later meeting
Obama as a high-ranking member of the Bush administration, Abel comes to
realize that his success in life has been contingent on a fractured self that is the
product of his response to Jim Crow violence. In symbolically vesting Obama
with Abel's mantle, Randall envisions a new way forward for both Black politics
and the Black community through the imagined "unhyphenated" then-Senator.
In its representation of Obama as an exceptional figure within the context of
both the racial restructuring of the post-9/11 era and the history of Black struggle
for equal citizenship, Randall envisions a profoundly optimistic American future,
despite the presence of a main character's suicide at the novel's heart.

ABEL JONES III AND THE BLACK ELITE

In the diverging fortunes of African Americans in the post–civil rights era, with
some individuals entering into the most exclusive corridors of power and many

others relegated to what Michelle Alexander (2010) calls the "New Jim Crow" of mass incarceration and perpetual poverty, the emphasis on disputing the monolithic nature of either the Black experience or Blackness itself accords with the legitimization of political views and allegiances once seen as anathema in the Black community. In many ways, what Edwards calls the "[normalization] of black conservatism" reflects the broader discourse on the implications of the increased access to power by African Americans in the present period (Edwards 2013, 191). Whether framed as evidence of the progress enabled by such movements or as a tokenistic accounting for changing social mores that does not undermine the real structures of white supremacy, the implications of access to elite institutions has become a central element of contemporary African American literature.

Randall's protagonist Abel Jones III's career illustrates the movement from segregated institutions into mainstream corridors of power. Her depiction of the character locates his personal history within a longstanding Black upper class that has developed its own institutions and power structures in response to segregation. Indeed, Randall's novel helps reveal what is unique about the shift in representations of the intersection of race and class in the post era. African American literature has always featured representations of the Black elite and the Black bourgeoisie. Those depictions, however, largely focused on intraracial class divisions and the political question of the relationship between the Black middle and upper class and the Black masses. The shift in the twenty-first century has been to take the demographic changes identified by scholars such as Karyn Lacy in which the black middle and upper classes have increasingly moved away from neighborhoods featuring members of several different classes (Lacy 2007, 22). Having gotten jobs in mainstream institutions, and having sent their kids to predominantly white schools, members of the Black elite during the post era understandably seek to differentiate themselves from cultural stereotypes of poverty and urban crime. The effect, though, is to highlight the problematic construction Emily Lordi (2009) noted in recognizing that the ascendance of a post-Black elite necessitates the marginalization of those she labels as "still-black." In other words, what is unique about the representation of class in post era African American fiction is not necessarily its focus on the black middle and upper class, but rather that the class identity these texts represent suggests a shift in the relationship to power in American racial hierarchies. Randall's novel typifies this broader shift by documenting the transfer of power from an entrenched elite descended from the pre-civil rights era upper class to Barack Obama, who represents a more complete incorporation of Black people into the American state.

In tracing this transformation, Randall frames her novel genealogically. Randall describes Jones's father, Abel Jones Jr., who is a major civil rights activist in Nashville, Tennessee, as part of an historical Black elite, providing Abel Jones III with a background in which he is connected to the pillars of both African American literature and Black politics.

> The day Abel was born, sweet tucked deep in the dark South, Langston Hughes, out west on a speaking tour, typed a little poem in celebration. In Paris, Richard Wright received three different postcards and a letter shouting the good news. . . . Abel was colored-baby royalty. Related by blood or marriage to both W. E. B. DuBois [sic] and Booker T. Washington, he was also reputed to be kin to Charles Drew by marriage. Adam Clayton Powell had been, and Thurgood Marshall was, a close personal friend of the family. (Randall 2009b, 14–15)

This Black elite is the product of segregated institutions and provides specific functions within the Black community itself. At one point, describing a slightly older group of young men who are friends with, and protect, Abel, Randall describes a "mythology of the Talented Tenth" in which the most successful men within the Black community move from elite Black colleges to elite Black medical schools, advancing the community by demonstrating their capabilities (Randall 2009b, 128).[3]

As members of the post–civil rights era version of this talented tenth, Abel's and Hope's education at schools like Harvard, and their subsequent integration into elite institutions within the government create fragmentation on a personal level and complicity with violence on a state level. The post–civil rights era saw the breakdown of many intraracial elite institutions—and the Black political organizing that they enabled. Randall depicts how characters like Abel and Hope represent a generation moving outside of the HBCUs and community power centers like churches and segregated schools and hospitals that provided the foundation for a past elite. Instead, the marginalization of the post–civil rights generation occurs within the context of predominantly white institutions, generating an ambiguous superficial inclusion. When critics and authors decry the lack of proper representation of Black professionals in literature and popular culture, what they frequently mean is the deficiency in representing the experience of this limited post–civil rights mix of integration and marginalization (see, for example, Touré 2009). Novels like Randall's trace this demographic and political shift, highlighting individuals like Abel whose identities fragment in the face of cross-cutting class-based and racialized interests. In this, Randall offers a sharply different portrait of the Black South from the one analyzed in chapter 2, further highlighting how class privilege structures the relationship to post era redefinitions of Black identity.

To imagine the preconditions for his ascent, Randall frames Obama as a figure alienated from the civil rights legacy of Abel Jones III. Because Jones is the child of a major civil rights leader, his fascination with Obama derives at least partially from the fact that, as Hope describes, Obama "didn't see everything in black and white, through the lens of being formerly enslaved" (Randall 2009b, 352). In articulating his afro-pessimist philosophy, Frank Wilderson III argues, "Slavery is the great leveler of the Black subject's positionality" (Wilderson 2003, 24). For Hope to claim that Obama stands outside the history of enslavement while being Black, then, argues for a new form of Black identity capable of moving beyond both the trauma of that history and the fundamental exclusion from the state that it enacted.[4] In other words, Hope's statement here is less about Obama as an individual and more about him representing a new kind of Blackness that is directly tied to, but not defined by, the history of civil rights. For Randall, therefore, Obama represents a transcendent future-oriented Blackness. While the novel is certainly not blind to the structures of white supremacy and racism, both historically and in the present, Randall presents Abel's interpellation of those structures as a burden he cannot escape. In contrast, Obama's memoir speaks of his desire to locate a racial inheritance he can claim and make "workable." Randall's novel suggests that such workability requires repairing the division concretized most famously in Du Boisian double consciousness. To imagine this new Blackness, Randall constructs a fictionalized Obama to serve as the vanguard of a post-post–civil rights generation of African Americans.

Throughout the novel, Randall specifically isolates her representation of Obama from the racial identity encapsulated by Abel's world both structurally and thematically. Obama is never named in the novel. Instead, Randall inserts him in the text principally through references to the 2004 Democratic National Convention speech that catapulted him to national awareness. For example, during a long conversation between Hope and Nicholas, who was both Hope's and Abel's lover during Abel's time as a spy in Manila,[5] Nicholas mentions one of the last times he spoke to Abel prior to his death: "He was strangely worried about some marine named Seamus" (Randall 2009b, 216).[6] Abel's worry over Obama's speech does not simply derive from the fact of Obama mentioning Seamus. Nor does it represent a rethinking of his conservative advocacy for war, or a statement of guilt over his participation in a national tragedy. Instead, Randall associates Obama's invocation of Seamus, and his explicit repudiation of the neo-conservatism that Abel represents, with his distance from the specific history of slavery and the Civil Rights Movement. While, as Erica Edwards points out, the novel attempts to both "render the black conservative as exception, as deviant" and "rationalize him, to claim him as a member of a clan, a wayward son" (Edwards 2013, 200), both these projects pivot directly on the contrast between Abel and the implicitly progressive future embodied by Obama. While Abel's politics are not, and were not, typical of African Americans during the first decade of the twenty-first century,[7] Randall makes it clear that he, and the various family members and friends present in the novel, exist as the legacy of the Civil Rights Movement. As mentioned earlier, Randall establishes this trajectory at Abel's birth, emphasizing his relationship to not only major literary figures such as Langston Hughes and Richard Wright, but also key figures in Black intellectual thought and politics, from W. E. B. Du Bois to Thurgood Marshall. In contrast, Randall's decision to not even name Obama isolates him from the novel's focus on the legacy of the movement. Hope's statement that Obama's own history is removed from the determinative role of slavery (and assumedly by extension Jim Crow) in Black identity suggests that he occupies a unique position as a Black man able to move forward relieved from the specific burdens of the past.

FATHERS, SONS, AND THE BURDEN OF THE CIVIL RIGHTS LEGACY

Randall frames the legacy of the Civil Rights Movement as a specifically masculine inheritance. While she signifies this most directly in the generational legacy of the Abel Jones name, carried on by Ajay (Abel Jones IV), she dramatizes the existential conflicts experienced by Abel as a direct consequence of who his father is. Much as Obama constructs *Dreams from My Father* around the twinned ideas of race and inheritance deriving specifically from his absent Kenyan father, the lineage of Abel Joneses constructs an inheritance of wealth, status, and privilege related to a specific ideology of racial uplift and responsibility. In both cases, the gifting of the name signals the burden of the father on the son. While, in Obama's case, it is precisely his father's absence that necessitates the search for the symbolic inheritance that his father has gifted to him, in Abel's case, his name, and the inheritance it marks, overdetermines people's perceptions of him, obscuring any possibility for individual subjectivity. Randall's patriarchal vision of race and inheritance reinforces the "talented tenth" logic of the Black community she constructs in the novel. Randall's vision of Black history is one of a sequence of great men and great leaders, who, though often connected to specific female activists, are always in the foreground.

In recounting the traumatic scene of his thirteenth birthday party, which the novel positions as the decisive moment in Abel's turn away from the legacy of his father, Randall portrays Abel as ashamed of the Civil Rights Movement of which his father is such a big part. "His big friends had not protected him. Abel hated them for that. He hated the Fantastic Four for not having protected him from his daddy. And he hated his daddy. He hated the people he trusted so much that he had no hate left over to hate the Klan" (Randall 2009b, 304–5). In the wake of a horrendous attack on his house during his birthday party, where a cross is burned on his front lawn, Randall makes clear that Abel's animosity is directed only at his own Blackness, the recognition of which "he didn't want to remember" (Randall 2009b, 302). The mechanisms of shame in this moment construct a post–civil rights era marked by a simultaneous desire to move beyond the struggles of the past and return to its sense of community. In this case, Abel's path towards conservatism is framed as that of a wayward black sheep distancing himself from both his literal father and the figurative paternity of the Civil Rights Movement itself.

When Edwards argues that the novel attempts to rationalize an increasingly vocal (though still statistically marginal) Black conservatism, she is right to point out how Randall renders ideological disagreement as a family melodrama, with Abel ultimately seeming less invested in the conservatism that enables American torture, extraordinary rendition, and indefinite detention than that he is subverting the legacy of his father.[8] However, by conflating family drama and political ideology, Randall suggests a dilemma faced by the post–civil rights generation between individual access to economically and politically powerful positions for a long-suffering elite and the idea of large-scale structural change in American society. In the novel, Abel's conservatism is only the most extreme example of the Black elite seizing positions of power as the rightful outcome of civil rights era organizing, in contrast to ongoing struggles by more radical activists for revolutionary change.

As the novel makes clear, the existential desire that Abel typifies, which is shared by many of the other African American characters in the novel, is to overcome the limitations structured around race in American society. As Hope puts it at one point, in vocalizing this desire, what Abel wanted was to become "an unhyphenated man" (Randall 2009b, 177). Randall's phrase speaks directly to Du Bois's formulation of double consciousness, with its statement of a split between racial identity and American citizenship. Furthermore, Randall's use of the term specifically comes in the context of Abel's (and Hope's) recruitment into the CIA, presaging Abel's further career in government and his rise to power. The association with the CIA clouds the wholeness evoked by the lack of hyphenation. Implicit in the term's repudiation of Du Boisian double consciousness is the idea that to be unhyphenated would mean to transcend this referenced sense of "twoness." Indeed, by referring to the desire to be "an unhyphenated man" in the context of Abel's CIA recruitment, Randall emphasizes that it is precisely Abel's skill with masking that makes him suitable for the job. When Hope refers to how "an abused black southerner presented all kinds of political possibilities" because "black southerners had a very complex relationship to law," she makes it clear that it is specifically because of Abel's "hyphen" that he is so capable as first a spy and later an administrator over the most egregious war on terror abuses (Randall 2009b, 94).

Late in the novel, Randall refers mysteriously to someone that Abel has met on a plane that he describes as "his first unhyphenated black man" who evidenced "not a single syllable or hint of race-based double consciousness" (Randall 2009b, 320). As representing the "unhyphenated black man" that Abel aspires to be, yet recognizes that he can never become, Obama serves as both a foil for Abel and a surrogate son, despite their being of the same generation. Randall frames Abel's suicide with the significance of a photo of him, Ajay and Obama: "Abel, who had spent time wanting to die and be born again as his own son, had captured the full brightness of this man *of his own generation* who made radically different things of this world's realities. Compared with the senator from Illinois, Abel was just too pale. Someone had taken a picture of the three of them together. Abel looked puffy and old-fashioned" (Randall 2009b, 353, emphasis in original). Randall's reference to Abel's own light skin color makes it clear that the path not taken signified by Obama represents a fuller realization of Abel's racial identity than Abel was capable of attaining. Further, Randall makes it clear that it is Abel alone who is "too pale," in contrast to Ajay, who Randall highlights as indicative of some coming importance: "everyone other than Ajay was less" (Randall 2009b, 352). In the case of the pictures of Ajay with Obama, the fact that someone other than Ajay is discussed, and indeed centralized, associates the two individuals. As opposed to Abel's paleness, Obama stands as a surrogate father to Ajay, one who more directly prefigures Ajay's brightness in the frame. By aligning the figures in this way, Randall constructs an alternate inheritance for Ajay, and a distinct legacy for the Civil Rights Movement.

Throughout the novel, Randall restages the relationship between Abel and Ajay as a toxic extension of Abel's hatred for his father. Consequently, that Obama's presence in the photo illuminates Ajay's brightness reveals that all Abel has been able to pass on to Ajay as an inheritance is his experience of trauma. Specifically, Randall's novel depicts the disruption of Abel's progression into manhood through the repeated ambiguous restaging of his thirteenth birthday party. During the initial narration of the birthday party, the events pivot on Abel's fear of the KKK's actions, culminating in his urinating on himself. Big Abel serves as a clear villain, angry towards his son for his fear more than he is at the KKK for burning the cross. As Big Abel says to Waycross about his son, "A Negro boy afraid of white folks is worse than dead" (Randall 2009b, 299). Retreating to his room, Abel questions the ultimate symbolic father/son relationship:

> It was getting so Abel didn't like church. He didn't like the preacher, didn't like the way they, the family, were all so visible, didn't like taking communion after singing that creepy song, *There is a fountain filled with blood drawn from Emmanuel's veins*, didn't like getting on his knees, didn't know for sure that Jesus was the son of God, wasn't sure there was a God to have a son, didn't want to be someplace where one person, the preacher, was free to stand up and tell what and why and how he was right about everything, while everyone else was free to keep their mouth shut and smile. (Randall 2009b, 300)

Abel's religious ruminations question not just the authority of the church but the charismatic Black male leadership typified by the pastor-fronted Civil Rights Movement of which his father is representative. Recalling "the day he'd been told" he was Black, Abel even questions his racial identity, wishing that he could be white in order to transcend the structures of terror embodied in the events of the day.

The scene culminates in the confrontation between father and son: "Big Abel closed the door. When the sun rose the next morning there were two men living under Abel's roof and they hated each other" (Randall 2009b, 304). Randall's representation of the scene positions this as a moment of trauma for young Abel. In the scene, not only is Abel fully brought into contact with the violence of white supremacy, he is also introduced to the full power of his father. Randall's use of third-person narration, which suggests objectivity, and the ambiguity of the end of the scene, when Abel's bedroom door closes, allows the reader to fill in the gaps of the narrative. Randall emphasizes that Abel welcomes such participatory readings of the scene, saying, "After a time, Abel let their stories [about the party] make him smile" (Randall 2009b, 304). Consequently, while the closing of the door removes the possibility of such knowledge, it allows the reader to follow through on the implications of the scene, inscribing Big Abel's violent abuse of his son and the sexualized dimensions of having Abel strip out of his urine-stained clothing. It is this mythology that Abel willingly perpetuates, and the fact that Hope and Abel ultimately divorce over her unwillingness to allow him to physically discipline young Ajay in the same terms inscribes a nearly clichéd cycle of abuse. Furthermore, this initial narration serves the dual purpose of positioning Abel as the inheritor of Big Abel's masculinity while the ambiguity of the scene signals the queerness associated with Abel's CIA tenure.[9] The party appears to be Abel's version of a bar mitzvah, introducing him to the myriad dangers of the adult world, including his father's own predation. However, the very ease with which a story of racialized trauma becomes indicative of what it means to be a Black man in America underscores the fragmentation resulting from trauma that Du Bois theorized as double consciousness. The novel laments the unique circumstances of Abel's particular transition into manhood, but does not question the necessity of the experience. In this context, even Big Abel's apparent victimization of the younger Abel forms part of an inheritance defined by suffering gifted to Abel on his birthday.

The novel's thematic emphasis on inheritance connects Randall's repetition of Abel's thirteenth birthday scene with the implications Abel's encounter with Obama has for his relationship with his own son, Ajay. Folding together the ideas of Abel's death and rebirth in Ajay, Randall positions Abel's subsequent embrace of his own death as an attempt at a redemption in which his deviation from the legacy of civil rights is reborn in Obama's presidency.[10] When Hope says that "Abel had prepared to act," it functions as the resolution of two interrelated strands of the narrative by positioning his death as a quasi-suicide, and explaining it in terms of his son: "Hope got it: earth without Abel was safer for his kid and her kid and all the kids being called to the big bad war" (Randall 2009b, 353). The idea of Obama as a kind of savior hovers over this entire culminating scene, which Randall makes even more explicit with Hope's preface to her realization, stating that Abel had "perhaps [confused] himself with Hannibal and the senator from Illinois with Jesus" (Randall 2009b, 353). Implicit in Hope's claim that "earth without Abel was safer" for "all the kids" is that his death, in the context of the war on terror, enables a direct substitution of the senator from Illinois for Abel. In this sense, Hope and Randall argue that for Obama to take his proper place at the head of the Black community, and America as a whole, the generation that fought for civil rights, those such as Abel's generation who are too intimately tied to that struggle, must die or otherwise recuse themselves to open space for Obama. Furthermore, by framing the entire novel, and this scene specifically, in terms of the inheritance of sons from their fathers, Randall generates a lineage in which Ajay's brightness indicates continuity through Obama rather than his own father. However, the removal of Abel from this lineage, while partially a corrective for Abel's neo-conservatism, further removes the direct associations that Abel carries to not just his father, but the Black elite who were invoked at Abel's birth at the start of the novel. In place of this historical Black community, Obama offers a possibility of being "unhyphenated" for not just himself but all the Black community.

A STORY OF RACE AND INHERITANCE

Randall constructs the meaning of unhyphenation through the revision of Abel's thirteenth birthday party, which connects the novel's thematic focus on race and inheritance with Barack Obama's depiction of his brief interactions with his father in his own "story of race and inheritance." These scenes, with their suggestion of maturing into manhood, center racial identity as a battleground for personal fulfillment and national belonging. Tracing the connections between them elucidates the fundamental importance of Obama as a character in Randall's novel and explains his presence at the plot's climax. As I detail earlier, a KKK cross burning traumatizes Abel during the party, leading to a bedroom scene with his father highly suggestive of sexual abuse. The final scenes of the book, however, transform the implications of both Abel's thirteenth birthday party, and the issue of what truly constitutes Abel's inheritance. While this is done partially through Hope's realization of the profound love that Abel feels for his son, it is the presence of Barack Obama that reframes the specific family drama as a fundamental transformation of racialization and Black politics.

To understand the implications of Obama's importance to the scene, it is critical to notice that Abel's thirteenth birthday party is a restaging of another traumatic childhood encounter between a father and a son: the single meeting between Barack Obama and his father recounted in *Dreams from My Father*. In this case, the central connection between the two texts comes in the form of a gift: a basketball. When the senior Barack Obama (who, like Abel Jones, gave his son his name in addition to any other inheritance) returned to Hawaii for over a month, his son had recently returned to the islands from Indonesia to attend Punahou School in Honolulu (Obama [1995] 2004, 63–71; see also Remnick 2010, 73–74; Maraniss 2012, 272–76). As in *Rebel Yell*, Obama's description of his paternal encounter outlines the dilemma of "inheritance" that he centralizes in the figure of his father. Describing the short month in only a few pages, Obama tantalizes the reader as he describes the only period of his life during which he meets his father face to face after his infancy. Within a memoir that Obama titles after his father, this scene promises to reveal a critical facet of his unique biography, to which his political speeches have returned again and again to both trace the contours of difference in America and attempt to transcend them. However, as with Randall's novel, the scene that should narratively offer insight instead remains obscure. The expectations of the brief month in 1971 on the part of both the reader and the young boy overwhelm the actuality of his memory. Within the body of the memoir, the description of the month takes up only nine pages, and opens with a line that undermines its implications: "After a week of my father in the flesh, I had decided that I preferred his more distant image, an image I could alter on a whim—or ignore when convenient" (Obama [1995] 2004, 63). By making this statement prior to his father's arrival in the text, Obama forecloses the idea that the coming scenes will offer substantial revelations in either "a boy's search for his father" or his search for "a workable meaning" in his Blackness. Instead, the quote substitutes the importance of the myth of his father over the actual man, suggesting that these sorts of moments will never offer explanations for either the writer or the reader. Just as Randall's description of Abel's birthday offers a tantalizing glimpse into the childhood of the inscrutable Abel before the novel later exposes the lies at the heart of the memories and narratives of the scene, Obama's statement prefaces the importance of the scene while asserting its limitations.

As scenes defined by the twin concerns of race and inheritance, these moments map the changing structures of racial identity as the two boys move into adulthood. However, while Abel's birthday party underscores the trauma that leads him to be ashamed of his Blackness, Randall's subtle invocation of Obama's autobiography in the scene suggests that Obama's unmooring from the specific legacy of his father opens the space for his "unhyphenation" and the movement away from the inheritance of the Civil Rights Movement. In each case, the ambiguity created by the specter of the absent father troubles the idea of inheritance. As Abel describes, he is usually anxious about his birthday precisely because his father is so absent from his life. Referring to his birthday parties specifically, he states, "his father had never come" (Randall 2009b, 301). Furthermore, Abel notes that this absence signals a behavioral pattern: his father's work as a lawyer and activist has always taken precedence over his family. While Abel's father is not several thousand miles away for most of his life, as Barack Obama's was, he is in many ways just as absent for Abel. Describing his father's visit, Obama states, "He remains opaque to me, a present mass; when I mimic his gestures or turns of phrase, I know neither their origins nor their consequences, can't see how they play out over time" (Obama 1995[2004], 70). Both scenes emphasize the ambivalence of simultaneous presence and distance. While Abel's father is often physically present, he remains a mysterious figure to his son precisely because his literal presence seems to offer the same opaqueness Obama describes with regard to his own father. The simultaneous absence and presence of Abel's father denies Abel either the clear inheritance of his father's civil rights legacy or a clean break from his shadow. Consequently, while Obama's meeting with his father resolves itself in the narrative mythmaking of the son even before his father leaves, Abel's transition into adulthood represents a trauma that he is never able to move beyond, asserting the broader presence of the civil rights era into the contemporary period.

In each scene, the physical sign of the basketball marks both normalcy and an accepted performance of Black masculinity. When Obama remarks on the legacy of his father's visit, he focuses on a series of pictures, "the only ones I have of us together, me holding an orange basketball, his gift to me." (Obama [1995] 2004, 70). In Obama's memoir, basketball functions as a marker of his Blackness, both as a means by which he demonstrates and performs his racial identity and the medium through which he attempts to assimilate into a larger Black culture.[11] Referring to his individual "costume" as his "armor against uncertainty," Obama states that "at least on the basketball court I could find a community of sorts, with an inner life all its own. It was there that I would make my closest white friends, on turf where my blackness couldn't be a disadvantage" (Obama [1995] 2004, 79–80). Obama's description here modifies his characterization of himself as performing "a caricature of black male adolescence" (Obama [1995] 2004, 79), which allows Obama to gain entrance within the multiracial social landscape of Hawai'i. The fact that it is his Kenyan father who gifts him the basketball highlights how Obama's search for a coherent racial identity is a direct substitution for the specific inheritance of his father. In place of that father, the basketball delineates the space wherein an interracial community can be imagined, one where his Blackness serves as a form of social capital.

In Randall's novel, the gift of the basketball represents a suburban middle-class identity that the KKK intrudes on; an intrusion that Abel blames on his father. As his slightly older Black male friends collect the basketball to give it to Abel, the act of terror occurs, with its violation marked by Opelika dropping the basketball and Abel watching it "bounce and roll into the gutter" (Randall 2009b, 296). Within the plot, this traumatic moment helps to explain Abel's fetishization of whiteness, which culminates in both his second marriage to a Southern white beauty queen and turn towards evangelical neo-conservatism. As in Obama's narrative, the basketball signifies a normalized Blackness, albeit one marked, as Obama suggests, by elements of caricature. When Abel insists that all that he wants is the "safe space" that he imagines whiteness provides (Randall 2009b, 305), that safety is specifically juxtaposed against the activism of his father, which has led to both Abel's feelings of abandonment and the sense of trauma that he blames on his father rather than on the white supremacists.

In Randall's novel, Abel's birthday party signifies the moment of fragmentation in which Abel is alienated from both his Blackness and his Americanness. Characterizing Abel in this way, Randall suggests a broader generational foreclosure of the necessary construction of new black identities in the wake of the civil rights struggle. Abel's trauma denies him access to any affirmative understanding of his Blackness, leaving him only to exploit his fragmentation through his work with the CIA and during the War on Terror. In contrast, Randall integrates Obama within the narrative in specific opposition to this fragmentation. At the end of the novel, Abel's recollection of the true events of his birthday intertwine with the staging of his death and the narration of Obama's birth. Through this imbricated narrative, Abel bequeaths his inheritance of the civil rights legacy to Obama as a means of constructing a new Blackness labeled as unhyphenation.

The revision of the birthday scene at the end of the novel specifically overturns the implications of paternal victimization, as Abel's narration informs the reader that his father, far from inscribing his own power as a figure to fear over and above the KKK, offered Abel a comfort and embrace that was, if anything, more traumatizing. As Abel is put into an ambulance for transportation to the hospital, the "redneck" EMTs slow down because they want to see Abel "get tortured a little" (Randall 2009b, 354; 360). Oddly, this racism reassures Abel; in fact, he imagines himself enrobed and protected by the whiteness he has adopted through his politics: "*White men are safer in enclosed spaces. Dark men are safer out in the open. I am a white man. I will be safe*" (Randall 2009b, 355, italics in the original). Abel's thoughts in the ambulance transform the actions of the EMTs from expressions of the same white supremacy that drove the KKK to burn a cross on his lawn on his thirteenth birthday to empty gestures of a dying regime. Abel willingly relinquishes himself to their ministrations, actively finding comfort in their predictability. Thus, when the ambulance driver slows down slightly to test the limits of Abel's suffering and ability to survive before reaching the hospital, Abel accepts the possibility of his death. The narrator explains: "Abel kept his face blank. Abel could use ten minutes. 'Good enough for a white prince, good enough for me,' mumbled Abel. Assassination was a king's death" (Randall 2009b, 358). In this moment, Abel aligns himself fully with the racial hierarchies represented by the EMTs. In doing so, he distinguishes his life from that of both his father and the movement he represents in the novel. Abel locates his heroism in the embrace of his abjection at the hands of the EMTs. The fact that Randall highlights Abel's anticipation of the EMTs' racism conjoins his willingness to die with his relinquishment of his fantasy of whiteness.

The final line's reference to assassination emphasizes the heroism of Martin Luther King Jr. as the charismatic figurehead of the Civil Rights Movement, and serves to fully cleave the possible inheritance suggested in an earlier flashback during which Abel meets King. During that flashback, a young Abel finds himself in awe of King as someone to whom his father shows deference. The eight-year-old Abel parrots back lines from King's "Letter from a Birmingham Jail" as a kind of performance, culminating in the repetition of Mother Pollard's famous statement that "my feets is weary but my soul is at rest!" (Randall 2009b, 118). In the context of this early flashback, the moment connects to the broader idea of patriarchal inheritance. Here, after all, is a figure to whom even Big Abel shows respect, a prospect that is somewhat frightening to Little Abel. King's presence in the fictional world of the novel also validates the assertions of Big Abel's prominence in the movement, positioning Little Abel as the direct repository of this legacy. When King hands Abel a candy bar, ostensibly to reward him for what he has learned about the Movement, it seems almost a passing of the torch because of the reader's knowledge that within a year King will be dead.

In this context, the final paragraphs of the scene highlight both Abel's youth, but also his somewhat casual disregard for the meaning of King's gesture. Turning back to speak to Abel, King says, "You don't know what that means now, but one day you will. And I predict when that day comes it will be as true for you as it was for that lady. If it's not, don't you eat my candy bar" (Randall 2009b, 118). Referring to Pollard's words when asked about her participation in the Montgomery Bus Boycott, King vests Abel with a significant burden. Predicting the continuation of the struggle for which he is soon to give his life, King's candy bar functions as a symbol of the burden he is placing on Abel, rather than a treat. While it is clear Abel will not hold onto the unopened candy bar, King's words suggest that the act of ingestion is a commitment to whatever form the future struggle takes. In that light, the fact that Abel cavalierly "gobbles" the candy bar down "quick" reflects his lack of awareness of the implications of King's words (Randall 2009b, 118). Consequently, the call back to King in Abel's rumination on his death at the end of the book has a double signification. On the one hand, it implies that Abel now does understand the words that he spoke as an eight-year-old, suggesting that his soul, on some level, is at rest. On the other hand, his statement that "assassination was a king's death" in contrast to his alignment of himself with the "white prince" demonstrates that it is precisely the relinquishing of King's burden, and his association with it, that provides that sense of peace.

The fact that the novel takes this moment to return to Abel's bedroom during his thirteenth birthday party, and then to Barack Obama, connects this racial reconfiguration with both generational change in the Black community and the seemingly generative implications of the election of the first Black president. It is only at this point in the narrative that Abel admits he fabricated the narrative of his father's abuse. In place of that abuse, his final memory of the scene depicts Big Abel as a strong and reassuring father who contrasts the callous and indifferent figure of earlier iterations. Paradoxically, in this context Little Abel, rather than his father, becomes the vessel of shame. When Abel's father tries to reassure him that he has "seen men in the war wet themselves," his "tenderness is a heavy weight" on Abel (Randall 2009b, 360). But Abel is not merely ashamed of his own fear in the face of KKK-inspired terror. Instead, this re-narration makes it clear that Abel's shame stems from his perceptions of both his Blackness and his connection to the Civil Rights Movement of which his father is a part. During the earlier description of the birthday party, Abel longs to forget his recognition of his own Blackness, saying, "Everyone in North Nashville except Abel knew that Abel was black. He remembered the day he'd been told. It had been in this very room, in his bedroom. He didn't want to remember" (Randall 2009b, 302). Abel's childhood recollections connect innocence with a sense of racelessness. In doing so, his desire to be "unhyphenated" takes on new meaning. Like Du Bois, Abel imagines that there is a moment of rupture during which the young Black child becomes aware of both their Blackness and what that Blackness means.[12] Here, Abel is sitting in his room, anticipating his father's discipline, longing for the racelessness and innocence he associates with whiteness. The end of the narrative makes his racial alignment even more explicit: Abel absents himself from his father's legacy through his suicide and concomitantly restores the integrity of that civil rights era inheritance through the honest retelling of the scene in his bedroom.

It is only during this late scene in the novel that Abel finally accepts his complicity in the broader structures of racial terrorism, thus linking himself to the same white supremacy with which his father was at war. Ultimately, Big Abel is fundamentally incapable of protecting and reassuring Little Abel, precisely because of his vulnerability as an African American: "It is not strange and dramatic occurrences that shatter; it is a shivering hug that can not [sic] matter enough" (Randall 2009b, 262). By substituting the lie of abuse for the fact of reassurance, Abel imagines himself as "[translating] an utter and tender, complete and mutual defeat into the oldest and most powerful male story you know—domination and transference . . . [elevating] you believe, father and son" (Randall 2009b, 362–63). Abel thinks that he transforms the story of him and his father into a version of the relationship between Christ and God, with Abel cast as the Christ-figure, both the victim and repository of his father's power. However, the self-awareness that he exhibits at the end of the story demonstrates the fallacy of his own agency over this past. Instead of translating the story into a useable history that he can ultimately pass on to his own son, Abel's shame renders him incapable of engaging with that same son, in whom he sees himself: "Later you fear your own son and the fun-house mirrors his eyes have become" (Randall 2009b, 362). Consequently, Randall ultimately positions Abel's suicide as a final act of love, a gesture of tenderness in the midst of failure. In place of Abel's shame over his Blackness and the self-fracturing experience of double consciousness, he leaves his son in the hands of the "unhyphenated man," Barack Obama.[13]

As Abel reflects on the end of his own Civil War at the same moment his ambulance symbolically approaches the site of the final shots of the actual Civil War, the last scene moves from the narration of Abel's death to a fictionalization of Barack Obama's birth. Randall contrasts Obama's birth with Abel's failures, characterizing Obama as both an alternate version of Abel himself, and representative of Abel's generation. Furthermore, the conflation of Abel's death with Obama's birth symbolically associates Obama with the inauguration of a new generation able to move beyond the burden of the post–civil rights era. The page-long scene is framed as a fairy tale, emphasizing the magic of Obama's birth and exoticizing both the Hawai'ian locale of the birth and his mixed-race background: "Once upon a time, with nobody watching, in the early days of August 1961, a skinny brown baby, six pounds and a few ounces, was born, unwitnessed, born with black eyes in the maternity hospital founded by Queen Kapi'olani, a woman who would birth no children from her own body, a granddaughter of Kaumuali'i, the last king of Kaua'i" (Randall 2009b, 363). Randall uses this passage to construct an alternative mystical legacy to the struggles of the Civil Rights Movement occurring in the South at the same historical moment. By exoticizing Obama, Randall locates him within both the legacy of racialized colonialism that eventually led to Hawai'ian statehood and the indigeneity represented by the native Hawai'ian rulers she mentions.[14] While this dual positioning would seem to promote identity fragmentation, Randall isolates Hawai'i from the dominant strains of the civil rights era to imagine Obama as free of the white gaze that produces a specifically Black double consciousness. In Du Bois's discussion of the concept, he locates fragmentation as the product of an interpellated "second-sight" that incorporates the external gaze into the self, thus denying the individual the capability of seeing themselves outside of the gaze of others (Du Bois [1903] 1999, 10). By establishing the space of Obama's birth as existing outside of this gaze, he is able to elude the fragmentation that defines Abel within the novel. Instead of "witnessing" representing the commemoration of some historically significant moment, Randall argues for the liberation of the unwatched: "*Unwitnessed is free-ey*" (Randall 2009b, 363, italics in original).

In the end, Randall's book argues that the power of Obama's rhetoric and person is sufficient to exemplify an updated version of an American exceptionalism that allows for the transcendence of race:

The earth does not require our wretchedness. Abel got the news via television. He watched the man the Hawaiian baby had grown to become give a speech in Boston. Heard him talk about the marine Seamus. Near to where pilgrims once sought to build a city on a hill, a new Jerusalem, Abel caught a glimpse of a new happily ever after. *My feets is weary but my soul's at rest.* (Randall 2009b, 363, emphasis in the original).

Randall's description of Obama's birth culminates in the intersection between Obama's life story and the fictional Abel's. In this moment, Obama stands as the extension of an idealized American tradition in which the dreams of the earliest pilgrims once again become possible. The quote's invocations of Frantz Fanon and John Winthrop offers a reparation for a history defined by the struggle against slavery, colonialism, and racism. The inversion of Fanon's *The Wretched of the Earth* (1963) repudiates his insistence that "decolonization is always a violent event" to vest, through Obama, the fullness of national citizenship (Fanon 1963, 35).[15] The fact that Randall mentions a "new happily ever after," which she imputes to Abel's perceptions of Obama, embodies the position he holds in the novel. By keeping his presence shadowy, never mentioning his name, Randall turns Obama into a broader signifier of a new Black politics and a new racial order.

As Adolph Reed points out, diverse movements and writers have appropriated Du Bois's concept of double consciousness for a range of political and cultural programs (Reed 1997, 92). By placing Abel at the CIA, Randall centralizes Abel's fractured self as the basis of both his professional and personal identity. She locates this fragmentation as the product of trauma that forces Abel to internalize and resent an imagined white gaze that prevents him, even at the height of his success, from viewing himself as anything other than a victim. Randall indulges in what Reed calls a "presentism" in which a transhistorical double consciousness is claimed as "an existential condition generic among Afro-Americans" (Reed 1997, 11; 124).[16] In doing so, Abel's fragmentation signals a broader dilemma of the post–civil rights era in which the genuine economic progress of a small (if growing) segment of the Black community is put in conflict with the continued structures of white supremacy. In this sense, Randall invokes Du Bois as a master trope connecting Abel's individual dilemma to African American literary history and a presumed universal racial psychology. It is precisely this presumption of the universality (or near universality) of fragmentation that generates Obama's exceptionalism in the novel.

Furthermore, there is a substantial literature on "unhyphenation" in theorizing immigrant assimilation in the United States. In imagining the resolution of the African American's double consciousness, Du Bois asks whether the

"Negro soul" is "bleached . . . in a flood of white Americanism" or whether it would require that one "Africanize America" (Du Bois [1903] 1999, 11). Similarly, discussions of assimilation debate the implications of the loss of a hyphenated American identity. In other words, by claiming that Obama is "unhyphenated," Randall imputes a broader Americanness of which Obama is now an unqualified part. However, the question remains, does she imagine this American identity as deracialized? As Tanya Golash-Boza explains, "The unhyphenated American label is reserved for white Americans" generally (Golash-Boza 2006, 27), suggesting that assimilation requires a process of losing one's distinct ethnicity. Toni Morrison makes a related version of this argument in her book *Playing in the Dark* (1992) saying, "American means white, and Africanist people struggle to make the term applicable to themselves with ethnicity and hyphen after hyphen after hyphen" (Morrison 1992, 47). As Morrison explains, hyphenation perpetuates the association between whiteness and Americanness, suggesting that what is necessary is the creation of an American identity that acknowledges the history of race but that would allow a full claiming of the label "American" by people of African descent. Morrison furthers this idea to argue that "W. E. B. Dubois's [sic] observation about double consciousness is a strategy, not a prophecy or a cure," and that it is possible to imagine beyond such fragmentation (Morrison 1997, 12). In this case, the contrast that Randall draws between Obama and Abel, whose desire to escape his racialization mirrors Du Bois's vision of a Blackness "[bleached] . . . in a flood of white Americanism," distinguishes the loss of double consciousness from a mere assimilation into whiteness (Du Bois [1903] 1999, 11). Instead, Randall imagines unhyphenation as representing a lack of opposition between Blackness and Americanness, such that a Blackness no longer defined solely by a narrative of struggle can be liberated to take new forms. In this sense, Randall's description of Obama's unhyphenated Blackness echoes Touré's claim that Obama's is a post-Black presidency, "the president whom America, in its multiracial glory, had created" (Touré 2011, 176).

Consequently, in the context of both Du Boisian double consciousness and the broader literature on assimilation, Randall's concept of "unhyphenation" directly ties to the issue of full American citizenship.[17] As mentioned, Randall links double consciousness to the history of racial slavery. The reference denotes the origins of a systemic exclusion from American citizenship experienced by African Americans that continues through Jim Crow and into the present, echoing Du Bois's lament that "the freedman has not yet found in freedom his promised land" (Du Bois [1903] 1999, 12). Furthermore, Abel's status as the inheritor of his father's civil rights legacy and his position within the Black elite constructs a continuous history of Black struggle for full citizenship.

Consequently, Randall's reasoning about Obama's lack of hyphenation suggests that he represents an alternative teleology that can enable transformative change absent the continuing burden of a double consciousness born of racialized trauma.

TO INHABIT, AT ONCE, MULTIPLENESS: OBAMA, HOPE JONES, AND THE TRANSCENDENCE OF RACE

In contrast to how Randall distances Obama from Abel to allow him to ultimately supplant him, she draws explicit connections between Obama and Hope to define his lack of hyphenation with her desire to "inhabit, at once, multipleness" (Randall 2009b, 196). Indeed, it is Hope who most directly parallels the uniqueness of Barack Obama's life experiences. Hope, like Obama, is raised by a single white parent. While, in Hope's case, that parent is a father rather than a single mother, it generates a similar sense of lacking some authentic Blackness, leading Hope to describe herself as being raised "whitish" (Randall 2009b, 252). As with Obama, Hope strives to conceal her "whitish" childhood, seeking to perform an authentic Black identity. While the novel emphasizes Abel's trauma and its connection to a specifically African American double consciousness, Hope is presented as a differently fragmented individual, seeking some ability to live within the complexities of her identity. In relation to her attempt to live "multipleness," Randall aligns her specifically with canonical post-colonial writers, rather than the Blackness of Abel: "She read Aime Cesaire and Frantz Fanon and thought about her own history in a whole and new way" (Randall 2009b, 196–97). In this passage, Randall depicts Hope as occupying a more broadly cosmopolitan Blackness than Abel, who is continually associated with the Jim Crow south and its racial caste system.

Randall connects Hope most explicitly with Obama through her name. Randall's choice to name the character Hope aligns her with both Obama's biography and the specific racial significance the word carries in the Obama campaign because of its derivation from the Reverend Jeremiah Wright. Hope (often paired with change) served as the central rallying cry of Obama's 2008 campaign, which Shepard Fairey immortalized in his iconic Obama poster. While "hope" is a generic abstraction common to political campaigns, Obama seized on the term even before officially announcing his candidacy by titling both his 2004 Democratic National Convention speech and his 2006 policy book with a phrase he borrowed from one of Wright's sermons, "The Audacity of Hope." Wright used the phrase in a sermon testifying to the ubiquity of suffering in the world, in the face of which it is audacious to remain faithful and maintain hope. Wright's sermon aligns his faith with an explicit politics typical of his roots in Black Liberation Theology. Obama, in contrast, expands the scope of Wright's usage to refer to "the best of the American spirit" that "joined us [the nation] as one people" (Obama 2006, 356).

Describing the work of writing the 2004 convention speech, Obama states, "It was that pervasive spirit of hope that tied my own family's story to the larger American story, and my own story to those of the voters I sought to represent" (Obama 2006, 356–57). In Obama's definition, "hope" serves as the foundation for unity and transcendence. Furthermore, Obama imagines hope as tying together his background with the larger fabric of America, providing the "workable" identity that he has sought in both his ancestry and race. When Abel Jones III would have watched the 2004 convention speech that led inexorably to his death, he would have heard Obama end his remarks with a stirring call for a unified future enabled by "hope":

> In the end, that's what this election is about. Do we participate in a politics of cynicism, or do we participate in a politics of hope? . . . I'm not talking about blind optimism here, the almost willful ignorance that thinks unemployment will go away if we just don't think about it, or health care crisis will solve itself if we just ignore it. That's not what I'm talking. I'm talking about something more substantial. It's the hope of slaves sitting around a fire singing freedom songs; the hope of immigrants setting out for distant shores; the hope of a young naval lieutenant bravely patrolling the Mekong Delta; the hope of a millworker's son who dares to defy the odds; the hope of a skinny kid with a funny name who believes that America has a place for him, too. Hope in the face of difficulty, hope in the face of uncertainty, the audacity of hope: In the end, that is God's greatest gift to us, the bedrock of this nation, a belief in things not seen, a belief that there are better days ahead. (Obama 2004)

These words, to which Randall refers in her novel through both Hope's name and Abel's obsession with this speech, map the contours of the utopianism Obama symbolizes in the novel. Arguing for the continuing need for struggle, Obama reimagines "hope" as a kind of stubborn persistence. Even in this early national oratory, Obama evidences how, despite the fact that his "inspiring message of hope and promise is balanced by a tragic sense of America's racial history," it is ultimately "too often diminished by his commitment to American exceptionalism" (Winters 2016, 27). In opposition to Abel's fragmentation in the face of trauma, Obama's words voice both an individual and national unity. In choosing Hope as the name for Abel's wife, the character who seeks out the meaning of his death, Randall embraces the version of hope that Obama describes and, in turn, memorializes Abel for recognizing his inability to do so.

However, while Randall's use of hope directly associates Obama with the character, the phrase's connection to Wright further highlights Obama's ambiguous position to the narrative of racialized struggle embodied by Abel. As mentioned previously, Obama's explanation for his use of Wright's phrase displaces it from a racialized narrative to generate a nationalist universalism. In addition, Obama's efforts to distance himself from Wright during the campaign parallel Randall's representation of him as a figure outside the traditional mainstream of Black politics. In the context of the campaign, videos of Wright disrupted the deliberate attempt to avoid focusing on racial issues. [18] As Remnick's biography makes clear, Obama attempted a strict balancing act during the campaign, not running wholly from his race, but reluctant to engage it directly. Such a balancing act reinforces Randall's embrace of Obama's repurposing of Wright's phrase. Randall, building on Obama, reorients an idea of hope rooted in the African American freedom struggle to transcend the terms of that struggle, and, in doing so, to imagine a new future for both African Americans and the nation overall. Distancing Obama, and Hope, from the history of the Civil Rights Movement constructs an alternative identity formation in which Blackness is not indexed solely to trauma. By aligning Hope with Obama in this way, Randall recontextualizes Hope's search for meaning in her ex-husband's death from being about the personal to that of a quest to understand the broader meaning of race in the twenty-first century. Through Hope and Obama, then, Randall characterizes this desire for meaning as a racial utopianism in which Hope seeks a way to imagine her stated "multipleness."

In connecting Obama with Hope and the transcendence of race, Randall picks up on something that is present throughout Obama's own writings on his identity. While he consistently reproduces the classic "tragic mulatto" genre question of "where did I belong?" (Obama [1995] 2004, 115), Obama's construction of belonging is, like his idea of community, the instantiation of a dynamic fluidity. He returns to the civil rights era as a useable past that he can pick and choose from to motivate his act of racial self-creation. The "hope" that was so important to his campaign, and that is mirrored in Randall's character naming and serves as a utopian ideal at the heart of her novel, is underscored by the necessity of approaching this past only as a starting point. For Abel, his Blackness is a straitjacket, confining his possibilities and his sense of self, no matter how successful he might be or how much of an opportunity he has for self-creation.

In contrast, Obama views race in terms closer to the privileging of individual agency analyzed in relation to "post-Blackness" in chapter 1. Instead of Abel's conception of his ancestry as a burden, an inheritance that paralyzes,

Obama's decision to consciously take on that inheritance becomes liberating: "My identity might begin with the fact of my race, but it didn't, couldn't end there. At least that's what I would choose to believe" (Obama [1995] 2004, 111). The very fact that Obama feels as if he can choose the nature and meaning of his identity illustrates the key distinction between Abel and Obama. Obama sees himself as able to build on the foundation of his Blackness through his own agency. While he spends much of his autobiography performing, reading, and learning Blackness (a process that his biographers emphasize as a key part of his actual life not just a theme in his autobiographical self-presentation), it is in the interest of enabling and expressing an individual identity that reconciles his "uniqueness" with a broader Blackness he views as somehow authentic.

THE LIMITATIONS OF RANDALL'S VISION OF RACIAL TRANSCENDENCE

Published soon after the inauguration of the nation's first Black president, Alice Randall's *Rebel Yell* encapsulates the sense of epochal change found in the idea that the nation has entered "the Age of Obama." In arguing for the appropriateness of this designation, Harry Elam asks, "What does the current moment and its reformed politics of race, in which we have elected a black United States president, tell us about the evolving meanings of blackness and who controls those meanings?" (Elam 2014, 257–58.) Randall's novel embraces the optimism voiced throughout the 2008 Obama campaign to highlight a core utopianism at the heart of such a question. Furthermore, with her characterization of Abel, Randall also, as Erica Edwards argues, represents the significant transformations of racial meaning in the post-9/11 world. Indeed, by inserting Obama himself as a character alongside thin fictionalizations of historical figures such as Condoleezza Rice and Colin Powell, Randall signals her novel's conscious attempt to answer Elam's question with regard to the rearticulations of race in a certain historical moment. To do so, Randall centralizes the trope of double consciousness by clearly distinguishing between the significance of Abel's struggle with his sense of self and Obama's status as "an unhyphenated man." In the novel, Randall represents Obama as an almost sui generis figure. While the parade of details in the narrative that I have mentioned indicate Randall's familiarity with Obama's biography, and his own writings in *Dreams from My Father* and *The Audacity of Hope*, the novel does not consider or address the significant struggles, particularly with regard to racial identity, that Obama went through during his life. Instead, Obama serves as both a repudiation of Abel and a figure that can and will supplant him. As the penultimate paragraph in the novel culminates with the recollection of the lines Martin Luther King

Jr. quoted from Mother Pollard and that Abel recites back to King in an early scene, Randall aligns Obama with King, positioning him as the true carrier of King's burden instead of Abel. Just as Abel's rest is enabled by his acceptance of his complicity with torture, the restatement of these words at the end of the novel becomes possible only because of the presence of Obama. Accordingly, Randall aligns the legacy of the Civil Rights Movement with the concept of becoming unhyphenated.

The idea of being unhyphenated makes clear the dimensions of Randall's post-racialism. To say that Randall's representation of Obama is post-racial is not to say that it seeks to diminish or erase the strength of the intraracial community structures and organizations of the Black elite she represents. Much like the integration of previous hyphenated white ethnic American groups, Randall imagines a future transcendent of the limitations of both Jim Crow segregation and its post–civil rights vestiges. Post-racialism in this sense neither demands nor desires the erasure of Black identity but instead hinges on the reparation of the irreconcilability of racial self and national citizenship that Du Bois conceptualized over a hundred years ago. Randall's Obama represents liberation precisely because she argues he exists outside the white gaze. While it is clearly not true, and it seems unlikely that Randall would suggest that Obama actually lives, or has lived, outside of a racialized societal gaze, his lack of hyphenation comes from his exemption from the comparative burdens of Abel's experiences. Abel feels terrorized, and then later terrorizes, precisely because he feels perpetually unsafe. His vulnerability is the direct product of his racialization, and, as the revision of his thirteenth birthday scene makes clear, he has spent his life both fleeing from that sense of vulnerability and blaming the fact of his Blackness, rather than the structures of white supremacy, for it.

In Randall's novel, it is both Obama's Blackness and the alienation from that same Blackness that generates the distinction she creates between him and Abel. Because of his Blackness, he stands as the inheritor of the civil rights legacy that has so haunted Abel. In this way, Randall's novel mirrors popular cartoons, editorials, and sayings that argue that the election of Barack Obama as the nation's first Black president is the culmination of the Civil Rights Movement (see Squires 2014). However, the fact that Randall withholds Obama's name throughout the novel, narrating his birth as a kind of fairy tale, makes it clear that the Obama whom she is referring to is a nearly mythological figure rather than an actual human being. Randall makes a similar argument in an essay describing the specific genius of Obama's unwillingness to view racism as "endemic," choosing instead to view it as "a past that can be undone" (Randall 2009a, 221). Randall argues that Obama's "A More Perfect Union" speech is transcendent precisely because, despite "[mitigating] his radical message that we

must let the past be past with a tone of felt cool," he is able to speak propheti-
cally, "[calling] on the led to make" his vision "real" (Randall 2009a, 216). In
contrast to her Vanderbilt colleague Houston Baker's statement that the speech
was a "pandering disaster" (Salon Staff 2008), Randall argues that Obama used
the speech to speak an uncomfortable truth about the need to move beyond the
"bogeyman of irrational racial passions—be they a sense of pervasive injustice
or a sense of being burdened by less competent or violent others" (Randall
2009a, 222). As in her novel, Randall aligns Obama with a sense of profound
change. *Rebel Yell* implies that one can take Randall's statement on the speech
that "the moment before the speech was different from the moment after" and
rephrase it generationally: the period before the election of Barack Obama
was different from the period after the election (Randall 2009a, 222–23). In
making such an argument, Randall indulges in the messianic. When she states
that "what was a wish when the speech began was a reality when it came to
a close," Obama becomes a figure of both immense power and persuasion,
capable with one twenty-minute speech of totally revolutionizing American
race relations (Randall 2009a, 223). Ultimately, Randall portrays Obama as
the true guardian of the civil rights legacy and the individual most capable of
transcending its necessity. In doing so, she contrasts Obama with the lost and
damaged post–civil rights generation represented by Abel and imaginatively
constructs a vision of "how things might be" (Randall 2009a, 223).

Appropriate to a novel published in the wake of an event as epochal-feeling
as the election of the nation's first Black president, *Rebel Yell*, while ending
with Abel's death, suggests the optimism of a new era. If Abel represents the
excesses and abuses of the Bush-era War on Terror, the fictionalization of the
newly elected president attempts to relegate the actions of Abel as torturer and
terrorizer to the same dustbin of history as the white supremacist terrorizers so
instrumental in making Abel who he is. However, the actual Obama presidency
pushes against the fairy tale glow of the novel's narrativization of the president's
birth.[19] Erica Edwards argues post-9/11 racial reconfigurations are complicit in a
neoliberal multiculturalism that reframes the implications of race in society to
mask the maintenance of exploitative hierarchies through the visible participation of individuals of color at the highest level (Edwards 2013, 192–93).

Randall feeds into this racial reconfiguration in two ways. First, her obsession with the southern Black elite tells a history of the Black community that
naturalizes their movement into national positions of power without engaging
the radical critiques of that elite by the Black community itself. Second, while
Abel's story re-centers the history of Black conservatism to critique it, the
replacement of Abel with the "unhyphenated" Obama at the end of the novel
constructs an idealized new era in which the privilege of the entrenched elite

remains unquestioned. To reframe both these points, Randall's novel does not imagine alternative forms of Black politics capable of engaging with the political realities of the post-9/11 era. Instead, she imagines that Obama, as simultaneous insider and outsider, will simply inaugurate transformative change through his presence and rhetoric. The shift that Edwards notes conceals its utter lack of transformation beneath the superficial appointment of Black faces to positions of power. While Randall could not be expected to anticipate the continued complicity of Obama-era foreign policy in the abuses of the Bush presidency, her novel indulges in the same idealization of the idea that the election of Obama signals "one of those singular moments that nations ignore at their peril" that Morrison discussed in her endorsement of his candidacy. In doing so, the novel crystallizes the fantasy of a culmination of civil rights era struggle. However, more importantly, it signals the desire for new conceptions of Blackness detached from the specific histories central to such a struggle.

Tying the potential for a post-racial future to Obama's election, as Randall does, demonstrates the attempt to crystallize new articulations of African American identity. In interviews following Obama's election, Morrison repudiated her optimism because of the sustained racialized backlash to the Obama presidency. Indeed, the election of Donald Trump as president, whose role in the racist "birther" conspiracy theory elevated his profile, has only further legitimized and prompted the growth of explicit white supremacy in the years since Randall's novel was published.[20] However, it is the desire for continued progress and change manifested in a candidate emphasizing hope and change embodied in his multiracial, cosmopolitan self that maps the tension between the continual attempt to imagine a new present, even in the face of evidence of the persistence of past structures. For African American literature in the present, both the possibilities and the inadequacies embodied by Obama illuminate the continual attempt to construct new forms of racial subjectivity. Seizing on Du Boisian double consciousness, Randall uses Obama as a character to imagine a path out of the trap Du Bois linked to the twentieth century's struggle with the color line. The backlash against that president, as well as the actions of Obama himself as president, reminds us that symbolic associations necessarily confront stubbornly persistent realities. Despite this, Randall's novel christens the possibility of reborn Blackness for the new century rooted in the symbolic conjunction of millennial change and the singular election of the nation's first Black president.

A NON-AMERICAN BLACK GUIDE TO AMERICAN BLACKNESS

Rearticulating Race through a Diasporic Lens

One of the questions underlying the tension that I am arguing defines the post era concerns whether there is such a thing as a "Black community." The answers to this question, presented across the post era fiction and criticism I have analyzed, take several forms: from the poststructuralist critique of labeling found in Colson Whitehead to the anti-essentialism of post-Blackness and post-soul aesthetics to the class-based criticism of Kenneth Warren. Across these works there is a broad emphasis on the sheer diversity of Black people in the United States; as individual texts focus on class, gender, sexuality, or individual experience, writers throughout the post era continually highlight such heterogeneity in trumpeting incremental racial progress. Emphasis on the heterogeneity of Blackness during the post era pivots around the tension between external categorization and self-definition. However, despite the presence of such an emphasis in African American writing, American racialisms remain largely dichotomous, admitting to exceptions, but more often simply distinguishing between race (Black/white) and ethnicity (Hispanic/Asian). Existing as what Jennifer Hochschild, Vesla Weaver, and Traci Burch call the current "racial order" (Hochschild, Weaver, and Burch 2012, 9), these structures have undergone shifts during the early twenty-first century. In particular, the new century has seen the growth of interracial marriage, with a resulting increase in the number of people claiming a distinct mixed-race identity, and increased immigration from the Caribbean and continental Africa, what historian Ira Berlin terms the "fourth great migration" (Berlin 2010). Substantial recent scholarship focuses on the history of mixed-race identity in the United States, highlighting signal events such as the 1993 publication of Dr. Maria P. P. Root's "Bill of Rights for People of Mixed Heritage" in constructing a political and social mixed-race subjectivity. Furthermore, works such as Michele Elam's

The Souls of Mixed Folk (2011) and Ralina Joseph's *Transcending Blackness* (2011) document the cultural representation of an emerging mixed-race identity that is not detached from structures of racialization but which does challenge the assumption of there being sufficient common experiences among those labeled as Black people to support claims that there is something definably Black about particular works of art or cultural practices. In contrast, less has been written about how the twenty-first century expansion in African diaspora narratives have "helpfully [countered] the hegemony of any single genealogy of blackness" (Goyal 2017, 642).

While, in this chapter, I analyze Chimamanda Ngozi Adichie's recent *Americanah* (2013), her work is but one major example of the expanded presence of African immigrant authors in twenty-first century African American literature. Dinaw Mengestu's novels *The Beautiful Things that Heaven Bears* (2007) (originally titled *Children of the Revolution*), *How to Read the Air* (2010) and *All Our Names* (2014) trace the unique experiences of African immigrants and their children who arrive as refugees of violent dictatorships and armed conflict. London-born, Boston-raised, Ghanaian-American author Taiye Selasi's *Ghana Must Go* (2013) traces the return of a diasporic family to Ghana in response to family trauma. Zimbabwean novelist NoViolet Bulawayo's (pen name for Elizabeth Zandile Tshele) award-winning *We Need New Names* (2013) follows a young girl who leaves Zimbabwe searching for a new life in Detroit. Nigerian-American Teju Cole's *Open City* (2011) is a novel that revels in the space of New York City as it traces the thoughts and experiences of a young Nigerian psychiatrist. Imbolo Mbue's *Behold the Dreamers* (2016) follows the struggle of an undocumented Cameroonian immigrant family in New York just prior to and during the 2008 financial crisis. Each of these novels, which are only a few examples from a larger corpus, attempts to understand the experiences of immigrants of African descent in the United States in the late twentieth and early twenty-first century amid the widespread changes in opportunities and structural racisms that the other chapters of this book have already detailed.

Louis Chude-Sokei (2014) argues that the recent proliferation of narratives by African immigrants to the United States reveals an ongoing "category crisis" in racial identity and politics. Discussing Mengestu's *The Beautiful Things that Heaven Bears*, Chude-Sokei describes this literature as inhabiting "a context overdetermined by multiple demands of affiliation and by the tensions between rival claims of trauma and memory, all within the crowded and obfuscating skin of racial classification" (Chude-Sokei 2014, 54). In other words, while these works address the issue of racial identity to different degrees, they all interrogate the implications of both the similarities and differences between the experiences of African immigrants, Caribbean immigrants, and native-born Black Americans within a continuing regime of white supremacy.

This chapter focuses on Adichie's *Americanah* (2013) to make two primary arguments: (1) Adichie's novel typifies just how widespread the attempt to rethink the meaning of race in the twenty-first century is; and, (2) the experiences of the immigrant characters she depicts show the power racial dichotomies continue to hold. Furthermore, Adichie's novel also underscores the central thematic role that the person of Barack Obama plays in the ongoing racial imaginary as an emblematic figure for a range of overlapping discourses on racial fluidity and transcendence. As an individual who identifies as Black— both through the census and in cultural traditions and institutions that he has adopted over the years (most fully expressed in *Dreams from My Father*)— and someone whose background leaves open the possibility of mixed-race and diasporic identities that can be and have been imposed on him, Obama embodies the optimism of ongoing racial rearticulation while revealing its limitations. Consequently, Adichie's ethnographic anatomization of race, across *Americanah,* illustrates how an optimistic emphasis on the heterogeneity of the Black community often represented through the figure of the mixed-race or Black ethnic individual confronts stubbornly persistent American racialisms.

Like that of many other political and demographic realities that have so strongly influenced twenty-first century African American literature, the prominent representation of the experience of immigrants of African descent from continental Africa and the Caribbean is also a product of the social upheavals of the 1960s. For more than half a century, American immigration policy had favored Europe through a policy of country quotas. Even in the case of special government exceptions used to admit political refugees, "the largest single group were political refugees from communism, mostly from eastern Europe" (Reimers 1981, 3). With explicitly racist immigration policies denying widespread immigration from Asia and national quotas that favored not just Europe but particular European nations (Italy, for example, had a quota of "slightly over 5800" while Greece had a quota of 307, see Reimers 1981, 3; 4), many nations had few individuals immigrate to the United States prior to the 1960s. President Lyndon Johnson's 1965 signing of the "Immigration and Nationality Amendments" radically changed such immigration trends. The amendments replaced the nation-based quotas with regional quotas to set in place a strong set of preferences that emphasized, among other things, family reunification and occupational needs in the United States.

As opposed to litigation that was the explicit product of civil rights organizing, lawmakers only partially saw the 1965 Immigration and Nationality Amendments, or Hart-Celler Act, in racial terms when it passed. In *Creating a New Racial Order*, Hochschild, Weaver, and Burch chart the large racial demographic changes that were the product of this legislation, but argue that it occurred "more or less accidentally" (Hochschild, Weaver, and Burch 2012, 21). The act had the effect of broadly expanding immigration to the United States, particularly from Asia. However, predictions in the legislative history of the bill show that legislators all broadly underestimated the expansion of immigration towards which the bill would lead (Hochschild, Weaver, and Burch 2012, 21–26; see also Zolberg 2006, 324–26; DeSipo and de la Garza 2015, 77–83; Shachar 2006).

Since the 1960s, the demographics of immigrants has broadly shifted from being predominantly European to now encompassing large groups from a variety of Asian, Latin American, African, and Caribbean nations. While there are still immigrants from Europe, their previous predominance has been replaced by a vastly more diverse mix of ethnic groups. Among these large-scale shifts, which have seen their largest effects in the expansion of Asian and Hispanic populations and identities in the United States, immigration from continental Africa is only a small subset. For many Black immigrants, arriving in the United States is a process of situating oneself within racial structures distinct from one's predominantly Black home country.[1] In response to a Haitian woman arguing that race was not an issue between her and her white boyfriend, Ifemelu, the protagonist of Nigerian author Adichie's *Americanah*, points out, "I came from a country where race was not an issue; I did not think of myself as black and I only became black when I came to America" (Adichie 2013, 293). The sense of "becoming black" that Ifemelu invokes here illuminates the tension between racial self-definition and external classification. The fact is that for Black immigrants migrating to the United States is a process of "becoming black" to such a degree that one cannot simply dismiss the power that such racial fictions have on the individual, regardless of their individual self-definition.

Indeed, there is considerable resistance by many immigrants to simply being classified as Black, either by the United States government or people on the street. The preferences for skilled professionals and family reunification in immigration in the 1965 immigration law (and subsequent immigration legislation) led to a population influx that is, like Ifemelu, generally well educated. For example, compared to native-born Black people, both naturalized Black immigrants and noncitizen Black immigrants show higher levels of both educational achievement and wealth (Hochschild, Weaver, and Burch 2012, 36–37). Canonical immigrant assimilation theory, which focused on the European ethnic groups who composed the bulk of immigrants prior to 1965, argues that immigrant groups seek to integrate into the white mainstream to gain social mobility and acceptance. Research by scholars such as Mary

Waters (1999), Christina Greer (2013), and Rachel Reynolds (2009; 2013), however, emphasizes that this is not true for Black immigrants. Migrants from the
Caribbean and continental Africa rightly recognize the racially dichotomous
structure of American society, meaning that if they were to assimilate in the
classic sense (i.e. lose their accents, change their names, fight to be perceived
as simply American), they would be perceived and treated as simply Black.
As Waters argues, being perceived as Black constitutes "downward mobility"
for such immigrants (Waters 1999, 5), especially given that many Black ethnic
groups arrive with high levels of education.[2] However, despite attempts to
disidentify themselves from Black Americans, "race as a master status in the
United States soon overwhelms the identities of the immigrants and their
children" (Waters 1999, 8). As Ifemelu's description of "becoming black" upon
arriving in the United States illustrates, coming to the United States requires
confronting the ubiquity of its deep-seated racialism, confusing many immigrants who may have left societies in which racism is present but which are
nonetheless predominantly Black demographically. Indeed, scholars such as
Waters and Reuel Rogers (2006) detail how even immigrants from societies
with both a history of slavery and colonialism in the Caribbean are surprised
by the sheer extent of racialism in the United States.

The process of "becoming black" then, is necessarily one of self-situating.
As I discuss throughout this chapter, *Americanah* extensively documents the
complex racialization of the Black immigrant. With Black ethnic groups, then, it
is wrong to assume that there is either a lack of solidarity with Black Americans
or that there is a complete agreement about the meaning and consequence of
race in the United States (Greer 2013, 6). Because of this, racial solidarity among
the diverse populations that make up Black America is fundamentally fluid
and contextual. Furthermore, individual ethnic groups have distinct histories
of immigration and unique demographic and experiential factors that alter
the contexts that determine their reaction to American racialisms. Nigerian
immigrants like Ifemelu arrive with atypically high class and educational backgrounds. They migrate for the specific purpose of gaining educational and
economic opportunities lacking in Nigeria (Reynolds 2013, 278). Consequently,
first generation immigrants like Ifemelu "have an almost anthropological sense
of what it means to be an immigrant," leading to a heightened perception of the
meaning of their otherness in society (Reynolds 2013, 281). One of the values,
therefore, of a novel like *Americanah* is that it operates in dialogue with research
on Black immigrants to show how they seek to both resist being perceived as
Black Americans while recognizing the erosive effects of American racism.

Increasing numbers of Black immigrant authors, therefore, share the experiences Adichie represents in her novel, one of the reasons that characterizing

Ifemelu as a writer resonates so strongly within the twenty-first century boom of Black diasporic writing in and about the United States. In a 2014 interview, for example, the Ethiopian-American author Dinaw Mengestu traces several interlinked racial narratives while detailing his childhood in the suburbs of Chicago:

> You know, when I was growing up, Forest Park was full of integrated families. It was amazing. One my best friends was Vietnamese. Another one was half-Mexican, half-black. Another one was from Colombia. Another one was born in the U.S. but his mom was from Germany and spoke with a German accent. So we all had multiple identities. None of us were just one thing or another. We were all of us aware that if you went to one person's house, you had Vietnamese food, or if you went to another person's house, you had tortillas. At my house you had Ethiopian food. It was a remarkably eclectic childhood. Later, in high school in Oak Park, things were more clearly delineated. It was overwhelmingly white, and the minorities who were there were mostly African-American. I was neither white nor "African-American" in that sense, which was more problematic. You were reacting to kids who were sometimes openly racist, but on the other side, you were different from the black kids as well because of your name and your cultural history. That's when I started thinking of myself as being more than "black" or "American," but as being a product of Ethiopia. (Mengestu 2014b)

In the first part of his reply, Mengestu describes an idealized cosmopolitanism, in which pluralistic ethnic identities are both merged and maintained in a dynamic creativity. His use of the word "eclectic" emphasizes diversity and multipleness, both within the self and the overall community. However, the second part of his answer reveals the anxious racialization underlying the first part's paean to diversity. As with Adichie's characterization of Ifemelu, Mengestu describes not quite fitting into American racial dichotomies, struggling to fit within both the white majority and the African American community. The two parts of Mengestu's response contrast the dynamism of the former community with the "clear delineation" of the latter to privilege cosmopolitanism. Mengestu, in assessing his own self-definition, posits that he reacted to the stultifying atmosphere by resorting to a kind of liminal identity: "being a product of Ethiopia." The sense of "being a product of" establishes an identity akin to *Americanah*'s concept of being a "Non-American Black," someone who resides within the structures of racialization but who cannot simply situate themselves within them. Indeed, many 1.5-generation and second-generation immigrants, particularly those of middle- and upper-class backgrounds, define themselves specifically as immigrants to counter assumptions of their Blackness (see Waters 1999, Chapter 8).

On the one hand, the shifting contexts that generate the fluid solidar-ity relationship between various groups racially designated as Black within American society aligns with the post era emphasis on shifting definitions of group identity. On the other hand, however, the experiences recounted by Ifemelu, in fiction, and by Mengestu, in relation to his own childhood, indexes how the fluidity of experience does not mirror a similar loosening of the current racial order. Consequently, demographic shifts resulting from the 1965 Immigration and Nationality Amendments map yet another terrain in post–civil rights racial rearticulation in which the experiences of Black immigrants signal the ongoing breakdown of conceptualizing Blackness as a monolithic community, even while highlighting the continuing oppressiveness of American racial dichotomies.

Consequently, this chapter focuses on Adichie's novel precisely because it is a self-conscious interrogation of the meaning of Blackness in the contem-porary United States through the lens of immigration. In addition, it focalizes its consideration of racial identity in twenty-first century America through the figure of Barack Obama, who, as the novel reminds its readers, is the product of the same kinds of immigration the novel depicts.[3] As the son of a Kenyan father who traveled to Hawaii on an educational visa and married a local woman, the experiences of Barack Obama Sr., whose arrival predated the 1965 Immigration and Nationality Act by several years but who is still a mem-ber of a vanguard generation for many of the characters in the novels listed earlier, provides a historical anchor that allows Black immigrants to claim a space within American racial structures.[4] *Americanah* specifically attempts to position such migrants within complexly interrelated racial regimes. Adiche traces the experiences of Ifemelu as a student and then as a fellow at both Yale University and Princeton University using her writing on racial identity in new media platforms to voice Ifemelu's conflicted feelings of exclusion and belonging. Ifemelu's blog creates a site of both conjuncture and disjuncture that Adichie aligns with Obama during the election campaign. Inserting her voice into the racial discourse marked as simultaneously distinct (Non-American) and connected (Black), Ifemelu seeks to delineate a definable perspective on race in the twenty-first century in the United States.

RACE BLOGGING "FUCK YOU"

Arriving as the follow up to her best-selling historical novel of the Biafran War, *Half of a Yellow Sun* (2006), a substantial portion of the initial press on *Americanah* described its explicit social commentary and focus on such topics as fashion and hair as somehow less weighty than the content of her previous work. This commentary resonates with Frederic Jameson's argument that the inevitable topic for non-Western novelists is a national allegory of the type contained in *Half of a Yellow Sun* (see Jameson 1986). However, with *Americanah*, Adichie specifically seeks to counter objectifying assumptions about African literature, and, in doing so, to situate herself within the complex, and overlapping, migratory regimes I have been outlining so far in this chapter. In interviews, Adichie declared that this was her "fuck you" novel, and the pleasure she shows in discussing it encourages readers to see the fun that the author had in writing the text (Parks 2014). The novel is a "fuck you" in several senses, but the one I want to focus on is the connection between the text's ethnographic lens (reflected most directly in Ifemelu's blog) and its invocation of kitsch. Implicit in Adichie's well-known "Danger of a Single Story" TED talk is a long history of reviewers and scholars engaging in reductive terms with the continent of Africa and its artistic production (Adichie 2009). In the case of literature, such racist assumptions led to celebrations of even the most canonical works as mere windows into the lives of African peoples and the politics of African nations. As Eleni Coundouriotis (1999) documents, the reception of novelists such as Ben Okri, Chinua Achebe, and Yambo Ouologuem reflects primary concerns with authenticity and the relationship between white readers and the text. Emphasizing authenticity positions novels by African writers as fundamentally ethnographic in nature. Indeed, a 1978 article on "Fact, Fiction, and the Ethnographic Novel" prominently lists Achebe's *Things Fall Apart* (1958) alongside works by anthropologists in a genealogy of the form (Langness and Frank 1978). Adichie nods at this racist framework with the identity Ifemelu takes on so that she can work illegally while on a student visa: "Ngozi Okonkwo." The assumed name's references to Adichie herself and the main character of Achebe's *Things Fall Apart* serve as Adichie's sly joke on the reception of African literature. Notably, Adichie herself has long been linked to Achebe, likely because she once occupied a house that he had previously owned (Sunday Times 2015). However, with this detail, and its attendant discussion of how Ifemelu and Ngozi Okonkwo look nothing alike (Adichie 2013, 121), Adichie notes the capital attached to submitting to racist assumptions. To resist such racialization, whether on the part of Ifemelu, or Adichie when she was an up and coming writer, risks expanding their economic and legal vulnerability, ultimately forcing them to accede to such assumptions.

Adichie's prominent anatomization of racial folkways in the United States in the form of Ifemelu's blog posts are, therefore, a significant part of the novel's "fuck you." While the novel is not subtle in these moments, it does not intend to be so. Consequently, beyond being a book that engages throughout with the concept of Blackness in the United States, it is also a metafictional account of what it means to write about race as an African immigrant in the United States.[5] The very title of Ifemelu's blog, *Raceteenth or Various Observations About American Blacks (Those Formerly Known as Negroes) by a Non-American Black*, illuminates Adichie's gently satirical approach to Ifemelu's writerly insights. The use of the term "Raceteenth" subtly invokes the holiday of Juneteenth, which celebrates the moment at which the news of the end of the Civil War, and the freedom it implied, reached the slaves in Texas at the most remote point from the nation's capital. Her transformation of the term localizes race as the primary focus of the blog and situates it within the broader consideration of progress. The use of the term suggests both valedictory optimism further reinforced by the reference to American Blacks as "those formerly known as Negroes" while at the same time satirizing that same optimism. The directionality of the "observations" also reinforces the ambiguous positionality of "Non-American Blacks" in relation to "American Blacks." Saying that the blog will be a place for observations about American Blacks by Non-American Blacks establishes a distinction between the two groups, granting Non-American Blacks a privileged position to comment on other Black people from a presumed position of insight. However, the shared racial category of "Black" collapses this distinction, suggesting the landscape of common experiences and struggles shared by the groups through the flattened nature of their racial categorization.

Indeed, the terminology of "Non-American Black" can be read as Adichie's entry in a broader conversation about how to label the identities of African immigrants. Taiye Selasi (then writing under the name Taiye Tuakli-Wosornu) describes this relatively well-educated wave of immigrants from continental Africa as a generation of "Afropolitans" in her 2005 essay "Bye-Bye Babar; or, What is an Afropolitan?" Adichie, who Selasi prominently mentions in defining her neologism, typifies a group that is the product of a long-scale, and much-debated, African "brain drain" facilitated by educational institutions and various governmental programs within the United States and various former colonial powers in Europe. Selasi's essay functions as a diasporic iteration of post era anti-essentialism. Where post-Blackness and related discourses push back on domestic Black nationalisms, Selasi rejects a post-colonial nationalism that emphasizes an authenticity tied to the African continent and its individual nations. She insists on a definition of "African" that embraces a growing diasporic elite population.

Like post-Blackness, "Afropolitanism" and those who embrace it have been accused of propagating a class-based elitism used to neglect the actual cultural work and experiences of those living on the continent. For my purposes, however, Selasi's essay usefully reveals how the writing of Black immigrants to the United States participates in the ongoing redefinition of Black identity in the post era. Selasi celebrates such "Africans of the world" for their "refusal to oversimplify" Africa and for their "effort to understand what is ailing in Africa alongside the desire to honor what is wonderful, unique. Rather than essentialising the geographical entity, [they] seek to comprehend the cultural complexity; to honor the intellectual and spiritual legacy; and to sustain our parents' cultures" (Selasi 2005).[6] In addition to the comprehension of the cultural complexity of their various home countries, Afropolitans occupy liminal spaces between national, racial, and economic regimes that allow them to feel at home within Western countries without being confined by the racism of such nations. With its images of Afropolitans at clubs in world capitals, the essay simultaneously reveals the vulnerability of a generation of immigrants and children of immigrants who lack concrete feelings of home either in their ancestral or adopted homelands while celebrating their hybridity and fluid ability to occupy different cultural regimes.[7] As but one sliver in the broad global attempt to define what Selasi, quoting Claude Gruzintsky, calls the "21st century African," novels such as Adichie's broaden the construction of race in the twenty-first century to incorporate this new diasporic experience while recognizing the limitations of such a perspective within nationally bounded racial regimes as the one within the United States.[8] Whereas Selasi's post era portmanteau seeks to locate the experiences of African immigrants within a broader cosmopolitanism, Adichie's designation of Ifemelu as "Non-American Black" focuses on similar issues within the racial structures of the United States.

Throughout the novel, Ifemelu's blog posts establish a dialogue between the events of the plot and Ifemelu's expression of and processing of those events. At various points, even prior to the creation of the blog, in the course of the plot, things that occur in the novel lead directly into Ifemelu's blog commentary. For example, upon arriving in the United States, she encounters Alma, the Hispanic babysitter for her Aunt Uju. Instead of taking this moment to represent Ifemelu's own confusion over American racial categorizations, invoked through a line that says, "If Ifemelu had met Alma in Lagos, she would have thought of her as white" (Adichie 2013, 106), Adichie transitions to a blog post that Ifemelu writes "years later" titled "Understanding America for the Non-American Black: What Hispanic Means" (Adichie 2013, 106). In doing so, Adichie puts Ifemelu's blog writing in dialogue with her own. Adichie indexes Ifemelu's negotiation of racial categorizations by subtly noting that in the moment, "She hardly noticed Alma," and that "she would remember Alma, years later" while writing the post in question (Adichie 2013, 106). Furthermore, the blog post's interruption of the text—throughout, Adichie sets the blog posts apart in a different font and indentation—highlights the issues of race explicitly discussed in the body of the post. In turn, in commenting on Ifemelu's understanding of herself by locating her interest in the topic in the future, she also subtly denotes their prominent role. The specific blog post in question, like most of the others contained in the novel, reflects a form of popular sociology common on many blogs that attempt to translate complex issues of racialization and ethnic identity into a forum of popular, academically inflected expression. While the blog posts that dot the text provide a certain level of metacommentary on the structures of race that Ifemelu and the other categories are navigating, they are not privileged over the experiences of those structures. In other words, the novel does not serve as a series of events illuminated by the commentary of the blog, with the blog acting as an authoritative account of race in America and a lens through which the reader can understand the rest of the novel.

Instead, Adichie constructs a dialogue between Ifemelu's experiences and the blog posts to reflect on what it means to write about race in America, particularly from Ifemelu's self-proclaimed position as a "Non-American Black." Ifemelu often seems herself to feel some discomfort about the role that her blog takes on. Specifically, she is discomfited by the idea of her blog, which she views as observational and sarcastic (her long term love interest Obinze comments that "the blog posts astonished him, they seemed so American and so alien, the irreverent voice with its slanginess, its mix of high and low language, and he could not imagine her writing them" [Adichie 2013, 374]), being subject to the standards of academia. Immediately after the novel introduces the fact of her blog on the second page of the novel (and the fact of her having just written the last post two days earlier), Ifemelu reflects on the totality of her blogging experience, noting,

> readers like SapphicDerrida, who reeled off statistics and used words like "reify" in their comments, made Ifemelu nervous, eager to be fresh and to impress, so that she began, over time, to feel like a vulture hacking into the carcasses of people's stories for something that she could use. Sometimes making fragile links to race. Sometimes not believing herself. The more she wrote the less sure she became. Each post scraped off yet one more scale of self until she felt naked and false. (Adichie 2013, 5)

The inverse relationship this quote establishes between the volume of her writing and her certainty about its content and meaning governs the entirety of her career as a "race blogger." Ifemelu's nervousness reveals her uncertainty over her relationship to the identity categories and experiences she catalogues. As the novel makes clear, Ifemelu begins blogging as an expression of her experiences as a "Non-American Black" woman, and the success of the blog provides both her and her words access to elite academic institutions. On the other hand, Ifemelu is suspicious throughout of the academic implications of her blog work. Here, she expresses nervousness about that segment of her readership through the figure of SapphicDerrida, whose name evokes an interest in Cultural Studies, Queer Theory, and Deconstruction, and whose use of terms like reify sets a presumed academic standard that Ifemelu feels unsure she has the capability to meet. Furthermore, in seeking to meet this unspoken standard, she begins to question the very complexities the blog expresses, calling the links between concepts and experiences increasingly fragile.

Adichie further reveals Ifemelu's difficulty situating herself within the academic analysis of American racial structures after she secures an appointment at Yale where she lives with her boyfriend Blaine, himself a professor of African American Studies with a specialty in "southern Africa." By giving Ifemelu's lover an academic specialty that could encompass research into experiences such as those of immigrants like Ifemelu, Adichie explicitly sets up a conflict between the esoteric and the lived. As their relationship goes on, Ifemelu finds herself "realizing she was using Blaine's own words" (Adichie 2013, 344) and bristles when he argues that she has a "responsibility" based on the popularity of the blog (Adichie 2013, 313). To push back, she draws a distinction between "explaining" and "observing," associating herself with the latter in contrast to Blaine's analytical persona. However, Blaine's assertion of her "responsibility" speaks to the tension embodied by the act of writing about race itself. As so many of the authors in this study have discussed, at the heart of contemporary discussions regarding the meaning of African American literature is a version of an old debate over the proper role and responsibility of the African American author to the broader African American community. That Adichie invokes this old debate situates her work within that of authors I discuss throughout this book such as Kenneth Warren and Charles Johnson who argue that there is no longer even a conceptualizable African American community through which to imagine such a responsibility as the one Blaine raises. Even authors with a more favorable approach to the continued instantiation of an African American literary tradition question the extent to which ideas of "responsibility" become compulsions that dictate static constructs of racial and ethnic identities. As an increasingly influential participant in the structures that she claims to "observe" and not "explain," Blaine argues that Ifemelu bears some responsibility to instruct her readers in ways that break down structural racism and divisions between communities and groups.

While he is likely unaware of such specifics, Blaine might easily be speaking to Ifemelu's earlier capitalization on her blog writing fame as a business consultant, paid to speak to employees of various corporations as part of their diversity training. After conducting the first of these trainings, where she felt "pleased with the fluidness of her delivery" (Adichie 2013, 307), she receives a tepid response and hate mail. However, instead of questioning whether to continue to conduct such seminars, she adopts a mask that flatters her corporate clients without undermining her income stream. Her reflection on doing this, while bitter, is troubling precisely because it abdicates any responsibility: "During her talks, she said: 'America has made great progress for which we should be very proud.' In her blog she wrote: *Racism should never have happened and so you don't get a cookie for reducing it*" (Adichie 2013, 307). As she points out, her performance as a "controversial race blogger" in these corporate settings has nothing to do with the content of her words: "They did not want the content of her ideas; they merely wanted the gesture of her presence" (Adichie 2013, 307). By ritualizing diversity, and dutifully trotting out a "controversial" writer, these corporations absolve and legitimize themselves, even as they dismiss, with their sarcastic clapping and hate mail, the specific content of her work. However, Ifemelu is clearly aware of the charade that this enacts, leading the reader to question the legitimacy of her continued capitalization on it.

Furthermore, Ifemelu's Nigerian background complicates the exact nature of her "responsibility." The blog title's satirical vacillation between racial connectedness and divergence manifests a broader tension over the nature of belonging and access in the novel overall. While Blaine does not question Ifemelu's right to speak in collective terms for Black people or about issues of race, he does assign her a concomitant obligation to break down the structures she describes, either analytically or politically. Blaine's sister goes further than he does to question Ifemelu's privileged position as an African "writing from the outside" (Adichie 2013, 337).[9] Shan specifically contrasts Ifemelu's writing on race with her own struggles to publish work reflecting her experience as an African American woman. "You can't write an honest novel about race in this country. If you write about how people are really affected by race, it'll be too *obvious*" (Adichie 2013, 336–37). As she does throughout the novel, Adichie uses the elasticity of pronouns to signify the dynamically shifting communities that each character occupies at various moments. While Ifemelu has often been included in the "us" and "we" labeling all Black people, Shan's "you" here refers specifically to African American authors in opposition not only to white writers (who her friend Grace also calls out, saying that "white writers can be blunt about race and get all activist because their anger isn't threatening" [Adichie 2013, 337]), but also to an ambiguous group occupied by people like Ifemelu, who are Black yet not Black in the same way as Shan. Feeling angry as she is forced to agree with Shan, Ifemelu acknowledges, "It was true that race was not embroidered in the fabric of her history; it had not been etched on her soul" (Adichie 2013, 338). Ifemelu's language here indexes the troubling essentialism and prescriptiveness embedded in the very question of responsibility. In doing so, Adichie questions the exact nature of Ifemelu's racial lens.

The anonymity of her blog platform only reinforces Shan's question. After all, what actually constitutes the racial identity of the "Non-American Black"? Put another way, even granting Blaine's statement about Ifemelu's "responsibility," who is she responsible to and for? There are several moments in the novel in which Adichie explores the implications of constructing a "Non-American Black" identity. For example, when she first meets Shan, Shan remarks that a Nigerian friend of hers was "sure the Non-American Black was a Caribbean because Africans don't care about race" (Adichie 2013, 319). Far from attempting to resolve this ambiguity, Ifemelu establishes it as a product of deliberate calculation. Talking about an encounter with a cab driver from the Caribbean, she mentions how she revises the experience in turning it into a blog post: "When, years later, she wrote the blog post 'On the Divisions Within the Membership of Non-American Blacks in America,' she wrote about the taxi driver, but she wrote of it as the experience of someone else, careful not to let on whether she was African or Caribbean, because her readers did not know which she was" (Adichie 2013, 208). Maintaining deliberate ambiguity about the national background of the "Non-American Black" constructs a liminal racial identity that is distinct from any particular national identity or the racial identity of American Blacks. Ifemelu's blog, then, serves as a node within the matrix of American racial regimes. When Blaine speaks to Ifemelu's responsibility, he undermines her perception of herself as external to those regimes. However, it is not correct to assert that she occupies a similar situatedness as he does. Consequently, instead of serving as a space to voice resistance to American racialisms, Ifemelu's blog ultimately speaks to the tension between the flattening effect of race and the diversity of viewpoints masked by the blanket appellation "Black."

To return to my argument from the beginning of this section, Adichie uses the blog platform for two main purposes in the novel. First, it provides a space for Ifemelu's social commentary on race in America in a voice distinct from that of the novel's main narration. The platform's lack of subtlety offers Ifemelu, and other immigrants like her, a space to voice their shifting place within racially dichotomous structures that risk erasing their distinct experiences. Second, it allows Adichie to turn the same ethnographic lens on American culture that has so often been presumed within the literary representation of Africa. When she declares *Americanah* her "fuck you" novel, the "you" to whom her ire is directed is the whole body of racist assumptions about the nature of African literature, and Africa as a continent, that seek to dictate the nature of her art. By combining an explicit social commentary about race in America with the metafictional reflection on twenty-first century stereotypical representations of Africa, Adichie is able to map Ifemelu's negotiation of her own racial identity in simultaneously individual and collective terms. As an inherently public platform, that, through its popularity, signals the ubiquity of the topics Ifemelu addresses, the blog constructs an ambiguous and fluid "Non-American Black" racial identity that calls attention to the power of American racism to entrap Black individuals, both American and Non-American.

BARACK OBAMA, RELATIONSHIP AID

At the heart of the novel's negotiation of racial identity is the figure of Barack Obama, whose presidential candidacy, and ultimate election, serves as a topic through which the novel's characters and Ifemelu's blog articulate the meaning of Blackness in the present. As in Alice Randall's *Rebel Yell* (see chapter 4), Obama appears as a symbolic, and almost otherworldly, figure, an object of hope for Ifemelu and her diverse group of friends. Ifemelu's initial skepticism about Obama (she is an early Hillary Clinton supporter) transforms into the zeal of the converted after reading Obama's memoir *Dreams from My Father*. Ifemelu tellingly describes Obama in idealized terms: "She was absorbed and moved by the man she met in those pages, an inquiring and intelligent man, a kind man, a man so utterly, helplessly, winningly humane" (Adichie 2013, 354). When she goes on to say, "If only the man who wrote this book could be the president of America" (Adichie 2103, 354), Ifemelu expresses a connection between the nuanced complexity of Obama's writerly persona and the man she desires the candidate to be. As I discussed in chapter 4, the Obama of *Dreams from My Father* situates himself squarely within the African American literary tradition, focusing his narrative on the ambiguity of his racial identity while ultimately affirmatively claiming his Blackness. Adichie's specific reference to the book at this moment focalizes the connection between Ifemelu and Obama as individuals whose Blackness is not identical to that of people like Blaine, who she describes as "a descendent of the black men and women who had been in America for hundreds of years" (Adichie 2013, 178).

Obama's presence in the novel specifically serves to temporarily repair Ifemelu's and Blaine's fracturing relationship, which begins to fall apart following a racial conflict related to a Yale security guard, named Mr. White, who is falsely accused of selling drugs on campus. In the book, Mr. White represents a previous generation of African American men with whom Blaine identifies.

Recounting her first experience with Blaine and Mr. White, Ifemelu confusedly reacts when Blaine changes his identity performance as he interacts with Mr. White. Blaine's self-described "code-switching" buttresses his description of Mr. White as "a history book" to illuminate his understanding of Blackness as rooted in a specific African American history Ifemelu does not immediately understand (Adichie 2013, 343). Their divergent responses to the false accusations against Mr. White only reinforce the different meanings of racial solidarity they hold. Specifically, Blaine, outraged at his employer's racism, organizes a protest march to support Mr. White, which Ifemelu, though in agreement with Blaine about the outrageousness of Yale's behavior, skips to attend a party thrown by a Senegalese colleague.

Up to this point in their relationship, Blaine and Ifemelu have seemed remarkably in tune in a way quite distinctive from her relationship with her earlier white boyfriend Curt. While Adichie does not simplistically imply that racial difference, and Curt's inability to recognize how his own actions highlighted those differences, is all that ends Ifemelu's and Curt's relationship, Adichie communicates the structural barrier that race imposes even between individuals who care deeply about each other. Indeed, Ifemelu starts her blog as a platform to try to work through what she describes to her friend Wambui as all the "things unsaid and unfinished" about their relationship (Adichie 2013, 298). In contrast to Curt's unreflective privilege, Blaine's academic interests enables him to speak to the particularity of her experience with his knowing joke about her being a "Bourgie Nigerian" that communicates a "surprising and immediate intimacy" (Adichie 2013, 179). As she describes during their first encounter on the train, "His use of 'they' suggested an 'us,' which would be both of them" (Adichie 2013, 179). Beyond the romantic sense of connection, Adichie's play with pronouns here comments on the way that race structures even our most intimate interpersonal relationships. While her relationship with Curt must necessarily contain the "things unsaid" that are the product of the "slipperyness" of race as a topic, Blaine establishes an immediate common group identity that bridges racial divides. Adichie makes it clear that to centralize race in her relationship with Curt would be to threaten its very existence, while doing so with Blaine only feeds intimacy. Furthermore, with the role her blog plays, as a way to voice that which remained "unsaid" with Curt, Blaine's own status as a blogger—they reunite at the "Blogging While Brown" conference in Washington D.C.—provides a common platform centered on racial identity.

To the point of the incident involving Mr. White, Blaine's initial "us" has remained relatively uncontested. However, immediately prior to false accusations of dealing drugs on campus being leveled at Mr. White, Ifemelu meets Boubacar with whom she shares a "mutuality" and "fraternal" affection rooted in their shared roots in Africa. When Boubacar tells Ifemelu about the Princeton fellowship she will later receive, he states, "we need to get into these places, you know" (Adichie 2013, 341), Boubacar's words situate Ifemelu within a shifting and dynamic intersectional community. While she shares certain common experiences and understandings with Blaine rooted in their shared Blackness, she shares others with Boubacar because of their common background as African immigrants. Importantly, Adichie does not make Boubacar Nigerian, suggesting that their commonality is not based on shared roots in any specific nation, but rather a "Non-American Black" racial identity borne out of their shared expatriation. While Adichie has Ifemelu speculate that Blaine felt jealous because they "shared something primally African from which he felt excluded" (Adichie 2013, 341), she is not actually arguing for any inherent commonality. Instead, her use of essentialist phrasing speaks to the way that racial and ethnic identity are naturalized. Blaine's resentment highlights that Boubacar's "we" labels a community of which he cannot be a part, in the same way that his own assertion of an "us" flattens Ifemelu's identity to construct a common Blackness. While his academic interest in Africa suggests his understanding of the distinctness of her experience, it also allows him to elide potential differences in their understandings of race beneath the cloak of an intellectual exercise.

In this context, the incident with Mr. White disrupts the apparent stability of the "us" that Blaine imagines. The accusations against Mr. White are clearly racial, and of a kind with the various microaggressions that Ifemelu has written about throughout the novel. In seeking to emphasize the racism of the university, Blaine organizes a protest involving students and presumes Ifemelu's involvement. However, during the protest, Ifemelu attends a party with Boubacar and his colleague instead of attending. While Ifemelu perceives this as a minor issue that Blaine blows out of proportion, Adichie makes it clear that the incident disrupts their intimacy through its relationship to racial identity. Blaine specifically imagines the protest as a version of the utopian pluralism that he believes America should embody. "It was like a mini-America. Black kids and white kids and Asian kids and Hispanic kids. Mr. White's daughter was there, taking pictures of his photos on the placard, and I felt as if that finally gave him some real dignity back" (Adichie 2013, 345). Echoing the idealized representation of civil rights era protests, Blaine's vision of the protest locates his own actions and identity in service of a teleological American progress that Ifemelu violates with her apparent indifference.

Through her response to the racist accusations against Mr. White, Adichie represents the ambiguity of Ifemelu's racialization as a Non-American Black

woman. Ifemelu has been subject to and is clearly aware of the structural racism that such events illuminate. Through her work as a "race blogger," Adichie
also makes it clear that Ifemelu could easily explain exactly how the incident
is evidence of institutional racism. However, on a fundamental level, Ifemelu's
relationship to the event is filtered through Blaine's filial connection to Mr.
White. Blaine sees the accusations against Mr. White as representative of a
regime of white supremacy to which he has been subjected his entire life. In
contrast, while she "became" Black upon arriving in the United States, Ifemelu's
experiences are mediated through the distinction of her diasporic experience,
one that she shares more with Boubacar than with Blaine. It is critical that
Blaine imagines the protest in nationalistic terms, as his vision of a "mini-
America" includes immigrants like Ifemelu but only through an assimilationist
ideology of American pluralism that elides ethnic and national difference.
Ifemelu is right to see in Blaine's anger an accusation of disingenuousness
towards her Blackness:

> "You know, it's not just about writing a blog, you have to live like you believe it.
> That blog is a game that you don't take seriously, it's like choosing an *interesting*
> elective evening class to complete your credits." She recognized, in his tone, a
> subtle accusation, not merely about her laziness, her lack of zeal and conviction,
> but also about her Africanness; she was not sufficiently furious because she was
> African, not African American. (Adichie 2013, 346, italics in original)

While Adichie makes it clear that Blackness is imposed on the African immigrant, Blaine reverses the agency of that formulation, accusing Ifemelu of
wearing a mask of Blackness testifying to fellowship in a racial community to
which she only pretends. In doing so, he suggests that the same unbridgeable
gap that Adichie imagines between Ifemelu and Curt because of their different
racial identities may similarly exist between Blaine and Ifemelu despite their
phenotypical similarities.

   In this context, Obama's presence in the narrative negotiates the relationship
between Ifemelu's Non-American Blackness and Blaine's African American
identity. On the most basic level, once again, the ability of Obama's background
to speak to both the specific and the universal allows for each of them to erect
a bridge through their shared affection for him. Adichie plays off of Obama's
simultaneous American Blackness and roots in Non-American Blackness to
erect a commonality that temporarily resists the dissolution of their relationship: "Their union was leached of passion, but there was a new passion, outside
of themselves, that united them in an intimacy they had never had before, an
unfixed, unspoken, intuitive intimacy: Barack Obama" (Adichie 2013, 353).

Adichie, then, recognizes the tendency to idealize Obama as a representative of cosmopolitan individualism potentially pointing the way towards a utopian future. The very fact that Adichie repeatedly locates discussions of his candidacy in dinner parties and other shared settings emphasizes the communal nature of the hope generated by the Obama candidacy. In doing so, Adichie associates Obama directly with Blaine's "mini-America," which foreshadows the multicultural jubilation of the Grant Park celebration of election victory. Like Alice Randall, Adichie seems less interested in Obama as an individual who governs, has policy positions, and whose decisions can and will have effects on people's lives. However, unlike Randall, Adichie emphasizes the danger of such utopianism. For example, responding to the claim by a Haitian poet and an older white man that "Obama will end racism in this country," Ifemelu uses her relationship with Curt as evidence of the limitation of the progressive narrative they are reading into Obama, which she labels "How Far We Have Come" in a blog post (Adichie 2013, 292). Relatedly, though Obama's presence temporarily repairs the gulf in Ifemelu's and Blaine's relationship created by the incident involving Mr. White, their particular efforts ultimately fail. As much as Obama provides her and Blaine with a symbolic site of reconciliation, his is an impossible symbolism that seeks to reconcile identities that are both overlapping and divergent. Instead of gesturing towards a totalizing distinction or a full commonality, Obama's presence in the novel illuminates the constant and dynamically shifting nature of Ifemelu's racial positioning in the novel.

In this regard, Adichie's invocation of Obama is instructive because his rhetoric serves as an intertext within the novel in dialogue with Ifemelu's experiences and her blog commentary. While she does not quote from Obama's "A More Perfect Union" speech, its specific mention interpolates Obama's conciliatory language that both emphasizes the legitimacy of grievances based in racial difference while charting a path forward towards a union that while it "may never be perfect . . . can always be perfected" (Obama 2009, 249). In the speech, Obama gestures towards a post-racialism rooted in the idea of difference as the basis for commonality. He constructs a multi-racial community that is capable of recognizing historical injustice, but which is also able to imagine the transcendence of the divisions through the reparation of those injustices. Far from serving as a simplistic endorsement of Obama's utopianism, which culminates in the heroic individualism of a young woman named Ashley overcoming any potential personal animus to inspire an older Black man in the common cause of an Obama presidency, Adichie uses the role Obama's candidacy plays in Blaine's and Ifemelu's relationship to cast that utopianism as a naïve unwillingness to seriously engage with the complexity of contemporary demographics and politics. However, while many critiques of Obama's rhetoric in the speech focus on his largely dismissive attitude towards Black grievance, and his placement of its justification categorically in the past, Adichie specifically shows that his universalism excludes Ifemelu, a fact manifested most directly in her inability to vote for him as she waits for the citizenship swearing-in ceremony.[10]

Instead of demonstrating the categorical distinction of Obama's America in the diverse nationalities, ethnicities, and racialisms of her novel, Adichie demonstrates how race in America continues to homogenize an increasingly untenable diversity of backgrounds and experiences. For Ifemelu, the most direct interrogation of this failure occurs at the college she migrated from Nigeria to attend. Adichie dramatizes the presence of both an African Students Association and Black Student Union on the Wellson campus[11] as a space for negotiating ethnic and racial identity. As her friend Wambui explains, "Please note that in general, African Americans go to the Black Student Union and the Africans go to the African Students Association. Sometimes it overlaps but not a lot" (Adichie 2013, 141). In this description, Adichie makes clear the complexity of the position of what Wambui describes as "American-African" students. As she makes clear, the distinction between American-African and African-American is far from obvious. For many students, it is untenable to categorize oneself as either suited to the Black Student Union or the African Students Association. For others, the racial assignation as Black is involuntary and violates affiliations rooted more in national identity. For still others, as Wambui humorously describes, Africa stands as a mystical motherland idealized through a popular cultural imaginary that objectifies and essentializes Blackness.

Adichie literalizes the dilemmas manifested by Obama's own personhood, and Ifemelu's individual tension within shifting racial and ethnic categories, in the character of Dike, the son of Ifemelu's Aunt Uju. Dike is a classic 1.5-generation immigrant, born abroad but brought to the United States as a child. Consequently, Dike faces the difficult prospect of seeking to define his own racial subjectivity within a society that primarily defines him as solely Black while residing in a home environment that emphasizes his distinctiveness as Nigerian.[12] As she leaves the ASA meeting, Ifemelu reflects on Dike's difficult position, wondering "which he would go to in college, whether ASA or BSU, and what he would be considered whether American African or African American. He would have to choose what he was, or rather, what he was would be chosen for him" (Adichie 2013, 142). With this quote, Adichie highlights the tension between self-definition and affiliation by choice with the imposition of racial identity that is the defining racialization experience for the immigrant. Here, Ifemelu emphasizes Dike's choice in the matter, suggesting the primacy of self-definition. However, the quote also notes the role that "what he would be considered" necessarily plays in determining the nature of that self-definition. Just as Ifemelu herself has some choice in whether she will attend ASA or BSU meetings and would likely be welcome, to one degree or another, in either, she questions the positionality that Dike will occupy in a hypothetical future in which his national identity as American is unquestioned but his position within American racial hierarchies remains ambiguous.

In negotiating this ambiguity, Ifemelu's blog posts trace a sociological understanding of race as a social construct that contains and invokes certain histories but is not determined by them. In other words, Barack Obama does not cease to become Black because his father was a Kenyan national rather than the descendent of slaves. However, the presence of the institution of slavery continues to mark the meaning of and performance of that Blackness. As Ifemelu argues in a blog post, "In America, you don't get to decide what race you are. It is decided for you. Barack Obama, looking as he does, would have had to sit on the back of the bus fifty years ago. If a random Black guy commits a crime today, Barack Obama could be stopped and questioned for fitting the profile. And what would that profile be? 'Black Man'" (Adichie 2013, 339). However, as much as you cannot choose your race in America, it does not mean that the race assigned to you accords with your subjectivity. As the novel traces throughout, the experiences of African immigrants call into relief the increasing distance between the meanings constructed in racial categories and the demographic realities those categories claim to encompass. Consequently, the shifting subjectivities of Adichie's characters map the topography of fragmented selves, shifting racial performances, and overlapping but distinct "we's" and "us's" occupied at various moments by each individual. In doing so, Adichie notes, and even highlights, the continuing structures of racial discrimination that mark the day to day lives of individuals of color, but also challenges the utopianism embodied in Blaine's vision of a multi-racial democracy echoed in Obama's candidacy.

In the novel, the conflict between Blaine and Ifemelu over her indifference reflects Chude-Sokei's point that "the very notion that racism is a suturing factor or a shared catalyzing burden is no longer to be taken for granted" (Chude-Sokei 2014, 55) as the basis for imagining a unified Black community in African immigrant fiction. In the wake of Mr. White's arrest, both Blaine and Ifemelu invest themselves heavily in Barack Obama's 2008 campaign, using this shared investment as a means to hold off the deterioration of their larger relationship. Ultimately, the fact that Blaine and Ifemelu invest in Obama for related but distinct reasons signals the continuing power of American racial dichotomies even as it highlights the overdetermination of Blackness as a category—for example, in the way Obama's own diasporic and mixed-race background is often subsumed by the label "first Black president." The arc of the text's central romance culminates in Ifemelu's return to Lagos and her lover Obinze. While this ending would seem to trace a reparative path of return, Adichie insists throughout the narrative on the untenability of static conceptions of both race and national identity. Designated as the titular "Americanah" upon her return, Ifemelu's position remains always liminal, dynamically shifting depending on the racial and national contexts within which she finds herself. The narrative of Ifemelu's experiences in America highlights what Michelle Wright describes as the "[insular] and the oppressively homogenous models for Blackness" produced in the United States while also demonstrating what she articulates as "the complex negotiation between dominant and minority cultures that all peoples of African descent in the West must make in order to survive" (Wright 2004, 226; 231). In emphasizing how "Blackness" is a signifier not of some stable self but instead a complex negotiation in constant flux, Adichie uses her non-American Black protagonist to illuminate the already present fluidity of racial and individual subjectivity in both the United States and Nigeria, subtly signaling the ongoing reconfiguration of racial categorizations and national boundaries in the twenty-first century.

THE MYTHIC BARACK OBAMA

Adichie's novel highlights the tension between ideas of progress and their limitations, regarding Barack Obama and, more generally, the post era itself. The novel provides an updated version of the American Dream narrative, depicting a Black immigrant who travels to the United States as a student, overstays her visa illegally, yet finds a modicum of fame through new technology and new media platforms. The text nods at the disproportionate use of social media platforms by African Americans, perhaps most famously in what is labeled "Black Twitter" (see Bonilla and Rosa 2015; Sharma 2012). In doing so, it indicates some of the extent of the incorporation of previously marginalized populations and discourses into academic, publishing, and cultural institutions. While, even by the time the novel was published, the prominence of blog platforms had waned in the face of the expansion of social media, Adichie's novel takes seriously the roles that technology, globalization, and migration play in transforming discourses around identity. Ifemelu feels liberated through the opportunities engendered by blogging. That liberation, however, was already a qualified freedom, as is revealed when her understanding of herself and her role butts up against the expectations and critiques of her readers.

In the twenty-first century, the figure of Barack Obama provided a platform through which to express a qualified optimism about American racial progress.

For many writers and critics, including the fictional Ifemelu and Blaine, his campaign offered an opportunity to express, and try to call into being, a more equitable and just world. Like the technologies that offer Ifemelu a pathway to economic security, the implications of the shifts instantiated by Obama's election are yet to be fully understood. Adichie's novel centers Obama as an archetypal figure for a world in which technology, transportation, and culture have grown only increasingly interconnected. Indeed, both Obama's defenders and his critics have positioned him as an avatar of a cosmopolitan world in which old boundaries are changing. As the ultimate failure of Ifemelu's relationship with Blaine signals, however, those same boundaries, whether between nations or racial categories, remain stubborn in the face of technological, cultural, and governmental shifts.

In that sense, the final three chapters of this book might be accused of glorifying what I have already referred to as a pernicious fiction: that the election of Barack Obama constitutes, in reality, a marker on the road to racial transcendence. The figure of Obama who cameos in Alice Randall's *Rebel Yell* and who provides a useful, if temporary, prop in Ifemelu's slowly deteriorating relationship with Blaine indexes a cosmopolitan future in which the racial individualism of post-Blackness enables diversity without collapsing identities into stifling expressions of collective responsibility. This mythic Obama, despite being consistently belied by the reality of the actual Obama presidency, provides the authors I have discussed with a proxy for post era literary discourses wherein claims of collective responsibility only serve to restrict creative expression. Emphasizing the diversity embedded within identity categories thus serves to militate against claims of any unitary agenda or experience.

Hopefully, through the course of the analyses here, my skepticism of the actuality of this progress has been clear. I say this not just to emphasize that a proliferation of metrics reveals just how little has materially changed for African Americans in the increasingly long period since the waning of "the Movement era" (James 2003; see also Jeffries 2013). The parade of headline-generating police shootings and revived social movements such as Black Lives Matter reveal that the mere passage of time is insufficient to delineate the meaning of as ambiguous an idea as progress.[13] Indeed, the same social media platforms that helped organize protests following the murders of Trayvon Martin, Michael Brown, and others have also been leveraged by governments and multinational corporations to create surveillance regimes unprecedented in history. In other words, post era efforts to idealize the present must always confront the persistence of historical structures of exclusion. On the other hand, as much as the optimism of some of these novels may be premature, the extensiveness of the desire to designate the present as "new" or "post" highlights the attempt to define the current moment in its own terms, not necessarily without reference to the past but without being restricted by it.

It is this desire that Adichie's novel emblematizes, however incompletely. In her declaration of this novel as a "fuck you" to critics and their expectations of African literature and literature by Black authors, she asserts a defiant, and intentionally vulgar, individualism that privileges her own choices and her own definitions for her identity and her art. In contrast to the complex crises experienced by Ifemelu as her responsibility as a writer is repeatedly called into question, Adichie echoes the other authors analyzed in this book in her refusal to accede to discourses of authenticity. This refusal is far from triumphal. As a diasporic analogue to post era theorizing, Selasi describes, in an interview, identifying her generation as "Afropolitans" "from that stranded place" of melancholy and loneliness in a world of overlapping exclusions (Bady and Selasi 2015, 159). Ifemelu, as a character, reflects a similar ambiguity with regard to belonging. She feels shifting forms of allegiance and marginalization that typify the broader post era representations of American racial identities in which the desire for agency and self-definition continually confronts the intractability of systemic and institutionalized racism in American life.

CODA

African American Literature Post-Obama

If the cover of the 2008 issue of *The American Scholar* which contained Charles Johnson's "The End of the Black American Narrative" asked the question of what kind of African American literature is suited to "a Barack Obama world," that question must now be rephrased to ask the same thing about a "post-Obama" world. It is already clear that both Obama as a person and Obama as an archetypal figure remain principal reference points for post-Obama Black aesthetics. Paul Beatty's *The Sellout* (2015), for example, frames its satire through a concluding image expressing skepticism about the progress narrative located in the first Black president. The high profile awards won in 2016 and 2017 by Colson Whitehead, Beatty, and Jesmyn Ward suggest that one avenue of resistance to the Trump administration and the visibility of explicit white supremacy will be the further incorporation of African American literature and culture into dominant institutions to construct a counter-narrative emphasizing cosmopolitanism and diversity.[1] Such incorporation will likely only deepen the tension over the power that institutions like publishing and the academy hold over the kinds of stories Black authors are able to tell. Furthermore, such celebrations of Black art risk instrumentalizing Black artists as tools in ongoing fights over the dimensions of American identity, an extension of the "neoliberal multiculturalism" critiqued by Jodi Melamed.[2] The social construction of race dictates that the boundaries of what constitutes whiteness and Blackness will continue to be in flux. However, demographic changes long predicted by social scientists and the ongoing racial polarization of American politics continues to center racial identity in any analysis of American culture (see Alba and Nee 2003). Post era interrogations of the multiculturalism and diversity discourses first institutionalized in the 1980s thus provide a framework for considering the meaning of these changes. In this context, the importance of identity (in both its individual and collective forms) as a battleground over personal and political agency is likely to persist.

The prefix "post" establishes a temporal distinction. It argues for a transition, in time, between one era and another. As I explained in the introduction, this implied categorical distinction is deceptive. Indeed, rather than marking a clear and definable shift from one moment to the next, the "post" in the post era gestures towards an opening up of definition itself, creating space for new performances of Black identity and new Black literary aesthetics. The implied temporal distinction, however, weights post era literature with questions of progress. Interviews with the authors analyzed in this book resound with frequent questions about how, and in what ways, the literature of the present represents a fundamental difference from the past and how it relates to the alleged progress that the United States has made in the post–civil rights era. These questions cite a relatively common menu of evidence: the expansion of the Black middle- and upper-class; matriculation at elite colleges and universities; the increased visibility of Black authors; the dominance of Black culture, especially hip-hop, in American popular culture; the prominence of African American literary studies; and, most obviously, the election of a Black president. Speaking to what Rolland Murray refers to as the "incorporation" of African American literature into publishing and academic institutions, these questions construct a post era discourse in which the current state of the nation can be described as distinct from its past (Murray 2017, 731). Even those critics and authors who counter this subtle triumphalism with pessimism presume the dominance of a cultural discourse of progress.

Like previous moments in which individual authors sought to interrogate the orthodoxies of Black politics and Black identity, the political backlash to even minimal Black advancement has curtailed some of this discursive emphasis on progress, highlighting the limitations of the post era. The use of social media to widely publicize the longstanding problem of Black men and Black women being subjected to disproportionate violence at the hands of law enforcement and the election of Donald Trump campaigning on an explicit white ethnonationalist platform have motivated even mainstream media outlets to reassess the prematurity of their embrace of post-racialism. In this climate, Touré's subtitle to *Who's Afraid of Post-Blackness?*, "What it means to be Black now," feels hopelessly naïve in its definitiveness (Touré 2011). That said, though the socio-political climate of the late Obama years and early Trump years have blunted the more triumphal strains of post era theorizing, terms such as post-Black name a set of ideas, assumptions, and experiences that persist, and which have prompted questions and controversies that continue to drive early twenty-first century Black aesthetics.

Because of the implied temporality contained in "post" as a term, these theoretical frameworks—whether post-Black art, the post-soul aesthetic, NewBlack, or other permutations—sit uneasily as mere aesthetic descriptors. They were always also political visions of progress towards greater freedom. Thus, as the political context has shifted with the backlash to Black advancement, no matter how superficial it was, aesthetic claims have had to shift to account for that context. Eddie Glaude argues that Michael Brown's murder in Ferguson, Missouri served as "an event that ruptured the illusion of another historic moment: the election of the nation's first black president" (Glaude 2014, n.p.). As Glaude's words indicate, events since Trayvon Martin's murder in 2013 have challenged those articulating post era discourses rooted in progress. In his piece, Glaude rejects the political scientist and media pundit Melissa Harris-Perry's claim that Black Lives Matter arose as an outgrowth of the Obama presidency, arguing instead that it serves as a repudiation of the dominant progress narrative constructed around and through Barack Obama's election. As the post era context makes clear, however, both Glaude and Harris-Perry speak to the uneasy tension of the early twenty-first century, in which the possibilities and limitations of the post–civil rights era coexist.

A split screen image from *CNN* on November 24, 2014, the night that St. Louis County prosecutor Bob McCulloch announced that Darren Wilson would not be indicted for killing Michael Brown in Ferguson, Missouri, elucidates these contradictions. On the left, Barack Obama stands, exercising his preternatural gift for political rhetoric. In this case, he delivers a disquisition on a divided America during a time of racial strife. As I've detailed in this book, President Obama has a complex racial legacy. As the first Black president, he serves as an icon in the Black community, the culmination of over a hundred years of arguments for uplift and exceptionalism. Images of Obama interacting with young Black children are a near cottage industry, the light in their eyes a stand-in for the symbolic importance of seeing people who are like you in positions of power in society. At the same time, Obama maintained much of the expanded post-9/11 security state, which perpetuated racialized bombing campaigns abroad and propped up ongoing American imperialism.

Domestically, the November 24 remarks follow a familiar pattern. As the first Black president, Obama dutifully offers concessions to ongoing structural racism and endemic poverty. He explains that Black communities live within a pervasive surveillance state that leads to mass incarceration. At the same time, the post-racial Obama of the "Most Perfect Union" speech returns, voicing tributes to law enforcement and enjoining Black communities from going beyond non-violent protest, defined narrowly with reference to an idealized myth of the Civil Rights Movement. Here, Obama traverses well-trodden territory. He embraces the distinctiveness of his role as a Black president, using his own experiences to claim authority to speak out against racism. Yet, at the same time, he flees from his racialization, playing the role of a president calling for peace and the dutiful subservience to authority. At the same moment, in the image to his right, people are in the streets. There is smoke or tear gas obscuring part of the screen. There are police and fire department lights.

The end of the Obama presidency offered a stark referendum on the naïve optimism of post-racialism. Donald Trump, though long famous, made his political name as the public face of "birtherism," a conspiracy that questioned the legitimacy of the Obama presidency by challenging his citizenship. If, as I have argued, the core progressive narrative of the post era sees the teleology of American history pointing towards the full incorporation of African Americans into the state, Trump's popularity testifies to the entrenched resistance to full Black citizenship. Trump's campaign ran on explicit racial animus, echoing Ronald Reagan's dog-whistle slogan of "Make America Great Again" as a way to signal that the nation was much better before all these different groups started critiquing it or asking for power. That Trump pulled off a surprising victory in the 2016 election led many to question whether the optimism of the Obama years was simply a naïve cover over lingering rot. It certainly led to the death-knell of the post-racial era. If Obama's election led editors across the country to green light news stories and opinion pieces declaring post-racial America's birth, then Trump's election led to a somewhat smaller but still significant declaration of its death (see, for example, Hannah-Jones 2016; Workneh 2016; Kendi 2016).[3]

Donald Trump's election, thus, prompts urgent questions about the enduring meaning of the post era. Explicit white nationalism is now present in volumes not seen in decades. Racial inequalities endure and deepen as the instruments of the violent Trump-led government terrorize immigrants, both documented and undocumented, and carry out imperialist violence on people of color abroad. Trump's reported declaration that African nations are "shithole countries" during immigration legislation negotiations only underscores the enduring power racial hierarchies hold in the United States (Hirschfield Davis, Stolberg, and Kaplan 2018). Despite that context, however, the post era continues to demonstrate its influence across the activism of the late Obama years and early Trump ones. Key characteristics of ongoing movements—including the rejection of essentialist identity discourses, elevating the experiences and the work of queer and trans activists, and the privileging of individual choices about how to perform Black identity—carry the traces of post era resistance to identity policing.

That said, the increasing visibility of racial violence and white supremacy has led to questions about whether the historical traumas that post era authors so often viewed as burdening are at all historical, and whether maintaining a sense of collective obligation to fight such injustices is necessary. Nearly a decade after mocking the "Southern Novel of Black Misery" as a compulsory script for Black writers (Whitehead 2009b), Colson Whitehead won the National Book Award and Pulitzer Prize for *The Underground Railroad*, a play on the slavery novel as a genre, with the twist that the Underground Railroad is an actual railroad. Whitehead is hardly alone in his return to historical trauma as subject matter in 2016. Paul Beatty's Booker Prize-winning *The Sellout* (2015) is built around a typical post–civil rights figure, raised by his father, a practitioner of "Liberation Psychology," who reinstitutes slavery and Jim Crow in the novel's thinly-veiled fictionalization of Compton, CA. Yaa Gyasi's *Homegoing* (2016), a key entry in the ever-expanding library of works by African immigrant authors in the United States, is a historical epic, traversing hundreds of years to encompass slavery, Jim Crow, and the post–civil rights eras in the United States, as well as colonialism and independence in Ghana. These novels, arriving in the twilight of the Obama years, indicate that some elements of post era theorizing will endure even as its more visibly optimistic visions (think Touré's *Who's Afraid of Post-Blackness?*) are whittled down by repeated reminders of the intractability of American white supremacy.

Despite a generation-defining economic recession (which helped usher in the Obama years), the post–civil rights class divergence in the Black community remains. The Civil Rights Movement, with its triumphant and tragic fifty-year anniversaries (the Civil Rights Act, the Voting Rights Act, the assassination of Martin Luther King Jr.) slips further into the past. New tributaries of Black fiction such as Afrofuturism have burst forth into full-fledged cultural movements, offering new templates for representing the present and envisioning futures that do not just contain Black people but which are defined by their experiences.[4] The triumphant and bold imaginings of Black futurity restructure relationships to historical trauma to allow for visions of liberation and empowerment. The presence of signs at the 2017 Women's March, held to protest President Trump on the day after his inauguration, declaring that "Octavia Warned Us," recognizes that Black writers have always balanced prophetic imagining and pessimism in assessing the possibility of freedom in America and will continue to play an ongoing role in detailing the nation's deficiencies.

Furthermore, the rapid adoption of new technologies has opened spaces for new counter-publics and new ways of articulating Black identity. New cultural institutions and networks such as "Black Twitter" and Afropunk have created avenues for political organizing and cultural discourse while maintaining spaces for nonnormative Blacknesses.[5] Such counter-publics have provided a foundation for the more traditional organizing of Black Lives Matter and a plethora of local movements, which have allowed for the creation of activist networks spanning the nation and the globe. Incorporation of social media and new media into African American literature has been relatively superficial—Adichie's portrait of Ifemelu as "race blogger" comes closest to acknowledging the importance of these platforms within the broader literature—but the ever increasing visibility of current Black genre fiction and revived interest in authors such as Octavia Butler and Samuel Delany that indicate its longstanding presence in the African American literary tradition speaks to a hunger for representations of Black identity not confined to mainstream genres and connected to the interrogation of technology.

Rather than returning to previous models of political organizing or espousing revived nationalist ideologies, Black Lives Matter, and other movements, articulate new visions of liberation that combine the anti-essentialism of the post era with a rigorous analysis of historical and current white supremacy (see Lebron 2017; Taylor 2016).[6] In other words, while Black Lives Matter serves as a galvanizing organizing principal, and a means of making plain the precariousness of Black life within the current white supremacist state, it ultimately demands recognition and incorporation within that same state. This is neither a new nor novel framework for Black politics, which, as Michael Dawson has shown, has made its principal claims on the state in relation to the nation's founding ideals (Dawson 2003, 14). That said, as much as Black Lives Matter signals broader revived protest movement(s) against police violence, economic inequality, sexual violence, and racial injustice, it also resists the problematic sexism and heteronormativity that have often characterized previous protest movements. Started and led by three queer women of color (one of whom, Opal Tometi, is the daughter of Nigerian immigrants), the movement affirms Derek Conrad Murray's argument that post-Blackness is capable of correcting how "the symbolic markers of normative heterosexual blackness fail to resonate with, or even speak to, the histories and lived experiences of female and queer subjectivities" (Murray 2015, 18–19).[7] The presence of Black Lives Matter has paralleled the mainstreaming of scholarly research on intersectionality and afro-pessimism. Intersectionality, coined by law professor Kimberlé Crenshaw in the 1980s, speaks to the invisibility of the experiences of groups such as Black women within traditional anti-discrimination frameworks. Because individuals occupy overlapping subjectivities and categories, the term highlights how political questions cannot be confined to narrow analyses focused solely on race or class or gender or sexuality. Despite backlash to "identity politics" that accuses contemporary activists of trafficking in essentialism, the turn to intersectionality refuses reductive identity policing while acknowledging multiple axes of difference.[8]

Afro-pessimism provides a critique of the temporality foregrounded, however tentatively, during the post era. During the waning years of the Obama presidency, such ontological analyses of Blackness that had been present in scholarly debates provided a philosophical foundation for some strains of Black activism and found popularity in mainstream form in the writing of Ta-Nehisi Coates.[9] Influenced by Orlando Patterson's *Slavery and Social Death* (1982) and philosophers including Lewis Gordon and Sylvia Wynter, afro-pessimism found expression in the writings of Frank Wilderson III, Jared Sexton, and Saidiya Hartman. Developed in dialogue with interlocutors, particularly Fred Moten, afro-pessimism articulates a wholescale critique of modernity as a project instantiated through construction of Blackness as non-being. These scholars argue that the very question of how and if one can measure racial progress is problematic. Afro-pessimist authors, such as Sexton, Hartman, and Wilderson in particular, not only push strongly against valedictory narratives of progress, they also argue against scholarly attempts to ascribe agency to the marginal and the disenfranchised.[10] This rejection of agency explicitly counters post era emphases on the link between the individual capacity for self-definition and the possibility of full Black citizenship in the United States.

As a philosophical critique of how Blackness has been constructed and articulated within Black politics and Black cultural expression, afro-pessimism specifically attacks the progressive teleological narrative that such scholars argue is embedded in the link between movement politics and cultural theorizing. Speaking of Charles Johnson's essay "The End of the Black American Narrative," Sexton argues that Johnson's titular thesis is "unoriginal, poorly drawn, and argued by assertion rather than evidence, but it resonates nonetheless with the political common sense I am attempting to challenge" (Sexton 2010, 42). Sexton encompasses this "political common sense" within his titular concept of "people-of-color-blindness." It is important to note that Sexton refers here not just to color-blindness itself as an ideology, but diverse forms of multiculturalism and even radical coalition building: "The call for paradigm shift has become the hallmark of the post–civil rights era, in which the initiatives of multiracial coalition politics, immigrant rights, liberal multiculturalism, and conservative colorblindness operate uneasily—and often unwittingly—within a broad-based strategic integration" (Sexton 2010, 43). To take just two of his examples, "liberal multiculturalism" and "conservative colorblindness" are, for Sexton, merely flipsides of the same coin, both part and parcel of a larger effort at a strategic integration designed not to overturn anti-Blackness but to mask its continued power. In this sense, Sexton's "color-blindness" is specifically a blindness to Blackness, which serves in this context as the ultimate signifier of race and color that, in its (non)being, makes real all other signifiers. Consequently, Sexton implicitly argues against the myriad of attempts to declare a "paradigm shift" in the post–civil rights era. The "strategic integration" to which he refers—which, in literary terms, speaks to the institutionalization of African American literature and Black studies, the increased publication of African American writers, and the blurring of racial lines with phrases such as "people/writers of color" (a particular target of Sexton's ire)—only re-inscribes anti-Blackness.

Any attempts to imagine new ways of being Black in the present that displace the persistence of anti-Black structures—the "Black American Narrative" in Johnson's terms—serve only to reinforce the very terms they struggle against. Moten refers to this contemporary aspect of Black studies: "The strain of black studies that strains against this interplay of itinerancy and identity—whether in the interest of putting down roots or disclaiming them—could be said, also, to constitute a departure [from black studies], though it may well be into a stasis more severe than the one such work imagines (itself to be leaving)" (Moten 2008, 1745). Moten notes the cyclical process of re-inscription embodied in the resistance to the supposed prescriptiveness of black identity performance. Everything from Golden's idea of "post-black art" to Ellis's "New Black Aesthetic" to post-soul and postrace aesthetics chafe against previous definitions of what it means to be Black, and what it means to make Black art. As Moten notes here, however, such a departure from the past does not ensure the liberation it seeks. It is this restlessness, however, that is so emblematic of twenty-first century African American literature, vacillating between pessimism and optimism over the position of African Americans in the American state in search of self-determination with regard to identity that has been so long denied.

Twenty-first century African American literature seeks to rearticulate the definition of Blackness in terms that allow for self-consciousness even when granting the overriding power of anti-Blackness. This attempt motivates narratives locating the individual within the constellation of racialized power structures in the present. When Valerie Oliver speaks to the central "question of blackness" in recent African American cultural expression, "how blackness manifested in cultural production and, more importantly, how artists could negotiate the paradox of race and identity without the debate of negation" (Oliver 2005, 25), she underscores an unwillingness to capitulate to even the "affirmative nihilism" of afro-pessimism in seeking an incomplete liberation for the blackness manifested in contemporary African American cultural production (Moten 2013, 774).

The post era's temporality, then, is far from definitive. It represents a series of tentative attempts to posit new ways of imagining the position of Black people within the United States. The visibility of Black people and Black culture within American and global popular culture and their incorporation into academic and media institutions has not waned even as it has generated cultural backlash. Though rejecting the essentialism that often exists within claims of collective identity, the post era has not questioned either the history or cultural traditions that form the foundation of racial filiation. Instead, African American fiction in the twenty-first century has attempted to connect political freedom with agency over racial identity performance. The dynamic dialogue this creates between continued anti-racist activism, the recognition of how racial, and other, identities shape an individual's positionality within society, and an emphasis on individual identity performance provides fertile soil for an era of new social movements as it responds to the explicit racism and ethnonationalism of Donald Trump and his supporters. Post era rearticulations of Black identity thus provide a necessary context for analyzing African American literature in a post-Obama world, though it remains unclear what its exact contours will be. Consequently, instead of closing with a concrete prediction of where African American identity and culture are going, I hope that this book serves as a roadmap for the diverse strains of Black thought that, through their conflict and interplay, will continue to help chart the way forward.

NOTES

INTRODUCTION. THE POST ERA

1. The question of whether the "posts" contained within the ongoing proliferation of "post" categories are related to each other is an important one, though somewhat beyond the scope of this book. Discussing the "post-(fill in the blank)" rhetoric that attended Barack Obama's election in 2008, Catherine Squires and other scholars debated (and ultimately dismissed) whether that moment was a "tipping point" on the long march towards America's perfectible future (Squires et al. 2010, 212). In doing so, these scholars affirmed the problematic relationship that "post" has with progress narratives and linked it to a utopian sensibility, not just an assertion of temporal distinction.

2. Fred Moten usefully distinguishes between analyzing Blackness, which is the focus of this book, and Black people when he explains that to "say that blackness is intrinsically experimental is not the same thing as to say that black people are intrinsically experimental" (quoted in Hayes and Shockley 2009, 130).

3. One major example is *The Trouble with Post-Blackness* (Baker and Simmons 2015), in which a version of Crawford's introduction first appeared. Though the volume is titled with a general reference to "post-blackness," it almost exclusively engages with Touré's book *Who's Afraid of Post-Blackness?: What It Means to Be Black Now* rather than the term's origins in visual art. This focus on Touré allows the authors to rebut his more explicit focus on a neoliberal "rugged individualism" that emphasizes individual success. These critiques broadly celebrate the present's expanded repertoire of Black identity performance but argue against the tendency among post-Black writers (especially Touré) to sever that expansion from the history of Black culture. They also dispute the value of an emphasis on Blackness in such individualistic terms absent a similar deconstruction of whiteness and the continued power of the white gaze to render Black people precarious.

4. For background on key predecessors to the post era, see McKnight, who actually coined the term "cultural mulatto" (1989), and argued for the inadequacy of the concept of Blackness in his essay "Confessions of a Wannabe Negro" (1993, see also Early 1993). Gates argued that the post–civil rights era shifts to which McKnight and Trey Ellis referred had provided the basis for a coherent aesthetic movement he labeled the "fourth renaissance" (Gates 1997). Nelson George published his book *Buppies, B-Boys, BAPS, and Bohos: Notes on Post-Soul Black Culture* with a preface opening "this book is about the culture of African-Americans who've come of age since the demise of the civil rights movement in the late '60s" (1992, xi). George's book celebrates post–civil rights Black creativity by emphasizing the diversity of its expression. Though all these writings refer to an earlier era of Black

literary and cultural expression than the twenty-first century authors that are my focus, their emphasis on aesthetics of hybridity, exploration, and play all presage the concerns which dominate the post era (see also Tate 1992).

5. Soyica Diggs Colbert discusses this idea with reference to Hamza Walker's essay in the *Freestyle* exhibition book in which Thelma Golden coins the term "post-black art." In his essay, Walker (2001) claims Blackness as a choice, despite its historical relationship to the marginalization his essay title, "Renigged," highlights. Colbert argues that Walker's emphasis on his own agency "amounts to a fundamental shift in the operation of blackness" because it moves from the "interracial exchange" that defined Du Bois's formulation of double consciousness to an "intraracial one" (Colbert 2017, 14–15).

6. In another clip, Wright excoriates the United States government for its racism, its imperialism and terrorism abroad, and its consistent lies used to defend such actions with the statement "No, no, no! Not God Bless America. God damn America" (Wright 2003).

7. As Carpio puts it, "We are nearly three hundred pages into the text at this point, having been presented with plenty of evidence for Obama's dark view of race relations in America. Only in this context can one understand why, for Obama, it takes *audacity* to hope that they will change for the better" (Carpio 2011, 79).

8. Interestingly, though Crawford also invokes a framework of "more than black" in reference to Carolyn Rodgers's 1970 poem "What Color Is Lonely," her usage of the phrase does not refer to Obama's words, but rather to the simultaneous "feeling of blacklessness and the sense that there is something more than black" that Rodgers evokes in her poem (Crawford 2015, 33). I take Obama's phrase as my title to suggest something similar to the idea that Crawford develops, the simultaneous sense of rootedness and transcendence gestured towards in the "more than."

9. While Obama has repeatedly argued that his election is not indicative of a post-racial America, and that he personally does not buy into the concept of post-racialism, Sumi Cho (2009, 1621–24) argues that Obama and his campaign operated within a post-racialist framework, allowing and encouraging the argument that he is indeed a post-racial figure.

10. Murray uses Ellis's essay to pose the question of "what happens to African American cultural expression once it is no longer an emergent subfield vying for legitimacy and becomes established at the center of the dominant culture" (Murray 2017, 727)? He employs the term "incorporation" to "[foreground] the consonance between corporate capital and liberal institutionalization" (Murray 2017, 731).

11. For the purposes of this book, I focus on the use of the phrase "post-black art" by Thelma Golden and "post-Blackness" by Touré because Womack's use of the term is confined to her title and a brief discussion in the introduction rather than specifically engaging in its theorization. However, her use of the term is thematically linked to Touré's expansion of Golden's more limited definition to cover a full generation of African Americans.

12. Paul C. Taylor documents a similar resistance among the visual artists that were a part of Golden's *Freestyle* exhibition and others in "Post-Black, Old Black" (Taylor 2007, 627–28).

13. As Levy-Hussen asks, "What would it look like to read contemporary black writing neither as the redemptive guardian of an 'ethical relationship to the past' nor as the nefarious guarantor of a prescriptive vision of black identity, forever tethered to the irredeemable wounds of the slave past?" (Levy-Hussen 2016, 16). Levy-Hussen's analysis gains its power through its focus on the ubiquitous contemporary narratives of slavery that have been the focus of so much of the scholarship on contemporary African American literature. That focus, however, misses how post era fiction navigates a similar question in an attempt to establish a temporal shift in Black culture.

14. As Melamed puts it, the presence of multiculturalist literature in colleges builds on ideologies that rely on "assumptions about the transparency of literature, the close and intimate access it offers to racialized others, its authenticity and representativeness, and its power to transform attitudes in a way that guarantees social progress" (Melamed 2011, 45).

15. As Squires details in *The Post-Racial Mystique: Media and Race in the Twenty-First Century*, "Post-racial rhetoric surged during the historic 2008 election" and is "widespread and ecumenical in media" (Squires 2014, 4–5). Squires's argument that "Post-racial discourses resonate with neoliberal discourses because of their shared investment in individual-level analysis and concern with individual freedoms" (Squires 2014, 4–5) supports my claims regarding both the possibilities and limits of the post era turn towards an individualistic understanding of Black identity. On the other hand, that post era discourses resonate with post-racial neoliberalism does not mean that they share a similar facile erasure of structural racism. Instead, post era discourses trace a shift in the relationship between individual Black artists and the acknowledgement of ongoing structural racism.

16. While the specific period covered by the Civil Rights Movement and thus the post–civil rights era remains a contested scholarly question (see Dowd Hall 2005), in rough terms, the post–civil rights era covers the period from the mid to late 1970s through the present. However, my analysis also argues that the era surrounding the election of Barack Obama constitutes the beginning of a new era transitioning away from the post–civil rights era.

17. Marable defined "postblack politics" as "the rise of African American political candidates who have relatively few connections with organic black social and political formations and institutions, and consciously minimise their identity as 'minority' or 'black'" (1993, 63). He premises this shift on the "regrettable, yet unavoidable fact" that most white voters will not vote for a Black candidate.

18. Marable identifies Obama as part of a cohort of postblack politicians who "were convinced that most whites would embrace, and vote for, a remarkable, qualified presidential candidate *who happened to be black*" (2009, 6, italics in original). Many of those politicians, such as Cory Booker, Deval Patrick, and others remain important figures in Democratic politics.

19. Obama's first bid for national political office was a primary challenge for the House of Representatives seat held by former Black Panther Bobby Rush. Although he lost this election, Obama positioned himself as representative of an ascendant multiracial coalition in contrast to Rush, who he argued was part of Chicago's black political machine (see Remnick 2010, 313–33).

20. Famously, Obama's speech refuses to condemn Rev. Jeremiah Wright's rhetoric as anti-American, but only through a context in which it is balanced against the legitimate grievances of white people who harbor potentially racist views. The end of the speech functions almost like a parable, wherein Obama details a meeting in which a young white woman named Ashley from South Carolina is organizing a "mostly African American community" (Obama 2009, 250). In doing so, she explains the struggles she had growing up with a parent's illness and poverty. As she asks the others in the room why they have come to the meeting, an elderly Black man hesitates, and then says, "I'm here because of Ashley" (Obama 2009, 250). Obama uses this story to model the intergenerational and interracial recognition that he sees his campaign as embodying. Rather than standing as a monument of a past struggle, or a reminder of still existent racism, the older Black man in the story authorizes a form of post-racial politics.

21. As Harris states, there is a certain irony in the presence of a Black man in the Presidency serving under the "condition that issues specific to racial inequality not be prioritized in his administration" (Harris 2012, 173). For more, see especially Harris 2012, chapter 6.

22. Asha Best (2012), for example, cautions against a body of scholarship "that arrives at an understanding of a post-race discourse through ontological studies of multiculturalism or mixed-race people" (Best 2012, para. 6). Ralina Joseph's book *Transcending Blackness: From the New Millennium Mulatta to the Exceptional Multiracial* (2012) traces how the twin archetypes her title identifies coopts mixed-race individuals into white supremacist hierarchies that perpetuate anti-blackness.

23. Schmidt discusses the exclusively "male protagonists" found within his sources on page 12 of his book. Interestingly, he provides a useful footnote (on page 16) in which he distinguishes the overriding maleness of literary post-Blackness from the greater gender diversity of other media forms.

CHAPTER 1. ON THE BLACKNESS OF POST-BLACKNESS: COLSON WHITEHEAD AND RACIAL INDIVIDUALISM

1. As Smith and King note in *Still a House Divided*, in selected high-status professions, "from 1940 to 2008, African Americans substantially increased their presence in various professions in both absolute and percentage terms, with the greatest increases coming after 1970 (the percentages of black doctors and college teachers actually declined from 1940 to 1970)" (Smith and King 2011, 269). However, "Although those numbers confirm striking advances for African Americans and Latinos after 1970, . . . they show that African Americans, who made up a little over 12.8 percent of the U.S. population in 2008, are still significantly underrepresented in relation to their population share in the higher paid educated professions, as in political offices" (Smith and King 2011, 269–70).

2. Recent work on linked fate shows its possible diminution in the new century (from around 80 percent or more of survey respondents agreeing that "what happens to black people in this country will have something to do with what happens in your life" to around 60–65 percent), as well as the fact that such sentiments exist across the full range of identity categories rather than being a unique driver of African American political trends (Gay, Hochschild, and White 2016, 121).

3. Whitehead aligns himself with Ishmael Reed, Jean Toomer, Clarence Major, and Charles Wright in constructing a lineage of the "black intellectual novel" in the course of the interview.

4. Golden coined the term in the exhibition catalogue for the *Freestyle* exhibition at the Studio Museum in Harlem in 2001. *Freestyle* centered on a diverse set of young African American artists to assess the meaning of Black art in the new century. The exhibition followed Golden curating several notable exhibitions at the Whitney Museum of American Art, including the 1993 Biennial and the "Black Male" exhibition in 1995, both of which generated controversy for their focus on race and racism in the art world (see Jones 2012).

5. Transcriptions from Golden's talk at the Tate were made by the author.

6. As Michele Elam beautifully puts it, "Passers, in their supposed orbit of a racial norm, in fact generate that very norm, define it as the circumference defines the circle" (Elam 2011, 99).

7. Two canonical examples of the "scene of instruction" are found in W. E. B. Du Bois's classic *The Souls of Black Folk* and James Weldon Johnson's *The Autobiography of an Ex-Colored Man*. In both cases, the young African American child is educated to the meaning of race in the context of the schoolyard. Du Bois, for example, describes the scene in the following terms:

I was a little thing, away up in the hills of New England, where the dark Housatonic winds between Hoosac and Taghkanic to the sea. In a wee wooden schoolhouse, some-thing put it into the boys' and girls' heads to buy gorgeous visiting-cards—ten cents a package—and exchange. The exchange was merry, till one girl, a tall newcomer, refused my card,—refused it peremptorily, with a glance. Then it dawned upon me with a certain suddenness that I was different from the others; or like, mayhap, in heart and life and longing, but shut out from their world by a vast veil. I had thereafter no desire to tear down that veil, to creep through; I held all beyond it in common contempt, and lived above it in a region of blue sky and great wandering shadows. (Du Bois [1903] 1999, 10)

In line with Du Bois, Johnson's description also emphasizes the school setting.

One day near the end of my second term at school the principal came into our room and, after talking to the teacher, for some reason said: "I wish all of the white scholars to stand for a moment." I rose with the others. The teacher looked at me and, call-ing my name, said: "You sit down for the present, and rise with the others." I did not quite understand her, and questioned: 'Ma'm?' She repeated, with a softer tone in her voice: "You sit down now, and rise with the others." I sat down dazed. I saw and heard nothing. When the others were asked to rise, I did not know it. When school was dismissed, I went out in a kind of stupor. . . . I looked up into her face and repeated: "Tell me, mother, am I a nigger?" There were tears in her eyes and I could see that she was suffering for me. And then it was that I looked at her critically for the first time. (Johnson [1927] 1989, 16)

8. It is worth noting here that, in addition to revising the scene of instruction, Whitehead revises a line from Langston Hughes's poem "Ask Your Mama." In that work, Hughes sug-gests that the verbal structure of the dozens, the statement "ask your mama," takes on the form of violence as a response to someone asking "would it rub off" about his blackness (Hughes 1995, 480). With the scene's nod to Hughes, Whitehead mirrors both his indebted-ness to the African American literary tradition and his revision of it. As opposed to Hughes's verbal play, neither the vernacular rhetorical strategies of the pre-civil rights era nor the literal resistance of the civil rights era present themselves as strategies to Benji. It is not that Benji is incapable of summoning or living within these traditions. Indeed, throughout the novel, Whitehead is quite attentive to the position of the new generation he represents in relation to African American literature. However, just as Whitehead draws on Hughes with-out mirroring his rhetorical response to racism, *Sag Harbor* signals that it is of the tradition but not bound by it.

9. Both Maus (2014, 108–12) and Andrea Levine (2011, 170–87) also center this scene in their analysis of the novel. They argue that the scene illustrates the violence and darkness under the novel's seemingly light surface and associate that violence with Benji's father and his precarious sense of what it means to have made it as a Black man of his generation. My analysis here is not meant to dismiss the violence of Benji's father, which indeed does structure much of the novel. Instead, my intent is to emphasize the importance of the shift in this scene from the structures of societal racism, located outside the family unit, to the more individualized trauma of abuse, which is related to structural racism (and patriarchy, as Levine illustrates) but in a less deterministic way.

10. As I mention above in note 2, recent research does seem to show some loosening in the sense of linked fate expressed by African American survey respondents. See Gay, Hochschild, and White 2016.

11. Sandra Adell argues that double consciousness serves as "a founding concept . . . for an ontology of blackness upon which is grounded the Black American literary tradition" (Adell 1994, 11).

12. The literary incorporation of Du Boisian double consciousness is a common strategy in African American literature at least as far back as James Weldon Johnson's *The Autobiography of an Ex-Colored Man*, published anonymously in 1912, only nine years after *The Souls of Black Folk*.

13. The two Greedos refers to George Lucas's digital revision of the original *Star Wars*. In the original, Han Solo shoots Greedo without provocation. In the digital rerelease of the film, Lucas controversially edited the film so that Greedo shoots first, thus diminishing Han Solo's responsibility for his actions.

14. For example, Lyndon Baines Johnson explained his support for affirmative action programs in his commencement speech at Howard University in 1965 using the race metaphor: "You do not take a person who, for years, has been hobbled by chains and liberate him, bring him up to the starting line of a race and then say, 'you are free to compete with all the others,' and still justly believe that you have been completely fair." For full speech, see Johnson 1965.

15. Whitehead has expressed a similar dislike of the post discourses that have surrounded the criticism of his work. He penned a satirical op-ed for the *New York Times* in 2009 called "The Year of Living Post-Racially," which specifically critiqued the claim that Barack Obama's election signaled a post-racial era, but he has also pushed back against descriptions of himself as a post-black artist in interviews, as Andrea Levine points out. See Levine, 181.

CHAPTER 2. "KATRINA IS THE MOTHER WE WILL REMEMBER UNTIL THE NEXT MOTHER": APOCALYPTIC STORMS AND THE SLOW VIOLENCE OF STRUCTURAL RACISM

1. Though much of the coverage of the storm focused on Black poverty, it is critical to note that "all strata of the black community was wiped out by the flooding" (Ya Salaam 2007, xiii).

2. The concert/benefit during which West made his remarks aired on NBC and NBC affiliated networks (including MSNBC and CNBC) on September 2, 2005. West's remarks deviated from a pre-written script. After his statement about President Bush, his microphone was cut off.

3. For a detailed examination of the various forms of neoliberal development that played out in the wake of the storm, see Johnson, *The Neoliberal Deluge*. Adrienne Dixson, in particular, documents the fundamental transformation of New Orleans public schools through the elimination of traditional public schools and the implementation of charter schools (Dixson 2011, 130–51). Since Dixson published her essay in 2011, the school district has become nearly entirely composed of charter schools. In 2016, control was returned from the post-hurricane Recovery School District (which took over "failed" schools) back to the local district after this transformation had taken place (see also Zernike 2016).

4. My use of "anti-Blackness" throughout this chapter is intended to invoke the distinction that Frank Wilderson III makes between anti-Blackness and white supremacy. As he argues, the reparative structure of white supremacy is political incorporation and "full

speech" (Wilderson 2010, 90–91). In contrast, anti-Blackness as a conceptual apparatus marks the totality of the marginalization explored by Wilderson and other afro-pessimist scholars, in which "the social distinction between Whites (or Humans) and Blacks can be neither assessed nor redressed by way of signifying practices alone because the social distinction between life and death cannot be spoken" (Wilderson 2010, 91).

5. Ward might be accused of feeding into many of the same stereotypes as those bell hooks blamed the popular independent film *Beasts of the Southern Wild* for perpetuating. hooks accuses the film of feeding into the image of Black people as closer to nature, the pathological representation of the violent Black father, of idealizing poverty and presenting it as an interracial utopia, and ultimately of imagining its setting, The Bottom, as a quasi-state of nature (hooks 2012). Zora Neale Hurston's *Their Eyes Were Watching God* ([1937] 1990), a novel that depicts the effects of the 1928 Okeechobee hurricane that hit the state of Florida that Ward references in *Salvage the Bones*, was similarly accused of feeding into negative stereotypes by other writers of the New Negro Renaissance. Richard Wright, for example, said in his review of the book that "Miss Hurston *voluntarily* continues in her novel the tradition which was *forced* upon the Negro in the theatre, that is, the minstrel technique that makes the 'white folks' laugh" (Wright 1937, 25).

6. Between 1953 and 1978, the National Hurricane Center used only feminine names for hurricanes before the adoption of a system of naming derived from lists created by an international body that alternates masculine and feminine sounding names.

7. Interview subjects for Spike Lee's film *When the Levees Broke: A Requiem in Four Acts* describe the wind in these terms. See, especially, interviews during acts one and two (Lee 2006).

8. Naimou also usefully links archival, recuperative, and salvage projects with the construction of legal personhood and citizenship. As I argue throughout this chapter, the marginalization experienced by the characters subject to the "slow violence" of racism and the hurricane and its aftermath marks the structural exclusion of Black people from the American state. In contrast to efforts geared towards inclusion within that state within other post discourses, Ward's and Laymon's novels emphasize a counternarrative that rejects the terms of that inclusion.

9. Christine Levecq maintains, "*Kindred* installs markers that profoundly question the process of discovering or recovering history. Yet it also depicts that very process at great lengths and in a realistic fashion, elaborately redeeming it from relativism, and consequently creating the space for the development of a speculative philosophy of history" (Levecq 2000, 526).

10. Marc Steinberg, for example, describes the relationship between Butler's themes and the novel's formal structure thusly: "Content and form intersect in the novel as the veiling of temporal boundaries blurs the notion of slavery transcended. By zigzagging the time frame of the novel from past to present, Butler points to ways in which past and present become interchangeable. She also writes of plausible historical actions and relationships, 'filling in' possible gaps that may be evident in classic slave narratives" (Steinberg 2004, 467).

11. As Larry Neal puts it "We can learn more about what poetry is by listening to the cadences in Malcolm's speeches, than from most of Western poetics. Listen to James Brown scream. Ask yourself, then; Have you ever heard a Negro poet sing like that? Of course not, because we have been tied to the texts, like most white poets. The text could be destroyed and no one would be hurt in the least by it" (Neal 2007, 653).

12. As Daniel Perlstein argues in a history of such schools, their pedagogical model was based partially on the Highlander Folk School in Tennessee, where so many SNCC

activists were trained. This model of "participatory education was based on the conviction that responses to oppression had to grow out of the experiences of the oppressed. In order to generalize from their experiences and discover solutions to their problems, oppressed people had to analyze them collectively. Highlander's task was not to dictate 'correct' answers to activists, rather staff asked questions in order to kindle exchanges through which grassroots activists could articulate concrete concerns, analyze them with others who had had similar experiences, and develop actions" (Perlstein 1990, 306).

13. The most visible example of this phenomenon comes with Barack Obama's frequent lectures directed at Black audiences for failing to preserve traditional family structures, to emphasize educational attainment, and violating the politics of respectability. His administration even launched the "My Brother's Keeper" initiative to address the very real barriers to success experienced by young Black men through an emphasis on individual initiative and traditional uplift rhetoric.

CHAPTER 3. "NEW AND BETTER STORIES": CRAFTING A LITERATURE TO FIT A BARACK OBAMA WORLD

1. Interestingly, just as Johnson argues that "many of Du Bois's remarks now sound ironic" given the progress over the past 80 plus years, his own remarks, a decade old as I write this, are almost humorous in the modesty of the declaration around then-candidate Obama. In this, Johnson's words say perhaps more than he intends, serving as a record of the continued doubt, right up until the moment it happened, that America would elect a Black president. Rather than forecast the legitimate chance that Obama would become president, Johnson signals that even the mere possibility of his major party candidacy is enough to instantiate a "Barack Obama world" in which the narrative of "victimization" is obsolete.

2. For example, the description of Soulcatcher's tattoo at the end of *Oxherding Tale*, a novel which otherwise superficially resembles the canonical Black American narrative, presents the vision of a palimpsest of interconnected souls in the person of the slave catcher, endlessly changing, layering, and shifting (Johnson [1982] 2005, 175–76).

3. Whitehead's choice of barbed wire as the product manufactured by the Winthrop company is also instructive. Barbed wire erects a passive barrier that works both through deterrence and injury if necessary. By associating the renaming of the town with the rise of Winthrop, Whitehead suggests that the very necessity of official naming (as opposed to the less formalized "Freedom") directly correlates with violent exclusion. In other words, the very act of naming is a drawing of a boundary that is policed in a manner that can directly cause injury. Furthermore, the association suggests that names and labels are "barbed," suggesting both their capacity to harm and their implicit aggression.

4. Jesse Cohn (2009) reads the limp as a reference to Oedipus, and the novel as a riff on Sophocles.

5. Whitehead's plot echoes real attempts to market "flesh-colored" band-aids to different racial groups. For example, see Malo 2013.

6. Chow argues that "The ethnic is both the universal, the condition in which everyone can supposedly situate herself, *and* the local, the foreign, the outside, the condition that, in reality, only some people, those branded 'others,' (are made to) inhabit" (Chow 2002, 28, emphasis in original). The Apex band-aids in Whitehead's novel echo the duality of universalism (i.e. everyone is ethnic because everyone marks themselves by association

with a particular band-aid color) and boundary-marking in violation of that universalism (everyone must declare their ethnicity and difference).

7. "Schwa," in linguistics, refers to the unstressed central vowel sound in a word. Beatty's use of the term to refer to Stone, then, analogizes his position to that of the off-beat, which produces syncopation in jazz through its emphasis.

8. For an ethnography of crate digging and sampling, see Schloss 2004.

9. Beatty's point here is interestingly directed at Black male authors. In the past, whole satires constructed around this idea have indicted the rise of Black women's literature with embodying a market for essentialist fiction. Ishmael Reed's misogynistic satire *Reckless Eyeballing* (1986), Trey Ellis's *Platitudes* (1988), and Percival Everett's satirical version of Sapphire's *PUSH* in his novel *Erasure* (2001) all portray the market for Black women's literature as distorted through essentialist fictions of abject Blackness. In this case, Beatty turns some of that satire around, pointing towards many of the "intellectual" counterparts to that genre category as participating in the same racialist narrative construction. By doing so, Beatty raises the troubling question of whether any form of African American writing can detach itself from the "Black American narrative."

10. As L. H. Stallings (2013) argues, Beatty's repeated satirical critiques of Wynton Marsalis throughout the novel interrogate the ongoing validity of the New Black Aesthetic. In that essay, Trey Ellis cites Marsalis as a representative artist. However, while I find Stallings's argument provocative, Marsalis's work has shifted towards a conservative traditionalism in the years since Ellis wrote his piece. Furthermore, he has become one of the most powerful figures in the institutionalization of Black culture through his role as the artistic director of Jazz at Lincoln Center. It is those shifts which Beatty critiques, not necessarily the more insurgent cultural role he played earlier in his life.

CHAPTER 4. THE AUDACITY OF HOPE JONES: ALICE RANDALL'S *REBEL YELL* AND THE IDEALIZATION OF BARACK OBAMA

1. Joseph R. Winters offers a book-length analysis of "hope" as a political construction in relation to contemporary Blackness in *Hope Draped in Black: Race, Melancholy, and the Agony of Progress*. In that book, he argues that hope need not imply either optimism or teleological progress (see Winters 2016, 4–7; 224–29).

2. Leonard Pitts, in his novel *Grant Park* (2016), also directly positions Obama as the culmination of the civil rights struggles of the 1960s, symbolically linking a plot to kill the newly elected president with the assassination of Martin Luther King Jr.

3. Du Bois writes in his essay "The Talented Tenth" (1903) that "the Negro race, like all races, is going to be saved by its exceptional men" (Du Bois 1903, 32). Randall's novel specifically focuses on those Du Bois includes in in this segment of the Black community. With the term "mythology," she underscores not only Du Bois's argument in his canonical essay, but also the self-identification of the Black elite she represents with its sense of being "exceptional," both in terms of personal worth and responsibility to the larger Black community.

4. Hope's statement feels especially dissonant in dialogue with Obama's memoir *Dreams from My Father*, which is subtitled "A Story of Race and Inheritance." Obama centralizes his struggle with the history of racial oppression in the United States and colonialism in Kenya. In his 2004 introduction to the reissue of his memoir, Obama states that the book, which was commissioned after Obama became the first Black editor-in-chief of the *Harvard*

Law Review, was intended to "speak in some way to the fissures of race that have characterized the American experience, as well as the fluid state of identity" (Obama 2004, vii). As
Obama's words make clear, experiencing one's Blackness "through the lens of being formerly
enslaved" is central to how racial identity is lived and performed in the United States regardless of one's own specific ancestry. Furthermore, while it is narrowly accurate to say that
Obama lacks an enslaved ancestor of African descent, some research suggests that he does
have enslaved ancestors through his mother, in addition to the enslaved ancestors of his wife
Michelle (Goldstein 2012).

5. It is no accident that Randall's characterization of Abel subtly alludes to his queerness.
There is a certain Orientalism at work in how the novel suggests that he feels free enough
to live his sexuality openly only in the context of imperialist missions in Southeast Asia
for the CIA. However, Abel's queerness underscores Derek Conrad Murray's argument for
post-Blackness as "a particularly queer phenomenon: one where the masculinist dogma
surrounding black authenticity has outlived its usefulness" (Murray 2016, 21). The civil rights
inheritance that Abel gets from his father is a specifically masculinist one, focalized in charismatic male leadership and the burdens of representing the race. Abel's suppression of his
sexual desires beyond his CIA tenure, and his adoption of an extreme heteronormative white
family structure after divorcing Hope, connects the confinement of his racialized inheritance
with an inability to acknowledge his sexuality. In other words, Abel is unable to participate in
liberating himself because of the stifling masculinism he inherits from his father.

6. In the text of Obama's speech, Seamus refers to the marine Seamus Ahearn, who
Obama met and befriended while campaigning in Illinois, and who he mentions rhetorically
to illustrate the consequences of the Iraq War, in which Abel has fictionally been such a large
participant. In the context of the speech, Obama's question, "Are we serving Seamus as well
as he is serving us?" balances his own stated opposition to the Iraq War, and his advocacy for
a candidate, in John Kerry, who voted for its authorization (see Obama 2004).

7. Even without an African American candidate running, President George W. Bush, who
Abel works for, received just 9 percent of the Black vote in 2000, and 11 percent of the Black
vote in 2004, according to the Roper Center at the University of Connecticut (for full data,
see Roper Center 2000 and Roper Center 2004).

8. Randall's novel provides one of the most visible examinations of Black Republicans in
contemporary African American literature. Leah Wright Rigueur argues, in her history of Black
Republicans, that critics of this "relatively small group of black men and women" (Rigueur 2014,
5) most often try to cast them as "traitorous" or "apologists" for oppressive governance (Rigueur
2014, 3). Randall takes a slightly different tack, however, in her novel. Rather than portraying
the Black Republican as some sort of "racial turncoat" (to use Rigueur's phrase), she characterizes Black conservatism as a legitimate strain of Black political ideology and Abel's party affiliation as a product of a son rejecting his father. For more, see Rigueur 2014.

9. Randall clearly implies that Abel conducts a sexual relationship with Nicholas, a fellow
spy, during his tenure with the CIA in the Philippines.

10. Randall's novel frames Abel's death as the product of a deliberate act on his part.
While he dies from an allergic reaction, and with the intervention (however slow, as I
discuss later in the chapter) of medical personnel, Randall makes it clear that the product
of Hope's investigation into Abel's death is the revelation of his suicide. My language in this
chapter seeks to emphasize the ambiguity of Abel's act, while making his choice to die clear.

11. Todd Boyd has argued that basketball and Black music provide the "two rarefied
spaces where the most fundamental elements of Blackness are articulated and played out,

both internally and for the masses" (Boyd 2003, 12). Boyd's argument typifies a broader association between Blackness and basketball that Obama invokes in his autobiography in choosing the basketball court as the symbolic space in which he seeks to negotiate his racial identity.

12. The scene of such a rupture is a recurring trope throughout the African American literary tradition. For example, Du Bois describes it as follows: "Then it dawned upon me with a certain suddenness that I was different from the others; or like, mayhap, in heart and life and longing, but shut out from their world by a vast veil. I had thereafter no desire to tear down that veil, to creep through; I held all beyond it in common contempt, and lived above it in a region of blue sky and great wandering shadows" (Du Bois [1903] 1999, 10).

13. Aida Levy-Hussen offers a sharply different reading of this scene than that which I have performed here. Using affect theory, Levy-Hussen argues that Abel's lie about abuse (which she goes as far as labeling "rape") serves as a way to "capture something authentic about how mercy felt like violence and likely also about Abel's adolescent feelings toward patriarchal power and disciplinary violence" (Levy-Hussen 2016, 127). Levy-Hussen, in other words, argues that the arc of the novel is not towards the revelation of untruth, but instead an exploration of how the multiple narratives that the novel contains "might entail something more like an art of approximation, whose success is measured through resonance with, or felt closeness to, an original expression" (Levy-Hussen 2016, 126). While I find her reading provocative and useful, incorporating the presence of Barack Obama as a decisive figure in Abel's character arc provides the novel's telos, connecting Abel's ability to reveal his lie with his own transfer of generational power to his son, who the novel connects directly with Barack Obama (see Levy-Hussen 2016, 119–29).

14. Randall's representation of Hawai'i fits into both the broad-based cultural myth of the islands as a multicultural utopia as well the exoticism that underlies the tourist industry. In doing so, Randall associates Obama with the indigenous individuals she mentions, without any substantial engagement with the United States government's illegal overthrow of the kingdom she invokes. Because of the unique history of colonialism in Hawai'i, J. Kēhaulani Kauanui argues that "civil rights, as a political project . . . is insufficient for indigenous and other colonized peoples and the ongoing and often pressing questions of sovereignty and nationhood" (Kauanui 2008, 636). Randall, however, does not symbolically isolate Obama from the political project of civil rights by invoking his Hawai'ian birth. Instead, she positions the state as simultaneously of the United States yet distinct from the history of the nation within which Abel resides, to construct a pathway for Obama's subsequent replacement of Abel within that history. For a further discussion of the complex relationship between civil rights politics and settler colonialism in Hawai'i, see Kauanui 2008 and, especially, Trask 1993.

15. This quote, along with the representation of Obama's birth in Hawai'i, reveals a disturbing dismissal of the history of settler colonialism in the United States. In this case, the invocation of Winthrop ignores the genocide and displacement of millions of indigenous peoples in early America just as the exoticization of the indigenous Hawai'ian king and queen elides the specific role of the United States government in overthrowing the independent kingdom of Hawai'i.

16. With regard to Reed's point, however, I concur with Joseph R. Winters that "because every idea travels and takes on new contexts during its journey," one cannot limit Du Bois's claims to their specific historical context, no matter how useful that exercise is in determining the concept's meaning to Du Bois (Winters 2016, 78).

17. The connection between citizenship and Randall's description of Obama as unhyphenated calls to mind repeated attempts to delegitimize Barack Obama by marking him as foreign, demanding the release of his birth certificate to prove his eligibility for office. Randall first published *Rebel Yell* on July 1, 2009, just less than six months after President Obama's first inauguration. While the degree of Randall's incorporation of the backlash to Obama's candidacy and presidency is unclear, false rumors of Obama's foreignness circulated throughout 2008, and as early as his Illinois campaign for Senator. Consequently, her portrayal of him as "unhyphenated" persists despite a likely familiarity with the presence of such a racialized backlash. For a history of "birtherism," see Smith and Tau 2011.

18. According to Remnick, Obama's campaign sought to distance itself from race as a topic, despite its relevance and presence in the larger discourse. Remnick explains that the Obama campaign had initially asked Jeremiah Wright to "deliver an invocation" at Obama's "announcement speech" (Remnick 2010, 468). However, following an interview with Wright that appeared at the same time in *Rolling Stone* magazine, the campaign sought to distance itself from Wright's racial rhetoric by retracting the invitation. The early stages of the Obama campaign suggest the twin struggles that Obama had faced as an individual throughout his life: first, demonstrating he was authentically Black, and second, showing that he was not Black in any radical way. Remnick recounts the steps that the campaign took to regulate the discourse on race. In the wake of the *Rolling Stone* interview with Wright, as well as statements condemning the campaign's decision to distance themselves from Wright by key Black intellectuals Tavis Smiley and Cornel West (Remnick 2010, 472–73), the campaign initiated an "advisory council on race that included Cornel West and Charles Ogletree" (Remnick 2010, 474). Further, as Remnick quotes Chicago political strategist Don Rose as saying, the campaign made an effort to distance themselves from "radioactive blacks" (Remnick 2010, 477). Rose further notes something that many political scientists have noted in the aftermath of the 2008 campaign: "Obama referred to race in his stump speeches infrequently" (Remnick 2010, 477).

19. Indeed, Rigueur notes that "President Barack Obama, the scourge of Republicans everywhere, has sounded a lot like the black Republicans of the 1960s and 1970s" (Rigueur 2014, 10), suggesting that the transition from what Abel represents in the novel to what Obama's presidency might signify may not be transformative after all.

20. For a detailed discussion of Donald Trump's role in perpetuating the lie that Barack Obama was not an American citizen, and thus an illegitimate president, see Barbaro 2016.

CHAPTER 5. A NON-AMERICAN BLACK GUIDE TO AMERICAN BLACKNESS: REARTICULATING RACE THROUGH A DIASPORIC LENS

1. "Phenotypically black immigrants, who now comprise about 10 percent of the Black American population, face distinct issues with regard to individual classification" (Hochschild, Weaver, and Burch 2012, 35). The 2016 report "The State of Black Immigrants" by the Black Alliance for Just Immigration (BAJI) also concurs on the 10 percent figure. See http://www.stateofblackimmigrants.com/.

2. As Rachel Reynolds explains in her ethnography of Nigerian Igbo community organizations in Chicago, Nigerians are, by some measures, the best-educated immigrant group in American history (Reynolds 2009, 212).

3. Adichie's novel contains the most explicit reference to Obama's background within these texts, but not the only one. Mengestu's *All Our Names* (2014), for example, traces a

love story between a young white woman from a small Midwestern town and an African refugee during the 1970s that culminates in a possible conception. As Aaron Bady (2014) points out, "'Barack Obama' looms over the story" and it is no accident that the novel, and the love story, end up in Chicago, the place that launched Obama's political life. The mythology of Ann Dunham and Barack Obama Sr.'s love for each other extends the fantasy of Obama's biography to trumpet an ideology of hope amid the traumas and violence that define the novel, and the history it represents. In the novel, interracial romantic love serves as a means of transcendence. Specifically, Mengestu imagines a scene of conception in which the comingling of bodies and fluids constructs a version of the old advertisement showing a white hand grasping a Black hand. The potential child born of this moment, who serves as a mythic version of Obama, instantiates an idealized potential future expressive of such a racial union. When Isaac and Helen end the narrative on the beach at Lake Michigan just north of Grant Park in Chicago, the novel invokes the transcendent possibility of the moment of Obama's victory rally, which, in the timeline of the novel, will take place in a few short decades. However, where Mengestu's references to Obama remain implicit throughout *All Our Names*, Adichie's celebrated anatomization of American racial norms specifically invokes Obama as an emblematic figure through which such structures of race can be negotiated.

4. Barack Obama Sr. matriculated at the University of Hawai'i through a scholarship provided by baseball star Jackie Robinson. While his scholarship was part of the same efforts by Tom Mboya and the African American Students Foundation (AASF), founded by William Scheinman, that led to airlifts between 1959 and 1963 that brought "nearly eight hundred East African students" (Shachtman 2009, 7), Obama Sr. received an individual scholarship and transportation rather than being a part of the larger airlifts. For the history of the AASF project, see Shachtman 2009.

5. My argument here differs from Caroline Levine's article "'The Strange Familiar': Structure, Infrastructure, and Adichie's *Americanah*" (2015), in which she locates the novel within the realist genre. While I agree with Levine that Adichie draws on the realist tradition, it is critical to contextualize that generic choice by Adichie in relation to the expectations that African authors will write either in the form of national allegories or ethnographically.

6. The postcolonial theorist Achille Mbembe uses the term "Afropolitanism" in a related manner to refer to already present cosmopolitanism throughout recent African history (Mbembe 2007). In doing so, Simon Gikandi argues that term serves to counter narratives of Afropessimism which claim that the continent cannot escape a past of violence, oppression, and economic underdevelopment (see Gikandi 2011).

7. Afropolitanism, as a term, has gained significant cultural cache and is used to market a range of products and experiences across the current diaspora. In response, there has been a proliferation of essays critiquing the term, and Selasi, orienting particularly around the implicitly high-class background necessary to live the lifestyle that Selasi celebrates as emblematic of the current generation. For further critiques, see Binyavanga Wainaina's talk "I am a Pan-Africanist not an Afropolitan," discussed in Santana 2013; Tveit 2013; Dbiri 2014; and Ogbechie 2008, which also discusses the Studio Museum of Harlem "F series" exhibition *Flow* in relation to Selasi's neologism. See also the recent forum on the value of the term in the *Journal of African Cultural Studies* (2015), which includes pieces by Grace Musila, Emma Dabiri, Stephanie Bosch Santana, Chielezona Eze, and Carlie Coetzee.

8. The small amount of criticism that has already been directed at Adichie's novel debates whether the novel is "Afropolitan" or not (see Hallemeier 2015; Guaracinno 2014).

9. Citing this scene in particular, Levine argues that Adichie uses this figure of the out-sider within the realist genre as a way of defamiliarizing racial structures (see Levine 2015, 595). In a similar vein, Goyal argues that Adichie's novel is centrally about the conflicts over identity between those Adichie labels American Blacks and Non-American Blacks. For Goyal, this leads to an oversimplification of such identities symptomatic of a wider inability to prop-erly account for diaspora in African American literary study (see Goyal 2017, 642–45).

10. Notably, while Blaine echoes many Black commentators who critiqued Obama's problematic equation of "black grievance" and "white fear" (Adichie 2013, 358), Ifemelu views such rhetoric as pragmatic, further underscoring their differing perceptions of the inherence of American racism.

11. Though I don't endorse an autobiographical reading of the text, Wellson possibly stands in for Adichie's own matriculation at Temple University in Philadelphia.

12. Mary Waters's research on Black Caribbean immigrants reveals the range of poten-tial positionings that Dike might inhabit as a 1.5-generation immigrant. While 1.5 and second-generation immigrants from lower class backgrounds were more likely to identify themselves as Black Americans, and very unlikely to view themselves primarily through their ethnic background, individuals from middle class backgrounds such as Dike—whose mother Uju is a doctor—were more likely to identify themselves primarily ethnically, fol-lowed by racially (see Waters 1999, chapter 8).

13. Furthermore, the necessary inclusion of individuals such as Amadou Diallo, the Guinean immigrant murdered by New York City police in 1999, in any list of the dead underscores how the vulnerability to state sanctioned violence is not confined to American Blacks but includes those depicted in novels such as the ones discussed in this chapter.

CODA. AFRICAN AMERICAN LITERATURE POST-OBAMA

1. My intention here is not to dispute the worthiness of Whitehead's, Beatty's, and Ward's novels, all of which are superlative. Instead, I seek to call attention to the way in which literary awards participate in the distribution of cultural capital and operate within literary power hierarchies.

2. As Melamed explains, "The idea that literature has something to do with antiracism and being a good person has entered into the self-care of elites, who have learned to see themselves as part of a multinational group of enlightened multicultural global citizens. Literary sensibility, redefined as an appreciation for the literature of other cultures, distin-guishes multicultural global citizens from others" (Melamed 2011, 45). In the face of revived domestic and international nationalisms, the multicultural global citizen specifically defines themselves through the appreciation and celebration of literature by Black authors and other people of color. The most visible version of this phenomenon during the Trump admin-istration was the widespread effort by booksellers and librarians to respond to the racist statement by the president that countries in Africa were "shithole" countries with displays highlighting the literary work from those countries. Though well intentioned, such efforts also reinforce neoliberal metrics of value that sees the worth of those countries through the lens of what they produce, literarily or economically. See, for example, *Electric Literature* 2018; Zimmer 2018; and Ransom 2018.

3. One of the major arguments for Obama's election constituting a real shift in American racial attitudes was that a significant number of white voters willingly and openly voted for

a Black candidate. Consequently, the most prominent data point mustered to declare the end of the post-racial era was the significant number of voters who voted for both Barack Obama and Donald Trump. In a more academic vein, Robert J. Terrill argues that Donald Trump's rhetoric participates in "a post-post-racial discourse—whereas rhetorics of post-racialism still express some obligation to address race, Trump very often does not. This rejection of a specifically racial burden establishes the context for, and thus enables, a wider rejection of the societal norms and expectations that provide the material for ethical speech" (Terrill 2017, 499).

4. In addition to the increased analysis of the genre in academic venues, Afrofuturism even received a triumphal write-up in the *New York Times* as a major stylistic trend (see La Ferla 2016).

5. Afropunk is just one example of cultural institutions designed to highlight nonnormative performances of Black identity. Founded in 2005 by James Spooner and Matthew Morgan in concert with their production of a documentary of the same name (which was released in 2003), Afropunk has expanded from its focus on Black punk rock fans to encompass multiple yearly music festivals. The figure of the Black punk rock fan joins other "cultural mulatto" archetypes such as the "Blerd" to trouble dominant stereotypes of Black identity. As Alexander Weheliye argued, figures such as the "black geek" function as imaginaries of "a blackness to come," remixing social categorizations and challenging essentialisms (Weheliye 2013, 226). That said, these archetypes, like other post era redefinitions of Blackness, have frequently revealed their limitations. With regard to Afropunk, Hannah Giorgis has documented how its expansion has undermined its institutional power as a space for community for Black punk fans specifically. For more on Afropunk see Giorgis 2015 and Pritchard 2017.

6. My brief discussion of Black Lives Matter is not meant to be either a comprehensive history of the movement's rise, nor is it meant to address the full complexity of its ideological roots.

7. As the organization declares in its "Herstory": "Black liberation movements in this country have created room, space, and leadership mostly for Black heterosexual, cisgender men—leaving women, queer and transgender people, and others either out of the movement or in the background to move the work forward with little or no recognition. As a network, we have always recognized the need to center the leadership of women and queer and trans people. To maximize our movement muscle, and to be intentional about not replicating harmful practices that excluded so many in past movements for liberation, we made a commitment to placing those at the margins closer to the center" (see Black Lives Matter nd).

8. I am speaking here about the circulation of "intersectionality" within activist and popular cultural circles. In academia, the institutional dominance of intersectionality within Gender Studies and in critical analyses of Black feminism has led to what Jennifer Nash describes as the "intersectionality wars" (Nash 2017; see also Puar 2007). For the original definitions of the term, see Crenshaw 1989 and Crenshaw 1990.

9. As the most prominent Black public intellectual of the late post era, Coates has been accused of being both too politically defeatist and ontological in his outlook (see Stephens 2017) and too mainstream and neoliberal (see West 2017).

10. Hartman goes so far as to describe these attempts as "obscene," describing them as: "the attempt to make the narrative of defeat into an opportunity for celebration, the desire to look at the ravages and the brutality of the last few centuries, but to still find a way to feel good about our selves" (Hartman and Wilderson III 2003, 185). While she is speaking here specifically about attempts by historians and literary critics, particularly during the early

post–civil rights era, to look back at slavery and locate the agency of the enslaved (such as in famous examples like Eugene Genovese's *Roll Jordan Roll*, whose subtitle "the world the slaves made" speaks directly to the agency of the enslaved in composing both individual and cultural experiences), Hartman's argument speaks to a more generalized distrust of American (and, more generally, Western) teleological histories that assign slavery to the past to differentiate the supposedly more progressive and less violent present from an admittedly horrifying past.

BIBLIOGRAPHY

Adell, Sandra. 1994. *Double Consciousness/Double Bind: Theoretical Issues in Twentieth-Century Black Literature.* Urbana: University of Illinois Press.

Adichie, Chimamanda Ngozi. 2006. *Half of a Yellow Sun.* New York: Anchor Books.

Adichie, Chimamanda Ngozi. 2009. "The Danger of a Single Story." *TEDGlobal 2009.* June 2009. https://www.ted.com/talks/chimamanda_adichie_the_danger_of_a_single_story.

Adichie, Chimamanda Ngozi. 2013. *Americanah.* New York: Knopf.

Alba, Richard, and Victor Nee. 2005. *Remaking the American Mainstream: Assimilation and Contemporary Immigration.* Cambridge: Harvard University Press.

Alexander, Elizabeth. 2010. "Today's News." In *Crave Radiance*, 36. Minneapolis: Greywolf Press.

Alexander, Michelle. 2010. *The New Jim Crow: Mass Incarceration in the Age of Colorblindness.* New York: The New Press.

Anderson, Benedict. 1983. *Imagined Communities: Reflections on the Origins and Spread of Nationalism.* London: Verso.

Anderson, Nick. 2010. "Education Secretary Calls Hurricane Katrina Good for New Orleans Schools." *Washington Post* (Washington, DC) January 30, 2010, http://www.washingtonpost.com/wp-dyn/content/article/2010/01/29/AR2010012903259.html.

Appiah, Anthony. 1991. "Is the Post- in Postmodernism the Post- in Postcolonial?" *Critical Inquiry* 17, no. 2 (Winter): 336–57.

Ashe, Bertram. 2007. "Theorizing the Post-Soul Aesthetic: An Introduction." *African American Review* 41, no. 4: 609–23.

Assensoh, Akwasi, and Yvette Alex-Assensoh. 2002. "Black Political Leadership in the Post–Civil Rights Era." In *Black Political Organizations in the Post–Civil Rights Era*, edited by Ollie A. Johnson III and Karin L. Stanford, 193–201. New Brunswick: Rutgers University Press.

Avilez, Gershun. 2016. *Radical Aesthetics and Modern Black Nationalism.* Urbana: University of Illinois Press.

Bady, Aaron. 2014. "The World and What It Isn't: Dinaw Mengestu's *All Our Names*." *The New Inquiry*, March 27, 2014. https://thenewinquiry.com/blog/the-world-and-what-it-isnt-dinaw-mengestus-all-our-names/.

Baker, Houston A. Jr. 1984. *Blues, Ideology, and Afro-American Literature: A Vernacular Theory.* Chicago: University of Chicago Press.

Baker, Houston A. Jr. 2002. "Blue Men, Black Writing, and Southern Revisions." *South Atlantic Quarterly* 101, no. 1: 7–17.

Baker, Houston A., and K. Merinda Simmons. 2015. *The Trouble with Post-Blackness.* New York: Columbia University Press.

Bakhtin, Mikhail. 1981. *The Dialogic Imagination,* edited by Michael Holquist. Austin: University of Texas Press.

Barbaro, Michael. 2016. "Donald Trump Clung to 'Birther' Lie for Years, Still Isn't Apologetic." *New York Times* (New York), September 16, 2016. https://www.nytimes.com /2016/09/17/us/politics/donald-trump-obama-birther.html.

Beatty, Paul. 2008. *Slumberland.* New York: Bloomsbury.

Beatty, Paul. 2015a. "Freedom to Create: An Interview with Paul Beatty." *Apogee* 5 (Spring). http://apogeejournal.org/issues/issue-05/freedom-to-create-an-interview-with-paul -beatty/.

Beatty, Paul. 2015b. *The Sellout.* New York: Farrar, Straus and Giroux.

Beatty, Paul. 2017. "Paul Beatty: 'Heartbreak Is Part of Doing Anything You Want to Do.'" Interview by Kate Kellaway. *The Guardian,* June 11, 2017. https://www.theguardian.com /books/2017/jun/11/paul-beatty-interview-the-sellout-booker-prize.

Berlant, Lauren. 2011. "Opulism." *South Atlantic Quarterly* 110, no. 1 (Winter): 235–42.

Berlin, Ira. 2010. *The Making of African America: Four Great Migrations.* New York: Penguin.

Best, Asha. 2012. "Post-Racial Ironies and Counterfactual Histories: a commentary on hipsters." *darkmatter* 9, no. 2. http://www.darkmatter101.org/site/2012/11/29/post-racial -ironies-and-counterfactual-histories-a-commentary-on-hipsters/.

Black Lives Matter. Nd. "Herstory." *Blacklivesmatter.com.* https://blacklivesmatter.com/about /herstory/.

Bonilla, Yarimar, and Jonathan Rosa. 2015. "#Ferguson: Digital Protest, Hashtag Ethnography, and the Racial Politics of Social Media in the United States." *American Ethnologist* 42, no. 1 (February): 4–16.

Boyd, Todd. 2003. *Young, Black, Rich, and Famous: The Rise of the NBA, the Hip Hop Invasion, and the Transformation of American Culture.* New York: Doubleday.

Brubaker, Rogers, and Frederick Cooper. 2000. "Beyond 'Identity.'" *Theory and Society* 29, no. 1 (February): 1–47.

Bulawayo, NoViolet. 2013. *We Need New Names.* New York: Little, Brown and Company.

Bullard, Robert, and Beverly Wright. 2012. *The Wrong Complexion for Protection: How the Government Response to Natural Disasters Endangers African American Communities.* New York: New York University Press.

Bush, George W. 2000. "Text: George W. Bush's Speech to the NAACP." *Washington Post* (Washington, DC), July 10, 2000. http://www.washingtonpost.com/wp-srv/onpolitics /elections/bushtext071000.htm?noredirect=on.

Butler, Octavia. [1979] 2004. *Kindred.* Boston: Beacon Press.

Byrd, Cathy. 2002. "Is There a 'Post-Black' Art?" *Art Papers* 26, no. 6: 35–39.

Carpio, Glenda. 2008. *Laughing Fit to Kill: Black Humor in the Fictions of Slavery.* New York: Oxford University Press.

Carpio, Glenda. 2011. "Race and Inheritance in Barack Obama's *Dreams from My Father.*" *Daedalus* 140, no. 1 (Winter): 79–89.

Chabon, Michael. 2012. *Telegraph Avenue.* New York: Harper Perennial.

Chiles, Nick. 2006. "Their Eyes Were Reading Shut," *New York Times,* Jan 4, 2006. https:// www.nytimes.com/2006/01/04/opinion/their-eyes-were-reading-smut.html.

Cho, Sumi. 2009. "Post-Racialism." *Iowa Law Review* 94, no. 5: 1589–1649.

Chow, Rey. 2002. *The Protestant Ethnic and the Spirit of Capitalism*. Durham: Duke University Press.

Chude-Sokei, Louis. 2014. "The Newly Black Americans." *Transition* 113: 52–71.

Cohen, Cathy. 1999. *The Boundaries of Blackness: AIDS and the Breakdown of Black Politics*. Chicago: University of Chicago Press.

Cohn, Jesse. 2009. "Old Afflictions: Colson Whitehead's Apex Hides the Hurt and the 'Post-Soul Condition.'" *The Journal of the Midwest Modern Language Association* 42, no. 1 (Spring): 15–24.

Colbert, Soyica Diggs. 2017. *Black Movements: Performance and Cultural Politics*. New Brunswick: Rutgers University Press.

Cole, Teju. 2011. *Open City*. New York: Random House.

Coundouriotis, Eleni. 1999. *Claiming History: Colonialism, Ethnography, and the Novel*. New York: Columbia University Press.

Crawford, Margo. 2017. *Black Post-Blackness: The Black Arts Movement and Twenty-First-Century Aesthetics*. Urbana: University of Illinois Press.

Crenshaw, Kimberlé. 1989. "Demarginalizing the Intersection of Race and Sex: A Black Feminist Critique of Antidiscrimination Doctrine, Feminist Theory, and Antiracist Politics." *University of Chicago Legal Forum* 1: 139–67.

Crenshaw, Kimberlé. 1990. "Mapping the Margins: Intersectionality, Identity Politics, and Violence against Women of Color," *Stanford Law Review* 43, no. 6: 1241–99.

Crownshaw, Richard. 2016. "Agency and Environment in the Work of Jesmyn Ward. Response to Anna Hartnell, 'When Cars Become Churches.'" *Journal of American Studies* 50, no. 1: 225–30.

Davis, Julie Hirschfeld, Sheryl Gay Stolberg, and Thomas Kaplan. 2018. "Trump Alarms Lawmakers with Disparaging Words for Haiti and Africa." *New York Times* (New York), January 11, 2018. https://www.nytimes.com/2018/01/11/us/politics/trump-shithole-countries.html.

Dawson, Michael. 1995. *Get Behind the Mule: Race and Class in African American Politics*. Princeton: Princeton University Press.

Dawson, Michael. 2003. *Black Visions: The Roots of Contemporary African-American Political Ideologies*. Chicago: University of Chicago Press.

Dbiri, Emma. 2014. "Why I Am Not an Afropolitan." *Africa Is a Country*, January 21, 2014. https://africasacountry.com/2014/01/why-im-not-an-afropolitan/.

DeSipio, Louis, and Rodolfo O. de la Garza. 2015. *US Immigration in the Twenty-First Century: Making Americans, Remaking America*. Boulder: Westview Press.

Dixson, Adrienne. "Whose Choice? A Critical Race Perspective on Charter Schools." In *The Neoliberal Deluge: Hurricane Katrina, Late Capitalism, and the Remaking of New Orleans*, edited by Cedric Johnson, 130–51. Minneapolis: University of Minnesota Press.

Douglass, Frederick. 1993. *The Narrative of the Life of Frederick Douglass, an American Slave*, edited by David Blight. New York: Bedford.

Du Bois, W. E. B. 1897. "The Conservation of the Races." Washington, DC: The American Negro Academy. http://www.gutenberg.org/files/31254/31254-h/31254-h.htm.

Du Bois, W. E. B. [1903] 1999. *The Souls of Black Folk: A Norton Critical Edition*, edited by Henry Louis Gates Jr. and Terri Hume Oliver. New York: Norton.

Du Bois, W. E. B. 1903. "The Talented Tenth." In *The Negro Problem*, 32–74. New York: James Pott and Company. https://archive.org/stream/negroproblemserioowashrich/negroproblemserioowashrich_djvu.txt.

Du Bois, W. E. B. 1926. "Criteria of Negro Art." *The Crisis* 32 (October). http://www
.webdubois.org/dbCriteriaNArt.html.

Early, Gerald. 2014. "What Is African American Literature?" In *Street Lit: Representing the
Urban Landscape*, edited by Keenan Norris, 3–8. Lanham: Scarecrow Press.

Edwards, Erica. 2011. "The Formidable Work of the Present." *Los Angeles Review of Books*,
June 13th, 2011. https://lareviewofbooks.org/review/the-formidable-work-of-the
-present.

Edwards, Erica. 2012. *Charisma and the Fictions of Black Leadership*. Minneapolis:
University of Minnesota Press.

Edwards, Erica. 2013. "Of Cain and Abel: African-American Literature and the Problem of
Inheritance after 9/11." *American Literary History* 25, no. 1: 190–204.

Edwards, Erica. 2015. "Sex after the Black Normal." *differences: A Journal of Feminist Cultural
Studies* 26, no. 1: 141–67.

Elam, Harry. 2014. "Black Theater in the Age of Obama." In *The Cambridge Companion to
African American Theater*, edited by Harvey Young, 255–78. Cambridge: Cambridge
University Press.

Elam, Michele. 2011. *The Souls of Mixed Folk: Race, Politics, and Aesthetics in the New
Millennium*. Stanford: Stanford University Press.

Electric Literature. 2018. "11 Incredible Books Written By Authors from 'Shithole' Countries."
Electric Literature, January 12, 2018. https://electricliterature.com/11-incredible-books
-by-writers-from-shithole-countries-aa68268e05c8.

Ellis, Trey. 1988. *Platitudes*. New York: Vintage Contemporaries.

Ellis, Trey. 1989. "The New Black Aesthetic." *Callaloo* 38 (Winter): 233–43.

Erickson, Steve. 2012. *These Dreams of You*. New York: Europa Editions.

Everett, Percival. 2001. *Erasure*. New York: Hyperion.

Fain, Kimberly. 2015. *Colson Whitehead: The Postracial Voice of Contemporary Literature*.
Lanham: Rowman & Littlefield.

Fanon, Frantz. 1963. *The Wretched of the Earth*. New York: Grove Press.

Favor, J. Martin. 1999. *Authentic Blackness: The Folk in the New Negro Renaissance*. Durham:
Duke University Press.

Fields, Barbara, and Karen Fields. 2012. *Racecraft: The Soul of Inequality in American Life*.
London: Verso.

Frey, William H. 2004. "The New Great Migration: Black Americans' Return to the South,
1965–2000." *Brookings Institution*, May 1, 2004. https://www.brookings.edu/research
/the-new-great-migration-black-americans-return-to-the-south-1965-2000/.

Gaines, Malik. 2005. "Black Spectacle: An Imitation of Life." In *Frequency*, 25–27. New York:
The Studio Museum of Harlem.

Gates, Henry Louis Jr. 1997. "Harlem on Our Minds." *Critical Inquiry* 24, no. 1: 1–12.

Gates, Henry Louis Jr. 2012. "Foreword." In *Black Cool: One Thousand Streams of Blackness*,
edited by Rebecca Walker, ix-x. Berkeley: Soft Skull Press.

Gay, Claudine, Jennifer Hochschild, and Ariel White. 2016. "Americans' Belief of Linked
Fate: Does the Measure Capture the Concept." *Journal of Race, Ethnicity, and Politics* 1
(March): 117–44.

Genovese, Eugene. 1976. *Roll, Jordan, Roll: The World the Slaves Made*. New York: Vintage
Books.

George, Nelson. 1992. *Buppies, B-Boys, BAPS, and Bohos: Notes on Post-Soul Black Culture*.
New York: Harper Collins.

Gikandi, Simon. 2011. "On Afropolitanism." In *Negotiating Afropolitanism: Essays on Borders and Spaces in Contemporary African Literature and Folklore*, edited by Jennifer Wawrzinek and J. K. S. Makokha, 9–11. Amsterdam: Rodopi.

Gilroy, Paul. 2000. *Against Race: Imagining Political Culture Beyond the Color Line*, Cambridge: Harvard University Press.

Giorgis, Hannah. 2015. "Gentrifying Afropunk." *New Yorker*, August 26, 2015. https://www.newyorker.com/culture/culture-desk/gentrifying-afropunk.

Glaude, Eddie Jr. 2014. "A Requiem for Michael Brown/A Praisesong for Ferguson." *Theory and Event* 17, no. 3: np.

Golash-Boza, Tonya. 2006. "Dropping the Hyphen?: Becoming Latino(a)-American Through Racialized Assimilation." *Social Forces* 85, no. 1: 27–55.

Golden, Thelma. 2001. "Introduction: Post . . ." In *Freestyle*. New York: The Studio Museum of Harlem: 14–15.

Golden, Thelma. 2009. "The Status of Difference: Thelma Golden—Post Black Art Now." *Tate Events* (Tate Modern Museum). March 12, 2009. http://www.tate.org.uk/context-comment/audio/status-difference-thelma-golden-post-black-art-now

Golden, Thelma, and Christine Y. Kim. 2005. "Introduction: Thelma Golden and Christine Y. Kim in Dialogue. Moderated by Ali Evans." In *Frequency*, 12–17. New York: The Studio Museum of Harlem.

Goyal, Yogita. 2017. "We Need New Diasporas." *American Literary History* 29, no. 4: 640–63.

Greer, Christina M. 2013. *Black Ethnics: Race, Immigration, and the Pursuit of the American Dream*. New York: Oxford University Press.

Griffin, Farah Jasmine. 2011. "At Last . . . ? Michelle Obama, Beyoncé, Race, & History." *Daedalus* 140, no. 2 (Winter): 131–41.

Guaracinno, Serena. 2014. "Writing 'So Raw and True': Blogging in Chimamanda Ngozi Adichie's *Americanah*." *Between* IV, no. 8 (November). www.betweenjournal.it.

Gyasi, Yaa. 2016. *Homegoing*. New York: Alfred A. Knopf.

Haggins, Bambi. 2007. *Laughing Mad: The Black Comic Persona in Post-Soul America*. New Brunswick: Rutgers University Press.

Hall, Jacquelyn Dowd. 2005. "The Long Civil Rights Movement and the Political Uses of the Past." *Journal of American History* 91, no. 4 (March): 1233–63.

Hall, Stuart. 1996. "Race, Articulation, and Societies Structured in Dominance." In *Black British Cultural Studies*, edited by Houston A. Baker Jr., Manthia Diawara, and Ruth H. Lindeborg, 16–60. Chicago: University of Chicago Press.

Hallemeier, Katherine. 2015. "'To Be from the Country of People Who Gave': National Allegory and the United States of Adichie's *Americanah*." *Studies in the Novel* 47, no. 2 (Summer): 231–45.

Hannah-Jones, Nikole. 2016. "The End of the Postracial Myth." *New York Times* (New York), November 15, 2016. https://www.nytimes.com/interactive/2016/11/20/magazine/donald-trumps-america-iowa-race.html.

Harris, Cheryl I., and Devon W. Carbado. 2006. "Loot or Find: Fact or Frame?" In *After the Storm: Black Intellectuals Explore the Meaning of Hurricane Katrina*, edited by David Dante Troutt, 87–110. New York: New Press.

Harris, Duriel E., Dawn Lundy Martin, and Ronaldo V. Martin. 2002. "Black Took Collective's Call for Dissonance." *Fence*: 124–42.

Harris, Frederick. 2012. *The Price of the Ticket: Barack Obama and the Rise and Fall of Black Politics*. New York: Oxford University Press.

Hartman, Saidiya. 2007. *Lose Your Mother: A Journey Along the Atlantic Slave Route*. New York: Farrar, Straus, & Giroux.

Hartman, Saidiya V., and Frank B. Wilderson III. 2003. "The Position of the Unthought." *Qui Parle* 13, no. 2 (Spring/Summer): 183–201

Hartnell, Anna. 2016. "When Cars Become Churches: Jesmyn Ward's Disenchanted America: An Interview." *Journal of American Studies* 50, no. 1: 205–18.

Hayes, Terrance, and Evie Shockley, eds. 2009. "African American Experimental Poetry Forum," *jubilat* 16: 115–57.

Henderson, Stephen. 1973. "Introduction: The Form of Things Unknown." *Understanding the New Black Poetry*. New York: William Morrow.

Higginbotham, Evelyn. 1992. "African American Women's History and the Metalanguage of Race." *Signs* 17, no. 2 (Winter): 251–74.

Hochschild, Jennifer, Vesla Weaver, and Traci Burch. 2012. *Creating a New Racial Order: How Immigration, Multiracialism, Genomics, and the Young Generation can Remake Race in America*. Princeton: Princeton University Press.

Holloway, Karla F. C. 2014. *Legal Fictions: Constituting Race, Composing Literature*. Durham: Duke University Press.

hooks, bell. 2012. "No Love in the Wild." *NewBlackMan (in Exile)*, September 5, 2012. http://www.newblackmaninexile.net/2012/09/bell-hooks-no-love-in-wild.html.

Hughes, Langston. 1995. *The Collected Poems of Langston Hughes*, edited by Arnold Rampersad. New York: Vintage.

Hunter, Tera. 1989. "'It's a Man's Man's Man's World': Specters of the Old Re-Newed in Afro-American Culture and Criticism." *Callaloo* 38 (Winter): 247–49.

Hurston, Zora Neale. [1937] 1990. *Their Eyes Were Watching God*. New York: Perennial Classics.

Ishiwata, Eric. 2011. "'We are seeing People We Didn't Know Exist': Katrina and the Neoliberal Erasure of Race." *The Neoliberal Deluge: Hurricane Katrina, Late Capitalism, and The Remaking of New Orleans*, edited by Cedric Johnson, 32–59. Minneapolis: University of Minnesota Press.

James, Joy. 2003. "Radicalizing Feminisms from 'The Movement Era.'" In *A Companion to African American Philosophy*, edited by Tommy L. Lott and John P. Pittman, 230–38. Oxford: Blackwell.

James, Joy. 2007. "Afterword, Political Literacy and Voice." In *What Lies Beneath: Katrina, Race, and the State of the Nation*, edited by The South End Press Collective, 157–66. Cambridge: South End Press.

Jameson, Frederic. 1986. "Third World Literature in the Era of Multinational Capitalism," *Social Text* 15 (Autumn): 65–88.

Jarrett, Gene Andrew. 2011. *Representing the Race: A New Political History of African American Literature*. New York: New York University Press.

Jeffries, Michael. 2013. *Paint the White House Black: Barack Obama and the Meaning of Race in America*. Stanford: Stanford University Press.

Johnson, Cedric. 2011. "Introduction: The Neoliberal Deluge." In *The Neoliberal Deluge: Hurricane Katrina, Late Capitalism, and the Remaking of New Orleans*, xvii–1. Minneapolis: University of Minnesota Press.

Johnson, Charles. [1982] 2005. *Oxherding Tale*. New York: Scribner.

Johnson, Charles. 1998. *Dreamer*. New York: Scribner.

Johnson, Charles. 2008. "The End of the Black American Narrative." *The American Scholar* (Summer): 32–42.

Johnson, E. Patrick. 2003. *Appropriating Blackness: Performance and the Politics of Authenticity*. Durham: Duke University Press.

Johnson, James Weldon. [1927] 1989. *The Autobiography of an Ex-Coloured Man*. New York: Vintage.

Johnson, Lyndon Baines. 1965. "To Fulfill These Rights." Commencement Address, Howard University, June 4, 1965, *Lbjlibrary.org* (Lyndon Baines Johnson Presidential Library).

Jones, Amelia. 2012. *Seeing Differently: A History and Theory of Identification and the Visual Arts*. New York: Routledge.

Joseph, Ralina. 2013. *Transcending Blackness: From the New Millennium Mulatta to the Exceptional Multiracial*. Durham: Duke University Press.

Kauanui, J. Kēhaulani. 2008. "Colonialism in Equality: Hawaiian Sovereignty and the Question of U.S. Civil Rights." *South Atlantic Quarterly* 107, no. 4 (Fall): 635–50.

Keizer, Arlene. 2004. *Black Subjects: Identity Formation in the Contemporary Narrative of Slavery*. Ithaca: Cornell University Press.

Kellner, Douglas. 2009. "Barack Obama and Celebrity Spectacle." *International Journal of Communication* 3: 715–41.

Kendi, Ibram. 2017. "The Death of Post-Racial America: How Obama's Presidency, and Trump's Election Killed an Idea that Never Made Sense." *New York Daily News* (New York), January 14, 2017. http://www.nydailynews.com/opinion/death-post-racial-america -article-1.2946137.

Kennedy, Randall. 2011. "The Fallacy of Touré's Post-Blackness Theory." *The Root*, August 11, 2011. https://www.theroot.com/the-fallacy-of-toures-post-blackness-theory-1790865279.

La Ferla, Ruth. 2016. "Afrofuturism: The Next Generation." *New York Times* (New York), December 12, 2016. https://www.nytimes.com/2016/12/12/fashion/afrofuturism-the -next-generation.html.

Lacy, Karyn. 2007. *Blue-Chip Black: Race, Class, and Status in the New Black Middle Class*. Berkeley, CA: University of California Press.

Langness, LL and Gelya Frank. 1978. "Fact, Fiction, and the Ethnographic Novel." *Anthropology and Humanism Quarterly* 3, no. 1–2: 18–22.

Laymon, Kiese. 2013. *Long Division*. Chicago: Bolden.

Laymon, Kiese. 2015. "Hypertext Interview with Kiese Laymon." Interview by Sheree Greer. *Hypertext*, Mar 31, 2015. https://www.hypertextmag.com/hypertext-interview-with-kiese -laymon/.

Lebron, Christopher. 2017. *The Making of Black Lives Matter: A Brief History of an Idea*. New York: Oxford University Press.

Lee, Spike, dir. 2006. *When the Levees Broke: A Requiem in Four Acts*. HBO Films.

Lee, Taeku. 2011. "Somewhere Over the Rainbow?: Post-Racial & Pan-Racial Politics in the Age of Obama." *Daedalus* 140, no. 2 (Spring): 136–50.

Levecq, Christine. 2000. "Power and Repetition: Philosophies of (Literary) History in Octavia Butler's Kindred." *Contemporary Literature* 41, no. 3 (Autumn): 525–53.

Levine, Andrea. 2011. "'In Our Own Homes': Gendering the African American Domestic Sphere in Contemporary Culture." *WSQ: Women's Studies Quarterly* 39, no. 1/2 (Spring/ Summer): 170–87.

Levine, Caroline. 2015. "'The Strange Familiar': Structure, Infrastructure, and Adichie's *Americanah*." *Modern Fiction Studies* 61, no. 4 (Winter): 587–605.

Levy-Hussen, Aida. 2016. *How to Read African American Literature: Post–Civil Rights Fiction and the Task of Interpretation*. New York: New York University Press.

Li, Stephanie. 2012. *Specifying Without Signifying: Racial Discourse in the Age of Obama.* New Brunswick: Rutgers University Press.

Locke, John. 1689. *Second Treatise on Government. The Founder's Constitution.* The University of Chicago. §49. http://press-pubs.uchicago.edu/founders/documents /v1ch16s3.html.

Lordi, Emily. 2009. "Letter to the Editor: The Post-Black Problem." *New York Times* (New York), May 20, 2009. https://www.nytimes.com/2009/05/24/books/review/Letters-t -THEPOSTBLACK_LETTERS.html.

Lott, Eric. 1989. "Response to Trey Ellis's: 'The New Black Aesthetic.'" *Callaloo* 38 (Winter): 244–46.

Madison, D. Soyini. 2009. "Crazy Patriotism and Angry (Post)Black Women." *Communication and Critical/Cultural Studies* 6, no. 3 (September): 321–26.

Mailer, Norman. 1957. "The White Negro: Superficial Reflections on the Hipster." *Dissent* (Fall): 276–93.

Malo, Sebastian. 2013. "The Story of the Black Band-Aid." *The Atlantic*, June 6, 2013. http:// www.theatlantic.com/health/archive/2013/06/the-story-of-the-black-band-aid/276542/.

Marable, Manning. 1994. "The Divided Mind of Black America: Race, Ideology, and Politics in the Post–Civil Rights Era." *Race & Class* 36, no. 1: 61–72.

Marable, Manning. 1996. *Beyond Black and White.* New York: Verso.

Marable, Manning. 2009. "Racializing Obama: The Enigma of Post-Black Politics and Leadership." *Souls* 11, no. 1: 1–15.

Maraniss, David. 2012. *Barack Obama: The Story.* New York: Simon & Schuster.

Maus, Derek C. 2014. *Understanding Colson Whitehead.* Columbia, SC: University of South Carolina Press.

Mbembe, Achille. 2007. "Afropolitanism." In *Africa Remix: Contemporary Art of a Continent*, translated by Laurent Chauvet, 26–29. Johannesburg: Jacana.

Mbue, Imbolo. 2016. *Behold the Dreamers.* New York: Random House.

McGeveran, Tom. 2008. "Toni Morrison's Letter to Barack Obama." *New York Observer* (New York) January 28, 2008. http://observer.com/2008/01/toni-morrisons-letter-to -barack-obama/.

McGrath, Charles. 2009. "Coming of Age in Sag Harbor Among Privilege and Paradox." *New York Times* (New York), April 27, 2009. https://www.nytimes.com/2009/04/28 /books/28cols.html.

McKnight, Reginald. 1989. "The Honey Boys." In *Moustapha's Eclipse,* 79–101. New York: Ecco.

McKnight, Reginald. 1994. "Confessions of a Wannabe Negro" In *Lure and Loathing*, edited by Gerald Early, 95–112. New York: Penguin.

Melamed, Jodi. 2011. *Represent and Destroy: Rationalizing Violence in the New Racial Capitalism.* Minneapolis: University of Minnesota Press.

Mengestu, Dinaw. 2007. *The Beautiful Things That Heaven Bears.* New York: Riverhead Books.

Mengestu, Dinaw. 2010. *How to Read the Air.* New York: Riverhead Books.

Mengestu, Dinaw. 2014a. *All Our Names.* New York: Knopf.

Mengestu, Dinaw. 2014b. "Dinaw Mengestu on *All Our Names.*" Interview by Kevin Nance. *Chicago Tribune* (Chicago, IL), March 21, 2014. http://articles.chicagotribune.com/2014 -03-21/features/chi-all-our-names-dinaw-mengestu-20140321_1_dinaw-mengestu -printers-row-journal-uganda/2.

Miller, Paul D. 2004. *Rhythm Science.* Cambridge: MIT Press.

Morrison, Toni. 1992. *Playing in the Dark: Whiteness and the Literary Imagination.* New York: Vintage.

Morrison, Toni. 1997. "Home." In *The House that Race Built: Black Americans, U.S. Terrain,* edited by Wahneema Lubiano, 3–12. New York: Pantheon Books

Moten, Fred. 2003. *In the Break: The Aesthetics of the Black Radical Tradition.* Minneapolis: University of Minnesota Press.

Moten, Fred. 2008. "Black Op." *PMLA* 123, no. 5: 1743–47.

Moten, Fred. 2013. "Blackness and Nothingness (Mysticism in the Flesh)." *South Atlantic Quarterly* 112, no. 4 (Fall): 737–80.

Murray, Derek Conrad. 2016. *Queering Post-Black Art: Artists Transforming African-American Identity after Civil Rights.* London: I.B. Tauris.

Murray, Rolland. 2017. "Not Being and Blackness: Percival Everett and the Uncanny Forms of Racial Incorporation." *American Literary History* 29, no. 4: 726–52.

Naimou, Angela. 2015. *Salvage Work: U.S. and Caribbean Literature amid the Debris of Legal Personhood.* New York: Fordham University Press.

Nash, Jennifer. 2017. "Intersectionality and Its Discontents." *American Quarterly* 69, no. 1 (March): 117–29.

Neal, Larry. [1968] 2007. "And Shine Sang On." In *Black Fire,* edited by Amiri Baraka and Larry Neal, 637–56. Baltimore: Black Classic Press.

Neal, Mark Anthony. 2002. *Soul Babies: Black Popular Culture and the Post-Soul Aesthetic.* New York: Routledge.

New York Times. 2005. "Barbara Bush Calls Evacuees Better Off." September 7, 2005. https://www.nytimes.com/2005/09/07/us/nationalspecial/barbara-bush-calls-evacuees-better-off.html.

Nixon, Rob. 2011. *Slow Violence and the Environmentalism of the Poor.* Cambridge: Harvard University Press.

Norman, Brian. 2010. *Neo-Segregation Narratives: Jim Crow in Post–Civil Rights American Literature.* Athens: University of Georgia Press.

Obama, Barack. [1995] 2004. *Dreams from My Father.* New York: Three Rivers Press.

Obama, Barack. 2004. "Transcript: Illinois Senate Candidate Barack Obama." *Washington Post* (Washington, DC), July 27, 2004. http://www.washingtonpost.com/wp-dyn/articles/A19751-2004Jul27.html.

Obama, Barack. 2006. *The Audacity of Hope: Thoughts on Reclaiming the American Dream.* New York: Vintage.

Obama, Barack. 2009. "A More Perfect Union." In *The Speech: Race and Barack Obama's "A More Perfect Union,* edited by T. Denean Sharpley-Whiting, 237–51. New York: Bloomsbury.

Office of Policy Planning and Research, United States Department of Labor. 1965. *The Negro Family: The Case for National Action.* March 1965.

Ogbechie, S. Okwunodu. 2008. "Afropolitanism: Africa without Africans." *Aachronym,* April 4, 2008. http://aachronym.blogspot.com/2008/04/afropolitanism-more-africa-without.html.

Oliver, Valerie Cassel. 2005. "Through the Conceptual Lens: The Rise, Fall, and Resurrection of Blackness." In *Double Consciousness: Black Conceptual Art Since 1970,* edited by Valerie Cassel Oliver, 17–27. Houston: Contemporary Arts Museum Houston.

Parks, Chanel. 2014. "Chimamanda Ngozi Adichie: I Felt If I Wear High Heels, Nobody Would Take Me Seriously." *Huffington Post,* March 7, 2014. https://www.huffingtonpost.com/2014/03/07/chimamanda-ngozi-adichie-high-heels_n_4921470.html.

Patterson, Orlando. 1982. *Slavery and Social Death*. Cambridge: Harvard University Press.

Patterson, Robert J. 2013. *Exodus Politics: Civil Rights and Leadership in African American Literature and Culture*. Charlottesville: University of Virginia Press.

Perlstein, Daniel. 1990. "Teaching Freedom: SNCC and the Creation of the Mississippi Freedom Schools." *History of Education Quarterly* 30, no. 3 (Autumn): 297–324.

Perry, Imani. 2011. *More Beautiful and More Terrible: The Embrace and Transcendence of Racial Inequality in the United States*. New York: New York University Press.

Pitts, Leonard Jr. 2016. *Grant Park*. New York: Agate Bolden.

Pritchard, Eric Darnell. 2017. "Grace Jones, Afro Punk, and Other Fierce Provocations: An Introduction to 'Sartorial Politics, Intersectionality, and Queer Worldmaking.'" *QED: A Journal in GLBTQ Worldmaking* 4, no. 3 (Fall): 1–11.

Puar, Jasbir. 2007. *Terrorist Assemblages: Homonationalism in Queer Times*. Durham: Duke University Press.

Randall, Alice. 2004. "Interview: Alice Randall." Interview by Robert Birnbaum. *Identity Theory*, July 14, 2004. http://www.identitytheory.com/alice-randall/.

Randall, Alice. 2009a. "Barack in the Dirty, Dirty South." In *The Speech: Race and Barack Obama's "A More Perfect Union*, edited by T. Denean Sharpley-Whiting, 205–23. New York: Bloomsbury.

Randall, Alice. 2009b. *Rebel Yell*. New York: Bloomsbury.

Ransom, Brian. 2018. "Celebrating Shithole Literature." *Paris Review*, January 12, 2018: https://www.theparisreview.org/blog/2018/01/12/celebrating-shithole-literature/.

Redmond, Shana. 2013. *Anthem: Social Movements and the Sound of Solidarity in the African Diaspora*. New York: New York University Press.

Reed, Adolph L. Jr. 1997. *W. E. B. Du Bois and American Political Thought: Fabianism and the Color Line*. New York: Oxford University Press.

Reed, Adolph Jr. 2010. "The 'Color Line' Then and Now: The Souls of Black Folk and the Changing Context of Black American Politics." In *Renewing Black Intellectual History: The Ideological and Material Foundations of African American Thought*, edited by Adolph Reed Jr. and Kenneth Warren, 252–303. New York: Paradigm.

Reed, Adolph. 2016. "How Racial Disparity Does Not Make Sense of Patterns of Police Violence." *New Labor Forum*, October 17, 2016. http://newlaborforum.cuny.edu/2016/10/17/how-racial-disparity-does-not-help-make-sense-of-patterns-of-police-violence/.

Reed, Anthony. 2014. *Freedom Time: The Poetics and Politics of Black Experimental Writing*. Baltimore: Johns Hopkins University Press.

Reed, Ishmael. 1986. *Reckless Eyeballing*. New York: Macmillan Publishing.

Reimers, David. 1981. "Post-World War II Immigration to the United States: America's Latest Newcomers." *Annals of the American Academy of Political and Social Science* 454 (March): 1–12.

Remnick, David. 2010. *The Bridge: The Life and Rise of Barack Obama*. New York: Knopf.

Reynolds, Rachel. 2009. "Igbo Professional Migratory Orders, Hometown Associations and Ethnicity in the USA." *Global Networks* 9, no. 2: 209–26.

Reynolds, Rachel. 2013. "Toward Understanding a Culture of Migration among Elite African Youth: Igbo College Students in the United States." In *African Migrations: Patterns and Perspectives*, edited by Abdoulaye Kane and Todd H. Leedy, 270–86. Bloomington, IN: Indiana University Press.

Rigueur, Leah Wright. 2014. *The Loneliness of the Black Republican: Pragmatic Politics and the Pursuit of Power*. Princeton: Princeton University Press.

Robinson, Zandria. 2014. *This Ain't Chicago: Race, Class, and Regional Identity in the Post-Soul South*. Chapel Hill: University of North Carolina Press.

Rodriguez, Dylan. 2007. "The Meaning of 'Disaster' under the Dominance of White Life." *What Lies Beneath: Katrina, Race, and the State of the Nation*, edited by The South End Press Collective. Cambridge: South End Press: 133–56.

Rogers, Reuel. 2006. *Afro-Caribbean Immigrants and the Politics of Incorporation: Ethnicity, Exception, or Exit*. New York: Cambridge University Press.

Roper Center Public Opinion Archives. 2000. "How Groups Voted in 2000." Voter News Service, a consortium ABC News, CBS News, CNN, FOX News, NBC News and the Associated Press. *Roper Center Public Opinion Archives*. Storrs: The Roper Center, University of Connecticut.

Roper Center Public Opinion Archives. 2004. "How Groups Voted in 2004." Edison Media Research/Mitofsky International for the National Election Pool (ABC News, Associated Press, CBS News, CNN, Fox News, NBC News). *Roper Center Public Opinion Archives*. Storrs: University of Connecticut.

Rushdy, Ashraf. 1999. *Neo-Slave Narratives: Studies in the Social Logic of a Literary Form*. New York: Oxford University Press.

Rushdy, Ashraf. 2001. *Remembering Generations: Race and Family in Contemporary African American Fiction*. Chapel Hill: University of North Carolina Press.

Salaam, Kalamu Ya. 2007. "Below the Water Line." In *What Lies Beneath: Katrina, Race, and the State of the Nation*, edited by The South End Press Collective, ix–xviii. Cambridge: South End Press.

Saldívar, Ramon. 2013. "The Second Elevation of the Novel: Race, Form, and the Postrace Aesthetic in Contemporary Narrative." *Narrative* 21, no. 1: 1–18.

Salon Staff. 2008. "What Should Obama Do about Rev. Jeremiah Wright?" *Salon.com*, April 29, 2008. https://www.salon.com/2008/04/29/obama_wright/.

Santana, Stephanie. 2013. "Exorcizing Afropolitanism." *Africa in Words*, February 8, 2013. https://africainwords.com/2013/02/08/exorcizing-afropolitanism-binyavanga-wainaina-explains-why-i-am-a-pan-africanist-not-an-afropolitan-at-asauk-2012/.

Schloss, Joseph. 2004. *Making Beats: The Art of Sample-Based Hip-Hop*. Middletown: Wesleyan University Press.

Schmidt, Christian. 2017. *Postblack Aesthetics: The Freedom to Be Black in Contemporary African American Fiction*. Heidelberg: Universitätsverlag.

Selasi, Taiye. 2005. "Bye-Bye Babar; or, What Is an Afropolitan?" *The Lip* 5 (March 3, 2005). http://thelip.robertsharp.co.uk/?p=76.

Selasi, Taiye. 2014. *Ghana Must Go*. New York: Penguin.

Selasi, Taiye, and Aaron Bady. 2015. "From That Stranded Place." *Transition* 117: 148–65.

Severson, Kim. 2015. "The New Orleans Restaurant Bounce, After Katrina." *New York Times* (New York), August 4, 2015. http://www.nytimes.com/2015/08/05/dining/new-orleans-restaurants-post-hurricane-katrina.html?_r=0.

Sexton, Jared. 2010. "People-of-Color-Blindness: Notes on the Afterlife of Slavery." *Social Text 103* 28, no. 2 (Summer): 31–56.

Shachar, Ayelet. 2006. "The Race for Talent: Highly Skilled Migrants and Competitive Immigration Regimes." *New York Univ. Law Review* 81, no. 1: 148–206.

Shachtman, Tom. 2009. *Airlift to America: How Barack Obama, Sr., John F. Kennedy, Tom Mboya, and 800 East African Students Changed Their World and Ours*. New York: St. Martin's Press.

Shapiro, Thomas. 2004. *The Hidden Cost of Being African American: How Wealth Perpetuates Inequality*. New York: Oxford University Press.

Sharma, Sanjay. 2012. "Black Twitter? Racial Hashtags, Networks and Contagion." *New Formations* 78 (Summer): 46–64.

Sharpe, Christina. 2014. "Black Studies: In the Wake." *The Black Scholar* 44, no. 2 (Summer): 59–69.

Sharpe, Christina. 2016. *In the Wake: On Blackness and Being*. Durham: Duke University Press.

Sharpley-Whiting, T. Denean, ed. 2009. *The Speech: Race and Barack Obama's "A More Perfect Union."* New York: Bloomsbury.

Smith, Ben, and Byron Tau. 2011. "Birtherism: Where It All Began." *Politico*, April 22, 2011. https://www.politico.com/story/2011/04/birtherism-where-it-all-began-053563.

Smith, Rogers M., and Desmond S. King. 2011. *Still a House Divided: Race and Politics in Obama's America*. Princeton: Princeton University Press.

Smith, Rogers M., Desmond S. King, and Philip A. Klinkner. 2011. "Challenging History: Barack Obama and American Racial Politics." *Daedalus* 140, no. 2 (Spring): 121–35.

Spaulding, A. Timothy. 2005. *Reforming the Past: History, the Fantastic, and the Postmodern Slave Narrative*. Columbus: The Ohio State University Press.

Spence, Lester. 2015. *Knocking the Hustle: Against the Neoliberal Turn in Black Politics*. New York: Punctum.

Spillers, Hortense. 1987. "Mama's Baby, Papa's Maybe: An American Grammar Book." *Diacritics* 17, no. 2 (Summer): 65–81.

Squires, Catherine, Eric King Watts, Mary Douglas Vavrus, Kent A. Ono, Kathleen Feyh, Bernadette Marie Calafell, and Daniel C. Brouwer. 2010. "What Is This Post- in Postracial, Postfeminist . . . (Fill in the Blank)?" *Journal of Communication Inquiry* 34, no. 3: 210–53.

Squires, Catherine. 2014. *The Post-Racial Mystique*. New York: New York University Press.

Stallings, L. H. 2013. "Sampling the Sonics of Sex (Funk) in Paul Beatty's *Slumberland*." In *Contemporary African American Literature: The Living Canon*, edited by Lovalerie King and Shirley Moody-Turner, 189–212. Bloomington: Indiana University Press.

Steinberg, Marc. 2004. "Inverting History in Octavia Butler's Postmodern Slave Narrative." *African American Review* 38, no. 3 (Autumn): 467–76.

Stephens, R. L. 2017. "The Birthmark of Damnation: Ta-Nehisi Coates and the Black Body." *Viewpoint Magazine*, May 17, 2017. https://www.viewpointmag.com/2017/05/17/the-birthmark-of-damnation-ta-nehisi-coates-and-the-black-body/.

Stepto, Robert. 1979. *From Behind the Veil: A Study of Afro-American Narrative*. Urbana-Champaign: University of Illinois Press.

Stepto, Robert. 2010. *A Home Elsewhere: Reading African American Classics in the Age of Obama*. Cambridge: Harvard University Press.

Sunday Times, The. 2015. "Chimamanda Ngozi Adichie Recalls Growing Up in Chinua Achebe's House." Books Live. *Sunday Times* (Johannesburg, South Africa), April 21, 2015. http://jonathanball.bookslive.co.za/blog/2015/04/21/from-the-archive-chimamanda-ngozi-adichie-recalls-growing-up-in-chinua-achebes-house/.

Tate, Greg. 1992. "Cult-Nats Meet Freaky-Deke." In *Flyboy in the Buttermilk*, 198–210. New York: Simon and Schuster.

Taylor, Keeanga-Yamahtta. 2016. *From #BlackLivesMatter to Black Liberation*. Chicago: Haymarket Books.

Taylor, Paul C. 2007. "Post-Black, Old Black." *African American Review* 41, no. 4: 625–40.

Terrill, Robert. 2017. "The Post-Racial and Post-Ethical Discourse of Donald J. Trump." *Rhetoric & Public Affairs* 20, no. 3 (Fall): 493–510.

Thomas, Michael. 2007. *Man Gone Down*. New York: Black Cat.

Tillet, Salamishah. 2012. *Sites of Slavery: Citizenship and Racial Democracy in the Post–Civil Rights Imagination*. Durham: Duke University Press.

Touré. 2009. "Visible Young Man." *New York Times* (New York), May 3, 2009. https://www.nytimes.com/2009/05/03/books/review/Toure-t.html.

Touré. 2011. *Who's Afraid of Post-Blackness?: What It Means to Be Black Now*. New York: Free Press.

Trask, Haunani-Kay. 1993. *From a Native Daughter: Colonialism and Sovereignty in Hawai'i*. Honolulu: University of Hawai'i Press.

Tucker, Boima. 2010. "The Scramble for Vinyl." *Africa Is a Country*, September 14, 2010. https://africasacountry.com/2010/09/the-scramble-for-vinyl/.

Tveit, Marta. 2013. "The Afropolitan Must Go." *Africa Is a Country*, November 28, 2013. https://africasacountry.com/2013/11/the-afropolitan-must-go/.

Walker, Hamza. 2001. "Renigged." In *Freestyle*, 16–17. New York: The Studio Museum of Harlem, 2001.

Walker, Rebecca. 2012. "Introduction." In *Black Cool: One Thousand Streams of Blackness*, edited by Rebecca Walker, xiv-xvi. Berkeley: Soft Skull Press.

Ward, Jesmyn. 2011. *Salvage the Bones*. New York: Bloomsbury.

Ward, Jesmyn. 2016. "Cracking the Code." In *The Fire This Time: A New Generation Speaks About Race*, edited by Jesmyn Ward, 89–95. New York: Scribner.

Ward, Jesmyn. 2017. *Sing, Unburied, Sing*. New York: Scribner.

Warren, Kenneth. 2011a. Interview with Henry Louis Gates Jr. "Live Chat: The End of African American Literature?" *The Chronicle of Higher Education*, February 24, 2011. http://chronicle.com/article/Live-Chat-The-End-of/126492/.

Warren, Kenneth. 2011b. *What Was African American Literature?* Cambridge: Harvard University Press.

Washington, Robert J. 2001. *The Ideologies of African American Literature*. Lanham: Rowman & Littlefield.

Waters, Mary. 1999. *Black Identities: West Indian Immigrant Dreams and American Realities*. Cambridge: Harvard University Press.

Weheliye, Alexander. 2013. "Post-Integration Blues: Black Geeks and Afro-Diasporic Humanism." In *Contemporary African American Literature: The Living Canon*, edited by Lovalerie King and Shirley Moody-Turner, 213–34. Bloomington, IN: Indiana University Press.

West, Cornel. 2017. "Ta-Nehisi Coates is the Neoliberal Face of the Black Freedom Struggle." *The Guardian*, December 17, 2017. https://www.theguardian.com/commentisfree/2017/dec/17/ta-nehisi-coates-neoliberal-black-struggle-cornel-west.

White, John Valery. 2006. "The Persistence of Race Politics and the Restraint of Recovery after Hurricane Katrina." In *After the Storm: Black Intellectuals Explore the Meaning of Hurricane Katrina*, edited by David Dante Troutt, 41–62. New York: New Press.

Whitehead, Colson. 1999a. "Going Up." Interview by Laura Miller. *Salon.com*, January 12, 1999. https://www.salon.com/1999/01/12/cov_si_12int/.

Whitehead, Colson. 1999b. *The Intuitionist*. New York: Anchor Books.

Whitehead, Colson. 2001. *John Henry Days*. New York: Anchor Books.

Whitehead, Colson. 2006. *Apex Hides the Hurt*. New York: Doubleday.

Whitehead, Colson. 2009a. *Sag Harbor*. New York: Doubleday.

Whitehead, Colson. 2009b. "What to Write Next." *New York Times* (New York), October 29, 2009. https://www.nytimes.com/2009/11/01/books/review/Whitehead-t.html.

Whitehead, Colson. 2009c. "The Year of Living Post-Racially." *New York Times* (New York), November 3, 2009. https://www.nytimes.com/2009/11/04/opinion/04whitehead.html.

Whitehead, Colson. 2011. *Zone One*. New York: Doubleday.

Whitehead, Colson. 2012. "Interview: Colson Whitehead, author of *Sag Harbor*." Interview by Jody Seaborn. *Austin American-Statesman*, Aug 31, 2012. https://www.statesman.com/lifestyles/interview-colson-whitehead-author-sag-harbor/vs31cU86EirFqv4MIgrPRI/.

Whitehead, Colson. 2016. *The Underground Railroad*. New York: Anchor Books.

Wilderson, Frank, III. 2003. "The Prison Slave as Hegemony's Silent Scandal." *Social Justice* 30, no. 2: 18–27.

Wilderson, Frank, III. 2010. *Red, White, and Black: Cinema and the Structure of U.S. Antagonisms*. Durham: Duke University Press.

Wilson, William Julius. 2018. "Don't Ignore Class When Addressing Racial Gaps in Intergenerational Mobility." *Brookings Institute*, April 12, 2018. https://www.brookings.edu/blog/social-mobility-memos/2018/04/12/dont-ignore-class-when-addressing-racial-gaps-in-intergenerational-mobility/.

Winters, Joseph R. 2016. *Hope Draped in Black: Race, Melancholy, and the Agony of Progress*. Durham: Duke University Press.

Winthrop, John. [1630] 1838. "A Modell of Christian Charity." In *Collections of the Massachusetts Historical Society* (Boston), 3rd series 7: 31–48. https://history.hanover.edu/texts/winthmod.html.

Womack, Ytasha. 2010. *Post-Black: How A New Generation is Redefining African American Identity*. Chicago: Lawrence Hill Books.

Workneh, Lilly. 2016. "This Election Has Completely Debunked the Myth of a 'Post-Racial' America." *The Huffington Post*, November 8, 2016. https://www.huffingtonpost.com/entry/this-election-has-completely-debunked-the-myth-of-a-post-racial-america_us_5821e158e4b0d9ce6fbea7f8.

Wright, Jeremiah. 2003. "Confusing God and Government." *BlackPast.org*. http://www.blackpast.org/2008-rev-jeremiah-wright-confusing-god-and-government.

Wright, Michelle. 2004. *Becoming Black: Creative Identity in the Diaspora*. Durham: Duke University Press.

Wright, Richard. 1937. "Between Laughter and Tears." *New Masses*. October 5, 1937: 22–25.

Young, Kevin. 2012. *The Grey Album: On the Blackness of Blackness*. Minneapolis: Graywolf Press.

Zernike, Kate. 2016. "New Orleans Plan: Charter Schools, with a Return to Local Control." *New York Times* (New York), May 9, 2016. https://www.nytimes.com/2016/05/10/us/charter-driven-gains-in-new-orleans-schools-face-a-big-test.html.

Zimmer, Ben. 2018. "Great Moments in 'Shithole' Literature." *The Atlantic*, January 12, 2018. https://www.theatlantic.com/entertainment/archive/2018/01/great-moments-in-shithole-literature/550472/.

Zolberg, Aristide R. 2006. *A Nation By Design: Immigration Policy in the Fashioning of America*. Cambridge: Harvard University Press.

INDEX

ABOUT THE AUTHOR

Cameron Leader-Picone is associate professor of English at Kansas State University. His research and teaching focuses on contemporary African American literature and culture. Leader-Picone received his PhD in African and African American studies from Harvard University. He has been a Sheila Biddle Ford Foundation Fellow at the W. E. B. Du Bois Center for the Study of Afro-American Research (now the Hutchins Center for African and African American Research) at Harvard University. His research has been funded by the National Endowment for the Humanities.